CONTACT!

A Tactical Manual for Post Collapse Survival

Max Velocity

Web: www.maxvelocitytactical.com

Email: info@maxvelocitytactical.com

Blog: maxvelocitytactical.blogspot.com

Copyright © 2012 by Max Velocity

ISBN-13: 978-1478106692
ISBN-10: 1478106697

This book is dedicated to The Fallen.

They went with songs to the battle, they were young.
Straight of limb, true of eyes, steady and aglow.
They were staunch to the end against odds uncounted,
They fell with their faces to the foe.

They shall grow not old, as we that are left grow old:
Age shall not weary them, nor the years condemn.
At the going down of the sun and in the morning,
We will remember them.

Lest we Forget.

The Ode of Remembrance

CONTENTS

Dedication
Contents
Disclaimers

INTRODUCTION 1
    The Anticipated Situation... 1
    Why.. 5
    About the Author... 6

Chapter One: Starting Points
    The Threat.. 9
    A Little More on Threat... 17
    The Mission.. 21
    Family/Group/Team... 22
    Mental Preparation & the Use of Force..................... 26
    Blog Extract: On Fighting 35
    Physical Preparation for Tactical Operations............ 28
    Weapons... 31
    Leadership.. 34

Chapter Two: To Stay or To Go
    Stay in Place.. 39
    Blog Extract: Long Term Security of Retreat Locations..... 53
    Vs. Bugging Out.. 62
    Timing.. 62
    Route Selection.. 63
    Location... 63
    Access & Concealment.. 64
    Numbers... 65
    Vehicles... 66
    Equipment.. 67
    Blog Extract: 'Camping after the SHTF'................. 69
    Surveillance Equipment... 73

Profile..74
Blog Extract: Body Armor.................................. 75
Law Enforcement Issues................................... 81
Situational Awareness...................................... 86
Mitigation...88

CHAPTER Three: Decision Making
Introduction...91
The Military Decision Making Process............. 93
The Combat Estimate...................................... 98
Combat Estimate... 99

Chapter Four: Training
Training Processes... 107
Blog Extract.. 111
Weapons Safety... 113
Shooting & Weapons Training........................ 115
Navigation..123

Chapter Five: Basic Principles
Introduction... 127
Basic Fieldcraft.. 128
Battle Preparation... 130
Observation... 130
Camouflage... 131
Countering Aerial Thermal Surveillance........ 133
Basic Movement.. 137
Taking Cover... 139
Basic Tactical Principles & Techniques......... 140
Maneuver Techniques................................... 145
Angles of Fire & Flanking.............................. 148
Tactical Terrain Terms................................... 149
Momentum... 153
Operational Tempo.. 155

Chapter Six: Casualties
Introduction..157
Tactical Combat Casualty Care (TC3).......... 160
Care Under Fire... 162

    Tactical Field Care………………………..………….. 163
    Casualty Movement……………………………………. 167

Chapter Seven: Post Event Vehicle Movement.
    Introduction…………………………………………..…...169
    General Movement Considerations…………………….171
    Vehicle Movement Basics……………………………… 178
    Specific Threats & TTPs………………………………….184
    Reaction to Contact Drills……………………………….190
    Actions on Halts………………………………………... 199

Chapter Eight: Dismounted Tactics
    Introduction……………………………………………….201
    The Squad………………………………….....…….. 204
    Satellite Patrolling……………………………………….206
    Communication & Movement……………………………. 210
    Squad Battle Drills & The Quick Attack…………..……. 213
    Casualties & Prisoners……………………………………227
    Grenades…………………………………………….. 228
    Bunker Drills…………………………………………….229
    Secondary Positions……………………………………...232

Chapter Nine: Defense
    Introduction……………………………………………….235
    The Principles of Defense………………………..………235
    Static (Point) Defense……………………………………248
    Mobile (Area) Defense………………………………….. 249
    Static/Mobile Combinations…………………………….250
    Defensive Operations in Built Up Areas (OBUA)…………. 250
    Entry Control Points (ECP)……………………………. 255
    Traffic Control Points…………………………………….258
    Key Point Defense Orders……………………………….262

Chapter Ten: Patrols
    Types of Patrol…………………………………………... 267
    Patrol Planning…………………………………………...268
    Patrol Execution………………………………………… 268
    Post Patrol Actions……………………………………… 276
    Patrol Equipment………………………………………...277

  'Actions on' 282
  Actions on Contact..285
  Offensive Drills... 285
  Break Contact Drills... 288
  Patrol Bases.. 292
  Infiltration... 300
  Patrol Orders.. 301

Chapter Eleven: Tactical Use of Vehicles.......................... 309

Chapter Twelve: Offensive Operations
  Introduction...315
  Principles of Offensive Operations......................317
  Advance to Contact/Hasty Attack....................... 318
  Deliberate Attack.. 323
  Fratricide..325
  Factors..326
  Cold Steel.. 329
  Raid..330
  Ambush..333
  Fighting in Woods and Forests (FIWAF) 343
  Offensive Operations in Built Up Areas..............345
  Squad Level OBUA.. 349
  Platoon Level OBUA.. 354
  Company Level OBUA.. 356

Chapter Thirteen: Withdrawal
  Introduction...359
  Withdrawal out of Contact................................... 359
  Withdrawal in Contact..360
  Exfiltration..361
  Vehicles...362
  Break Out.. 362

Chapter Fourteen: Conclusion.. 365

Disclaimers

This is an instructional manual on tactical techniques and procedures; the information contained in this work stems from extensive training and experience, including operations in combat theaters and areas that have experienced a societal collapse. The conduct of some of the techniques described in this book may entail risk to your personal safety; they are intended solely for extreme survival situations. When utilizing weapons or any of the activities described in this book, including vehicle and dismounted movement, utmost care must be taken and safety is paramount. Do not participate in any tactical maneuvers with weapons without receiving instruction on correct operation and safety procedures.

This manual explains techniques with weapons, explosives, vehicles and other tactical procedures that would not be morally, ethically or legally acceptable to conduct outside of a survival situation and/or a lethal threat to your life. The making or possession of some of the devices mentioned in this book, as well as the conduct of the tactics, techniques and procedures so described, are possibly illegal in some jurisdictions. Even possession may be construed as criminal intent. Consult you state and local laws. The content of this book is for informational purposes only and is intended to allow persons to prepare for a potential collapse of society and the absence of the rule of law. You are responsible for any training you conduct, and actions you may take, based off the information in this book. Safety and abiding by your state and local laws is paramount!

Nothing in this book constitutes legal advice. Consult an attorney or legal resource if you have any legal questions. The medical component of the book does not constitute medical advice. Consult a doctor or qualified medical person if you have medical questions. The tactics, techniques and procedures component is merely the opinion of the author. The author shall have neither liability nor responsibility to any citizen, person, or entity with respect to loss or damage caused, or alleged to be caused, directly or indirectly by the information contained in this manual.

INTRODUCTION

"Utrinque Paratus"
Ready for Anything

This manual is the result of a detailed consideration of a societal collapse and the civil shift and aftermath that would impact individuals and families who are intent on survival. The purpose of this manual is to provide information to enhance security, tactics and survival skills of law-abiding citizens who are faced with civil disorder, lawlessness, violence and physical threat in a post-collapse environment.

The information in this manual is derived from years of experience gained from service with special operations forces (SOF) followed by years of employment as a security contractor in hostile environments including Iraq and Afghanistan. It is a distillation of military and security training, principles, and tactics, techniques and procedures (TTPs) adapted to the threat and environment anticipated in this type of scenario in order to provide knowledge needed to train to survive in a world turned upside down. It is no longer just survival of the fittest but survival of those prepared.

The Anticipated Situation

This manual is primarily intended to be used by those who have given consideration to an event that has led to a societal collapse (or post-event) situation. These individuals, groups or families are commonly termed 'preppers' or 'survivalists'. Such people will have given consideration to the need to be prepared for situations where an 'event' has caused some form of disaster, or system collapse, which has led to a breakdown in society and the rule of law. This can be regional, country, continent or worldwide. Lawlessness, mobs, looters, gangs and starving desperate individuals, groups and families will be examples of the challenges to be faced.

This situation is commonly termed 'The End Of The World As We Know It' or TEOTWAWKI and WTSHTF (When the 'Schumer' Hits The Fan). Preppers will have taken steps to insure themselves against the breakdown in the system of law and the supply system, by stocking up on items such as food, water, weapons and ammunition and other survival goods and equipment. Such preparations vary on a sliding scale from simple short term disaster preparedness to living full time in a defendable 'retreat' in a remote location.

You do not need to be living in a fully stocked remote retreat to utilize this manual, but having the basic weapons and equipment will give you the gear to enable you to better carry out the techniques, thus improving your chances of survival. In fact, it may well be that most of the techniques described in this manual are more likely to be used by those who are not securely located in a remote fully stocked retreat, because you will have a greater need for them in order to survive. Therefore, this manual does not pretend to exclusivity among the prepper community: rather, in preference it would be read, assimilated and acted upon by a wider audience of law-abiding folk in order to provide a better defense against lawlessness and the inevitable starving horde post-collapse.

Responsible citizens should all be taking action to make sure that they have the basics available to survive at least a short term disaster, but the great majority will make no preparations at all. What they do not realize is that once the infrastructure starts to shut down, for whatever reason, they will not be able to live the convenient lives that they do right now.

As a whole, we have become a society dependent on the conveniences that technology has provided us. For the most part we have become a 'fast food society' driven by immediate gratification and less focused on the ability to provide for ourselves. When disaster strikes we are reminded about how woefully unprepared we really are.

As technology advances so too does our dependence on that technology. If it were to fail, so to would we. During the Great Depression people did not have the safety net of the Federal Government to bail them out of hard times therefore they were more self-reliant. We did not have unemployment, social security, Medicare, Medicaid, etc. and most people were able to grow some of their food. Today most people cannot even cook their own food much less grow it.

For instance, if the electricity grid were to fail, there would be a knock on effect across all services. Fuel would not get to gas stations, supply trucks would not get to supermarkets. Supermarkets and restaurants use a 'just in time' system whereby they do not have an extensive stock room. Once the shelves are bare after a short period of panic buying, that's it. Without grid power, services will not work. Communications will go down, especially the mobile phone system; once the relay stations run out of diesel for the usual site standby generator - that's it.

Historically, many public workers, including police and fire service, will go home to look after their own families in the wake of a disaster, thus exacerbating the problem. The government and public services will not be there to help people or bail them out. Fast food restaurants will not be able to serve food. The masses will not be able to find food or gas and they will soon get desperate.

Remember when you last had an unexpected power-cut; the odd realization that none of the 'stuff' in your house worked anymore? Did you go and break out the flashlights and then realize that, if this was the moment, if that was it and the power was not coming back on, how woefully prepared you would be?

You cannot rely on the government to bail you out in such a situation because the government will be overwhelmed and many of the workers will be looking to themselves. At least in the short to medium term you will have to look after yourself and whatever group you have prepared to survive with. The attitude of relying on others or emergency services is dangerous because you expect someone else to come to your aid rather than being self-sufficient and prepared to not be a burden. If help does come, then great; if it doesn't, or takes a long time, maybe even years, then be ready to survive in the meantime.

Importantly, this manual deals with topics of defense and violence. It does not advocate violence as a way of life, or advocate that post-event groups should make their way by the 'power of the gun'. Rather, it anticipates a situation where the lives, safety and freedom of your family or group are threatened and seeks to pass on knowledge to better prepare you to deal with, and survive, such situations.

The perspective is one of parents concerned for their kids and family, or friends concerned for their friends, or such combinations. The premise is that those utilizing this manual will be law abiding preppers who will take measures to be ready for a post-event situation should one occur. A large part of the tactical message is AVOIDANCE. The smaller part of the message is controlled use of VIOLENCE for the purpose of DEFENSE.

The hope is that preppers will conduct themselves with dignity and grace post-event in an attempt to continue, as best as possible under the circumstances, to provide a level of quality of life for their groups, families, and children. There should be space for forming alliances, building relationships between groups, charity, barter, cooperation, education and reconstruction. We are not talking Zombie Apocalypse, where everyone out there is the 'undead'! The people out there are fellow citizens; some will have become victims, others will be poorly prepared and desperate. In such situations, it is imperative to maintain the safety of the group, but if there is room for charity or to aid others, then do so.

Seek out the 'good', decent people who have survived the event. Be mindful that some of these people may simply be starving and desperate and afraid for their families and children. This can make them a threat to you, but given some precautions and charity they may also make great allies. Be welcoming of the decent people in society and be prepared to see the good in people across cultural, ethnic and religious boundaries.

There is no place now, and there is no place post-event, for bigotry and exclusion. It is the tribal racist type view that will increase violence and exclusion both in the ongoing collapse of society and after a specific event. There will be elements out there that are very dangerous. They will seek to survive by armed strength and taking from others by force. They may simply be amalgamated groups, but they may also be more organized around political, religious or racist agendas and motivated by exclusion and bigotry. Whatever the specific motivation, it is for those threats that this manual is written.

Remember, to a certain extent we will all become 'looters', or a better term 'foragers': If your health relies on a certain drug prescription, at some point you will need to get more. In a societal collapse, you may need to raid the pharmacy to get it, along with supplies of essential broad-spectrum antibiotics. Perhaps 'foraging' or 'scavenging' would be better words: when faced by starvation, most would agree that taking food is ok; similarly for other essential supplies.

When your kids grow out of their clothes and shoes, would it be ok to go to an abandoned children's store to pick up more, when no harm appears to be done? If such a store is actually occupied, or someone has opened a store stocking such items, then perhaps it would be ok to barter for such goods? However, this does not advocate the attacking of other groups in order to take or loot supplies; it is against this kind of threat that the book will prepare you.

Why?

The reason why this manual was written is therefore to prepare citizens with the tactical knowledge that they will need to survive a post-event situation where lawlessness has broken out and where they may find themselves facing a physical threat with only their own resources available to protect them.

There are many books and resources available that educate and describe in great detail the various aspects of prepping. These are detailed and involve topics that are beyond the scope of this book. The scope of this book is concerned with security, tactics and the ability to utilize controlled violence as necessary for the defense of you, your loved ones and your group.

Thus this book will not advocate the rights and wrongs of your prepper philosophy; the rural retreat (or castle) approach versus staying in your house in the suburbs, or going mobile and camping or in an RV or whatever other situation you may plan for or find yourself in come the day. You may in fact have an ideal prepper philosophy but be unable to attain it, such as not yet being in possession of a fully stocked retreat.

Thus, this book deals with the realities of the situations in which you may find yourself, the decisions that you may have to make, and the tactics, techniques and procedures that you will need to train and prepare for. The techniques described in this book are also not just relevant for the initial event or the immediate days that follow; they can be trained and utilized for multiple situations that your group may find itself in as time goes on. It is also not the purpose of this book to re-hash military publications which are freely available, such as the Ranger Handbook.

About the Author

The author is a British born U.S. Citizen with extensive military experience. He has served in both the British and US Armies. He served with British Special Operations Forces, mainly with the Parachute Regiment which is Britain's elite quick reaction force and which also provides support to the UK Tier 1 Special Forces, the Special Air Service.

The author served on six operational deployments, including to Afghanistan immediately post-9/11, and also a tour training and selecting recruits for the Regiment. In explaining what the Parachute Regiment is, it is easiest to compare it in role to the 75th Ranger Regiment, although it is of course its own unique and elite force. The author passed both

Parachute Regiment selection and also UK Special Forces Aptitude Selection during his career. He retired from the British Army in 2003.

Following retirement, the author spent five years serving as a security contractor in both Iraq and Afghanistan. This included working on contract for the US Government in Iraq, a year of which was based out of Fallujah, the rest variously based out of Baghdad and country-wide, and also two years working for the British Government in Helmand Province and Kabul, Afghanistan. These roles were operational security roles that included exposure to multiple different training methods and operational schools of thought, as well as both high profile and low profile mobile operations across Iraq and Afghanistan. The author then joined the U.S. Army and trained as a Combat Medic and Civil Affairs Specialist, he is a U.S. Citizen and lives in the United States.

The author is a family man with a strong interest in prepping. This comes from a desire to prepare for the worst while living to the best in our current society. This book springs from the author's ruminations on the need to keep his own family safe and survive any coming apocalyptic event, and a desire to share this knowledge with other law abiding folk. The intent is not at all to train you as a special ops team; much of the manual is written with the presence of young kids in mind. However, as the manual progresses it will give you the skills to train and operate a tactical team that will be able to conduct necessary operations beyond the family sphere.

The author can be contacted at: info@maxvelocitytactical.com or via www.maxvelocitytactical.com. Blog: maxvelocitytactical.blogspot.com

CHAPTER ONE

STARTING POINTS

The Threat

For the purposes of this manual the threat is considered to be hostile individuals or groups who are intent on endangering the safety of you and your group/team/family. They are doing this because we are in a post-event situation, lawlessness has broken out and supplies are limited. Their purpose will be to take from you, by force, whatever it is that they want: whether it is food, fuel, water, vehicles, equipment, weapons, your children or your spouse or partner.

The fact that you may be identified as a prepper makes you a target, because you are able to remain healthy and well fed and you have supplies that others will want to get hold of. The purpose of this manual is not to discuss in detail what may have led us to this situation, but by form of introduction let us consider some situations that may form 'The Event' and that may have led to a situation of post-societal collapse. Some of these will feed, relate to, or be caused by the others.

The list is not intended to be exhaustive:

- Economic decline/collapse: resulting in a collapse in currency and the economy.
- Environmental collapse: resulting in shortages of resources.
- EMP attack or Solar EMP: this could have a widespread destructive effect on the power grid, causing the knock on effect alluded to above.
- War or terrorist attack
- Natural Disaster: i.e. storm, earthquake, flood, volcano or combination of these events.

- Cyber-Attack: a very real threat which can be 'weaponized' in the form of physical results against infrastructure and notably including the power grid. A threat from national or non-national actors.
- Chemical, Biological, Radiological or Nuclear attack.
- Failure of the political system; widespread civil disorder and rioting.
- Viral outbreak or disease.
- Slow slide societal collapse brought about by increasing use of violence by the video game generations, lacking family and societal structure.
- Zombie Apocalypse: yes, of course this has to be included! Joking aside, of course we all love zombie shows, but is it really a metaphor for those starving unprepared masses trying to break through your front door, allowing us to disassociate ourselves mentally from the requirement to use lethal force against our fellow citizens?

The specific threats that this may result in that are the purview of this manual are:

- Assault, with or without a deadly weapon.
- Mob violence or civil disorder.
- Home invasion or assault onto your group's base or retreat.
- Illegal Traffic Checkpoints (ITCPs) or roadblocks.
- Ambush.
- Raid by hostile forces.
- Hostile use of firearms.

The types of weapons that may be used against you are whatever is available for sale in the US today or in the past. This may include military weapons taken by looters or deserting military personnel. However, for the purposes of this document the main threat we will be concerned with is the use of standard firearms against your group by hostile elements, up to and including automatic assault rifles, machine guns and sniper rifles.

Some types of weapons to be considered:

- Knives
- Sticks/clubs/bats
- Handguns
- Rifles
- Assault rifles
- Automatic weapons and machine guns
- Vehicles: ramming and with weapons mounted
- Explosives & Improvised Explosive Devices (IEDs)
- Military 'liberated' gear examples:
    - Grenades
    - Grenade launchers
    - Heavy machine guns
    - Anti-tank rockets
    - Mortars
    - Armored Vehicles

You should not just consider the situation at the time of the collapse but also give thought to how things will develop as time goes on. If there is a total collapse then people will get desperate very quickly. It may be that the government is still functioning to some degree and there may still be troops under command trying to restore order under martial law. Criminal gangs may coalesce to loot for supplies and exploit the lawlessness of the situation.

Groups will form for defense, such as around towns or neighborhoods, and they will likely be very suspicious of 'outsiders'. Your better defense will be in numbers, preferably selected, trained and of sufficient size and ability to be able to defend against raids by armed and motivated enemy groups.

It is likely that most people will be averse to the dangers of physical injury in a post collapse scenario, but that may be a simplistic view; you can't assume that a raid will not progress onto your property or location simply because you are armed. People will be desperate, and if they feel confident with their group, perhaps buoyed by other successful raids, they will be emboldened. They may already be committed to an attack before they realize that your defense is effectively putting some of their number down. It depends on the exact circumstances if they are already too committed to go back by then.

It is also true that a group of amoral looters may well have become a raiding band and, in a similar way to a criminal band or drug cartel, they may be very well organized as a group. This situation will result in relationship, group and leadership dynamics that will make it hard for them to:

1) Not seek to exact retribution from a prepper location that has mauled the gang and

2) Create a 'group think' and unwillingness of individuals to countermand orders (along with machismo) that may allow an attack to be pressed despite the theory that personal survival should be their paramount consideration.

Thus, some groups have dynamics that override our feeling that it would be 'suicidal' or 'crazy' to keep pushing forward under such circumstances. You would not do it, but don't discount the possibility that others will.

By all means, you have to be able to defend your home or location, which will include your family and friends. But before you decide to make a stand you have to consider if making a stand at that location, and with the resources that you have, is going to be effective against the threat you face. If you feel in any way that your location is not defendable against the threat, then you need to bug out. You need to have a plan to be able to withdraw or escape.

It may be that you decide to stay, but then perhaps a new threat from strong well-armed looter gangs emerges; you will be better served by leaving. Any defended location needs an escape route, but one of the most difficult maneuvers is to withdraw while in contact with the enemy. Getting out and breaking contact may be hard, may leave you without vehicles, equipment and means of transport. Imagine trying to do this while surrounded and under fire, with your children?

The alternative, staying in an Alamo kind of situation, could be fatal for your family. Historically, any city that defended itself against siege was raised to the ground when finally taken by assault. The people were raped, killed and taken into slavery. What you do will all come down to judgment and assessing the situation and threat. Don't become tied to a location if you feel that staying there will become untenable. Make a decision early and make a planned withdrawal with all your gear and vehicles. You may not be able to take it all, but don't be tied to a location simply because your painstakingly acquired stash is there.

Even if you prepare to stay, have extraction plans and routes ready in case you have to go; try and assess and make the decision early so that you can get away in safety with as much of your survival gear as possible. You may not have a retreat, and you may decide to initially stay in your home and assess the severity of the event. If you do, have a bug out plan ready, with locations to go to (even if it's a remote wood to camp and hide in) and routes to get there. Make a load carrying plan involving the ability to load gear onto vehicles with roof racks and trailers so you can get out with your supplies.

No-one really knows how the situation will develop post-event: a lot will depend on the type and severity of the event. We can know that it is a good thing to be trained and prepared. We can also know that it will be important to be self-sustaining and self-reliant so that your group can fend for itself and not become victims or refugees. Although we can expect that post-event both federal and local aid and response will be insufficient, don't expect that an event will suddenly 'wipe the slate clean' and suddenly we are in a total 'post-government' environment.

Yes, we will have to provide for ourselves and we will be up against huge dangers from looters and desperate people, of both the organized and disorganized types. But don't expect federal and state government to simply go away. Uncle Sam doesn't give up that easily. Whatever is left after the event, expect efforts to regain control, return law and order, and bring aid and disaster assistance in whatever way is feasible. Consider the possibilities of martial law, federal and state disaster relief and aid; also consider the possibility of international aid and perhaps international assistance.

Also, if Uncle Sam is mortally wounded, consider other nations taking advantage of that and bringing more than aid, perhaps even 'peacekeeping or stabilization aid' which could be an invasion masked as assistance. Don't become a freedom fighter/insurgent at the expense of your family. Don't shoot at those Chinese troops from your house! Don't involve your family in the fight, if you choose to fight. Establish a safe, protected, location for your family and then take off with your band and fight the invaders, if you so choose.

There is an element to the prepper mentality where, after all the expense and preparations, you can almost hope that something would happen so you can go ahead and implement it all – get to your retreat and survive etc. Some of this may come from a desire for change for changes sake, or the tiredness with the 'rat-race' of modern living and a desire for the freedom of some kind of apocalyptic situation. How cool would it be if we really had a Zombie Apocalypse?

But think about it: if it really all did go away, and we were back to the middle-ages with guns, would that really be that cool? There is another disturbing side to this that will need to be paid particular attention post-event: 'militia' groups. Many preppers get together and plan to defend a location, and we can expect that small towns will form some sort of militia or defense force. But there is a danger of extremism and fanaticism and in fact there are, today in America, many groups that are styled as militia but which are in fact extremist groups with political agendas.

A Militia at its basic level is a historical part of American history and tied in closely with the right to bear arms in defense of Citizen Liberty. Some 'militia' activity is politically motivated by extremism and it would definitely not be cool to encounter such a group post-event and not be someone included in their view of 'the right sort of people'. Be aware of this. Some of these groups are anti-federal government and would actively welcome a collapse; they would most likely try to establish a sphere of influence around their area.

While the efforts of genuine Militia and defense groups to establish a security zone are admirable, what is not acceptable would be an agenda that discriminates against groups within society. It may also be possible that, emboldened by collapse, such groups will become insurgents against federal government and fight efforts by such to get the country back on its feet.

Although many preppers have opinions on topics such as the size of government and State versus Federal powers and rights, the 'Feds' are not ultimately the bad guys. At least, they are not supposed to be. Yes, we worry some about sinister thoughts concerning martial law, seizure of our supplies post-event, and increasingly restrictive gun laws. These things are to be worried about. But remember, a government reflects its society, in the same way that an army reflects its society – many people don't get the gun thing, in the same way that they don't get prepping.

To harp on a little about the Federal Government and post event thing, consider that if you are a Patriot, then your loyalty is to the United States of America and the Constitution. That is the federal government, so long as it remains true to the Constitution, rule of law and liberty of the Citizens: unless you are an anarchist or extremist and are simply all about your own 'freedom'.

When you watch zombie movies, the general assumption is that there will be no more authority and the characters are operating in an apocalyptic scenario. Consider that it will not likely be so cut and dried. The television series Jericho (you can find it on Netflix) is an excellent show, very well informed, and thus not so surprisingly it disappeared after a rushed finale mid-season two. It is a testament to the state of modern America that it is easy to believe in a conspiracy to remove this TV show because it got 'too close to the truth'.

It is easy to wonder about our liberty in today's political climate. James Wesley, Rawles' excellent book 'Patriots' also touched on some of these issues of a more complicated situation post event. Some of the themes touched on by these two media:

- Serious collapse events affecting the whole of the country.
- Community defense and warfare between communities based on scarce resources.
- Continuing existence or emergence of a form of centralized government.
- Peacekeeping/occupation forces.
- Federal troops operating on home ground.
- Legitimacy of government issues: divergence from the constitution and the values of the United States of America.
- Troops/agencies/companies taking control in a 'fascist' like way.
- Martial Law.
- Creation of insurgents, in a very close to the mark observation of how insurgents are created by occupying forces: Jericho deputy sheriff: "Either we start shooting or they will take our houses." Also: "This is not a country, it's a company."

These media contain a lot of food for thought for preppers envisaging a post-event situation.

A Little More on Threat

This manual is not primarily designed to be used to train hostile environment security operators, SOF or the military for deployment. The author has written 'Rapid Fire!: Tactics for High Threat, Protection and Combat Operations' for that purpose. One of the problems with a document written by a military person is that it may not be targeted at the right audience; you don't need to know how to do 'underwater knife fighting' and the intention is to ensure that this manual keeps the subject matter relevant.

The reason for this following section is to outline the kind of threats faced in combat theaters like Iraq and Afghanistan simply to make you aware of them, in case similar threats emerge in the Continental United States as a result of a long term collapse situation.

Improvised Explosive Devices (IEDs) are not covered extensively in this manual, but there is definitely the capability to make them in the US and it may well be that this kind of threat emerges in a post event scenario.

Therefore, to introduce this topic, let us look at some of the main threats that may be faced in an insurgent type hostile environment. The threat outlined is generalized to asymmetric warfare and taken from the historical threat on OIF/OEF in Iraq and Afghanistan. The following is an account of general threats:

- Improvised Explosive Device (IED). IEDs come in various sizes and the effectiveness of an IED depends on large part as a function of size and placement, as well as accurate targeting. IEDs can be connected in a 'daisy chain' and usually placed to match the anticipated spacing of vehicles in convoys, to cause maximum damage. IEDs can be initiated in a number of ways:

    o Command Wire (CWIED). A physical connection between the initiation point (Firing point (FP)) and the CWIED itself (Contact Point)); the need for this connection can aid in detection of the device and the FP.

- o Remote Control (RCIED). The RCIED is detonated remotely using any one of multiple options. It can be anything from a cell phone to a garage door opener. This increases the enemy's options for placement and FP, without the need to be physically connected to the device. This can make it harder to detect the device.

- Vehicle Borne Improvised Explosive Device (VBIED). Simply put, the IED is inside the vehicle. This type of IED will usually be remotely detonated, or can be on a timer (exception: see SVBIED, below). The VBIED allows for mobility and placement of large IEDs. However, they can be detected: a simple example can be a car that is packed with Home Made Explosives (HME) and therefore the suspension is weighed down, making the vehicle suspicious as it sits parked at its placement point.

- Off-Route Mine or Explosively Formed Penetrator (EFP): A targeted IED capable of defeating armor:

  - o The EFP is very effective and can defeat many types of armor. The EFP is effectively an 'off route mine', using the 'Miznay-Chardin' effect to create a molten slug or spray of metal that will pierce armor, causing damaging effects inside the vehicle as it passes through. The Miznay-Chardin effect places explosives behind a metal cone or dish: on detonation, the cone inverts and forms into a slug of metal. This is a similar effect to that used by a standard RPG (the 'Monroe Effect'), with the exception that an RPG detonates on contact with a vehicle, whereas the EFP goes off several feet away by the side of the road. Whereas an RPG can have its lethal effect dissipated by the use of a mesh cage around vehicle and bunkers, to disrupt the molten jet effect of its warhead, the EFP is harder to defeat and will penetrate through armored vehicles, although it will be disrupted as it passes through parts of an armored vehicle.. It is not usually defeated by the use of a cage; an RPG is a contact warhead whereas the EFP is a standoff penetrator.

- o The effect of an EFP can be devastating but usually limited in scope. An EFP will pass through armor, and there have been multiple circumstances of EFPs causing traumatic lower limb amputation of personnel in the driver and front passenger seats of vehicles, but personnel in other compartments being left unscathed.

- o EFPs have historically been initiated with the use of an Infra-Red (IR) beam that crosses the road; effectively a tripwire. When the vehicle breaks the beam the EFP detonates. The impact point on the vehicle depends on the aspect the EFP is placed at and also the distance between the IR trigger and the device itself. How the insurgent sets this up will determine placement on the vehicle. Multiple EFPs can be tied to one IR trigger to hit one vehicle in numerous places, or be spaced in the hope of the 'daisy chain' hitting multiple vehicles in convoy. The EFP has to be armed - i.e. the IR trigger switched on – otherwise the device would initiate on the next vehicle along the route, which may be a civilian vehicle or otherwise not the target. Thus, the EFP is armed remotely, turning on the IR trigger. This also has the advantage of allowing arming while outside of any ECM 'bubble' that would defeat the remote arming device. This makes the EFP to an extent a remote controlled device, but also a Victim Operated (VOIED) device. There are ways of mitigating risk: see Mitigation, below.

- Victim Operated Improvised Explosive Device (VOIED). This type of IED is detonated by the actions of the victim. In order to be effective the IED will usually target a location that is known to be used by coalition forces (see vulnerable points, below). VOIEDs can be anti-personnel or anti-vehicle. The type of location targeted would usually be somewhere that locals could avoid, but that forms a channel for military personnel or vehicles. These devices, or the corresponding safe routes, may also be marked, often in unusual ways, similar to the way that mines are often marked in the Balkans i.e. piles of rocks, sticks, cloth tied to markers etc.

- Sniper. More likely to be a 'sharpshooter' rather than a trained sniper; defined by accurate rifle fire.

- Small Arms Fire (SAF).

- Rocket Propelled Grenade (RPG).

- Complex Attack/Ambush. An attack utilizing any or all of the individual threats listed.

- Close Quarter Assassination (CQA). May be planned or opportunistic; a threat at leader engagements or while otherwise interacting with local population.

- Kidnap/Capture. As per CQA; Isolated Personnel (IP) at risk of capture or a deliberate kidnap attempt. A concern if personnel are isolated following contact.

- Indirect Fire (IDF) – Rocket: 107/120mm rocket attack. Not a key threat in the scope of this document, more concerned with FOB/static location security, but could be employed by insurgents.

- Indirect Fire (IDF) – Mortar or artillery. As per rocket, may also be utilized as part of a complex attack. Accuracy varies widely. Personnel noticing that they are being 'bracketed' by IDF should be concerned that an observer is targeting them with accurate, observed and corrected IDF.

- Suicide Vehicle Borne IED (SVBIED). The employment of Rules of Engagement (ROE) & Escalation of Force (EOF) measures is necessary in order to mitigate this threat. We hope that we do not face this kind of threat post-event in the Continental United States.

- Suicide Bomber. A particular threat to dismounted personnel; additionally, the use of screening procedures is required at any type of organized meeting. Again, we hope that we do not face this kind of threat post-event in the Continental United States.

- In addition to this, and last but not least, is the generalized threat from attacks against protected locations from vehicle mounted and dismounted personnel determined to assault and overrun that location, for whatever spectrum of motives.

The Mission

The mission is to become tactically proficient and prepared in order to best ensure the safety and survivability of your group, team or family in a post-event scenario.

Intent: Defend to survive and thrive.

Purpose: Add tactical skills to a preppers skill-set so that in a worst case scenario of a physical attack the group or family will be able to deal with it, survive and continue to concentrate on building a quality of life post-event; to not have to live in fear of violent or predatory elements.

Family/Group/Team

The premise of this manual is that your group will be based around your family or small group of preppers. This will include persons of all ages (babies, kids, teens and the elderly), physical ability, training and perhaps physical disability and illness. This is not a manual for 'Delta Force'; this is what makes consideration of the situation inherently terrifying. We have to protect the weaker and more vulnerable members of our group and it may come to a situation where hostile fire is coming down onto your group and your kids. Shocking and terrifying. Therefore, we must do all we can to mitigate the threat.

This can be achieved by training, preparation, situational awareness, experience and above all AVOIDANCE. It is very important that those in the group that are physically capable do all they can to increase their ability to protect the weaker members. This means getting physically fit and strong, training in weapons and tactics, and being ready and maintaining that state of readiness.

Sexism has no place here: male and female alike need to be trained and ready. It may be that in some group individual's fall into common gender roles, and this is fine: a mother will be primarily concerned for the supervision and protection of the kids. The father will be as well, but he may be operating as the outer protection while the mother stays in close with the kids, but she must be able to defend them like a lioness if they are threatened; not only having the intent and will to do so, but having the capability to effectively do so as well.

As you progress through this manual, you will note that it moves on from a specific discussion about family or small groups with children and the elderly in tow, to more complex skills and techniques. Therein is a problem in making the connection between the 'husband/wife/family defense and survival scenario' and the well-developed tactics and procedures that we then progress to.

These more advanced tactics imply a well-trained, disciplined, fit, motivated and equipped team. This is certainly a possibility but either implies the ability to train in advance or to conduct training post-event, which may or may not be possible depending on the situation. There is definitely an advantage in numbers, by which is meant numbers of suitable candidates rather than simple 'mob' numbers. Therein lays another problem: getting buy in from suitable neighbors and suburban/town folk who perhaps have no idea or desire to consider the implications of an event.

So, best safety practice for your family implies getting with other families and personnel, a suitable number of people that would allow you to develop a tactical team that goes above and beyond simple protection of your family. You may or may not be able to achieve that, hence the two levels described in this book, the one being simple tactical defense for a small unit such as family group, the other being more advanced techniques when you can create a tactical group that can operate above and beyond the necessity for close protection of the group.

To conjecture for a moment on post-event scenarios, it's a big problem, a central problem. If a mob of 50-100-200 rampaging crazies turn up with 'heavy weapons' in 'technicals' they are just going to roll-up any number of brave but isolated families. In the summer of 2011 there was a mob on the loose in London, United Kingdom. Politicians called for the British Army to be called out, but there are not enough Army Reserves in the UK to defend any serious area against large numbers of extremist groups. How would the National Guard do in the USA?

It is most desirable and effective to have a community response; at least in the US there is the ability to have weapons, unlike in the UK where the population is defenseless and reliant on the military.

We often talk about a collapse taking us back to the middle or dark ages: In another post collapse situation, that of Britain once the Romans withdrew and took law and order with them, Alfred the Great saw this as the Vikings rampaged and ravaged ancient Britain; reducing it to a devastated wilderness. He made people build fortified towns, burghs, and he made them live in them. He ordered that the population provide an armed man for each five yards of the town wall. The Saxons were able to conquer Britain and then, later, survive the Vikings because they had a martial tradition based on the family, the extended family, the 'hundred' etc. War bands could be quickly assembled for attack or defense.

It is true that there are a huge amount of firearms in America. There are a lot of people who shoot and hunt, and those that have weapons for security and self-defense. That is not even to mention those that have them from criminal purposes. Because the bad guys have guns, it is necessary for the good guys to have them also, which is why any attempt to take away or diminish the right to bear arms will only hurt the law-abiding good guys; the genie of weapons proliferation is out of the bag and will not be stuffed back in.

There is also a strong tradition of bearing arms in America for the defense of citizen liberty, and when the government is unable to protect its citizens in a post-event scenario it is essential that those citizens are armed and equipped to do so themselves. Without getting into a spin off discussion about weapons ownership, second amendment rights, Federal and State government, the point being headed to is essentially that there is a lot of weapon ownership but not necessarily tactical ability.

Think of the hunter stereotype that has weapons and can sit in a hide or shoot from a truck, but is hugely overweight and unfit, unable to maneuver his body tactically? How about the homeowner who owns guns and desires to protect his family but has no real practice or training beyond a few rounds fired at his local indoor range?

The destruction of society and our youth through social breakdown, violent media and video games has conditioned society to a higher threshold of violence; we live in a violent society where role models and exposure to media has lowered the threshold of the willingness to act violently. This includes our law enforcement, both as a result of the increased threat they face but also the same exposure to media portraying justification of violence from pseudo law-enforcement role models.

The tradition of the Militia and citizen soldiers, now more institutionalized in the form of the National Guard but also among local militias, many of which are well intentioned with others that have political and extremist motives, is something that has value if such forces can be trained among law-abiding citizens and become the basis for civil defense groups post-event. If the National Guard isn't going to cut it in a crisis, then perhaps we need to consider supplementary forces.

To use Britain as an example again: Lord Roberts VC (of Kandahar fame), dissatisfied with Britain's defenses, set up the National Rifle Association (NRA) to teach citizens to shoot. Baden Powell having seen the lamentable state of Britain's city-bred citizen Army's fieldcraft in South Africa set up the Scout movement. In the 1950s virtually every man in Britain was 'trained' and could use arms. Even school cadets were proficient on the .303 rifle and the Bren Gun. Now hardly any adult male has handled a weapon; it is amazing how alarmed civilians get when they see a gun.

In contrast, the US public is 'gun toting' by comparison, although there are a huge amount of people out there who are alarmed by weapons in the same way as in the UK. Given the threat of weapons in the hands of the bad guys, they need to 'get over it' and get trained and equipped if they expect to be able to survive the assault of these same bad guys post-event.

It is very important to stay on the right side of the law; there is definitely a scope for small groups and Militia (being careful with that name due to some of the negative connotations associated with it nowadays) or alternatively civil and neighborhood defense groups, to be trained, equipped and ready for small team tactics. It can even be very fun and satisfying to conduct pre-event valuable and demanding training, promoting bonding and teamwork. Perhaps even to conduct fundamental 'Phase 1' training for groups of like-minded friends, from local streets and neighborhoods?

Think of these two images: The sad columns of tractors and trailers in the Former Yugoslavia; the man driving the tractor, the family in the trailer: Road block, the men taken away and shot. Then, fast forward to Libya and the utterly hopeless tactical standard of the militias. An interesting scenario in that NATO air power stopped the use of tanks, artillery and heavy weapons by government forces and the rebels were able to take out the rifle men and RPG men with longer-range 57mm AA cannon mounted on 'technicals', negating their tactical incompetence. Sad to say, as will become apparent later in this book, it's virtually impossible to defend a house by yourself against any sort of number of determined adversaries equipped with assault weapons.

Mental Preparation & Use of Force

A post-event situation is a survival situation. It is important to maintain a positive mental attitude and the will to survive and win. Post-event, there will be a huge dislocation of expectations and people will have to adapt to the new reality. Be open to that reality and don't remain in denial.

Decisions will have to be made and they may be hard ones, such as to stay at home or to go somewhere else. Specific to this manual, you have to be ready to fight and to use lethal force if necessary. In a post event situation there is not the luxury of fanciful moral dilemmas; you are effectively in a self-defense situation and when presented by a threat of force or lethal force you must act proportionately to stop the threat, in order to protect yourself, your family and resources. There is no room for hesitation.

For those who have never before been in a combat situation, you must mentally prepare yourself to be in combat. Reactions to combat situations will vary: we can exhibit the fight, freeze or flight responses. Denial is a problem; the dislocation of expectations leaves the individual in a denial of the true situation and they are reluctant to act in a way that may have been alien to them pre-event. The law and rules of society can also act in a negative way: self-defense in a lawful society is fraught with legal dangers, and therefore in a pre-event society the law can create an inherent hesitation because the person does not want to risk committing an illegal act. Fear of legal situations can be a problem. All this could hang over post-event. A good way to visualize a use of force would be by the following self-defense principles:

- The force used must be reasonable under the circumstances.
- The force used must be proportional to the threat.
- Use force to stop the threat, but no further.

A response using these principles to a violent threat including that of lethal force would be legally justifiable pre-event and during the down-slide when some law & order remains.

Research and consider the law in your state in terms of the castle doctrine and whether or not there is a stand your ground law. These are all relevant pre-event and will also help justify your actions post-event should there be an ultimate legal reckoning after a return to normality. However, consider alongside those principles that post-event your immediate concern is the survival of your group and there is no real time to consider the legal niceties.

Be prepared to act appropriately in response to violence and take a course of action to STOP THE THREAT. Such an action would be justifiable, given that you can't risk waiting and perhaps sustaining casualties and fatalities within your group. Don't hesitate to 'make sure it really is a lethal threat'; there will likely be no law enforcement coming round after the incident to decide whether you committed a crime or not: the important thing is to ensure the safety of yourself and your group, don't take a risk with risk!

When you go beyond stopping that threat, into vindictiveness and revenge, then you are overstepping the 'reasonable man' approach i.e. what would a reasonable man do under such a circumstance? Of course, to quip about it, what would a reasonable man/woman do in a post-event societal collapse? Get armed and prepared to defend his/her family!

There is another legal issue here; that of 'brandishing'. Brandishing your weapon is not allowed under most jurisdictions. What this means for a concealed carry permit holder is that the weapon must remain concealed at all times unless it has to come out and be used in response to a lethal threat. You can't take out your weapon to 'keep the peace' in response to what you perceive may be ramping up to a lethal threat. You would be brandishing, and brandishing is a crime.

You can legally carry your loaded weapons openly in certain places, such as your property and place of work if allowed by your employer and if you are legally allowed to carry. Generally, to legally carry a loaded weapon outside of these places it has to be carried as a concealed weapon with a CCW permit. Some places will allow you to carry a handgun unloaded, as 'open carry', which is not brandishing. Brandishing is getting the weapon out in such a way that (this is not a legal definition!) someone can feel threatened by it.

So, research the law and permits in your home state. The point of this is that not only do you have to be careful and research the law pre-event, but the flip-side is that post-event we will likely be a lot less concerned about these issues and we may be carrying handguns, shotguns and assault rifles openly. Such an act is in itself a deterrent and can be useful: you will not appear to be a soft target. Thus, brandishing under these circumstances can be useful as part of an escalation of force continuum.

Escalation of force is where you ramp up your actions as a response to a perceived threat. So long as you perceive it and feel threatened, you can escalate your response all the way up to the use of lethal force to stop a lethal threat. Escalation of force is not the same as rules of engagement; because we are not military i.e. we have not been deployed to engage in combat with the foreign enemies of the nation.

Rather, we are acting in self-defense (including defense of others: our family/team) and as such we have the right to ramp up our response as a reaction to perceived aggression. Escalation of force is often described (U.S. Army) as 'shout, show, shove, shoot' (4 S's) where you:

- Shout a warning
- Show your weapon
- Use non-lethal; physical force
- Shoot: lethal force.

However, shove comes a little bit too far up the scale and it would be better to have distance, so better would be shout (verbal warning), shove (non-lethal force to create stand-off), show (draw or raise weapons to show capability to use lethal force) and shoot (use lethal force).

When driving in vehicles, Iraq is a good example: escalation of force would take the form of visible signs on the vehicles, then signals such as visible flags, and then the firing of pen-flares (mini-flares) followed by shots into the engine block and then the cab of the vehicle.

The escalation of force measures were specifically designed to maintain stand-off (100 meters) between convoys and civilian vehicles due to the threat from suicide vehicle borne improvised explosive devices (SVBIED). The 4 S's was more suited to dismounted operations.

Whichever escalation you used, it is important to note that depending on the speed of the threat coming at you, you can skip steps and immediately ramp up to lethal force if the situation warrants it. So, what this really all says is that you should be able to escalate your response through a series of warnings towards the use of force or lethal force in order to stop the threat, and the level to which you will take this will depend on the nature of the perceived threat that develops.

Hesitation and denial can be a big problem in a combat situation. There are recorded statistics of large numbers of soldiers in combat either not firing their weapons or firing them in the general direction of, but not specifically at, the enemy. People don't want to kill. If you are a family unit and you are getting attacked, you have to kill or be killed. You have to run this over in your mind, and visualize it.

Realistic training builds muscle memory and will help you do the right thing when the SHTF. A combat situation is traumatic and creates the fight, freeze or flight response. It creates fear; adrenalin and other chemicals will course through your body in response. What this does is make you lose your fine motor skills and give you tunnel vision. Training will help you act, and act in the right way: shoot, move and communicate.

Your memory will play tricks and you probably won't have a clear memory of what happened afterwards. You may also feel guilt, because in retrospect you realize that tunnel vision meant you did not see A, while you concentrated on B, while therefore C happened. Or maybe you could not get the tourniquet tightened around D's leg, or get the stalled car started, because you had lost your fine motor skills. But you are under a great deal of stress and you have to do the best you can under the circumstances. Train and visualize as much as you can to create the muscle and mental memory to help you do the right thing and not freeze.

Try and train yourself in situations where you are creating muscle memory and the right response to a threat. You should be taking some action. It is one thing, for example, to witness and be a spectator to a fight outside of a bar, but when that guy gets in front of you, and his attention and aggression is focused on you, it is a different matter. What if you are a female confronted by an aggressive male?

What can happen is the freeze response, the paralyzing result of the fear that is your body's emotional response to the situation. You also can't hide in denial – it is definitely happening and that guy is really in your face and threatening bodily harm. Try and train and visualize so you will respond in the right way to a threat situation; make fear your friend.

A brave person is not one who is absent fear, but one who can continue, and act in the right way, while feeling the fear and controlling and overcoming it. There is also a certain refuge in action; thinking about and dwelling on possible threats beforehand can increase fearfulness unless you are doing it, as per this manual, in order to better prepare.

Initially freezing when confronted is a problem, but once you start taking action the fear should slip into the background and you can concentrate on doing the right thing. Training and muscle memory can help with this; otherwise, how to know what is the right thing to do when a threat confronts you? If you have trained and mentally and physically prepared, you will have a set of drills and responses and so long as you can get past the hesitation stage and get into doing it, you will respond in the right way.

Now, all of this does not advocate fighting or getting into trouble situations. Post-event medical care will be limited and anything that puts you at risk of death, wounding or disability will significantly negatively impact you, and your family who relies on you, chances of survival. The overriding principle when in a threat environment is AVOIDANCE. Mitigate the threat.

This does not necessarily mean run at all times, if this means, for instance, abandoning essential shelter or supplies, but mitigate and avoid threat as much as possible. When the time comes to stand your ground, be prepared and do the right thing to stop the threat. Be prepared for the worst and hope for the best. AVOID trouble. Run away from a fight if you can. Hit the assailant hard and then run away if possible. You need to develop an attitude of controlled aggression.

The good news is that violence can often solve a problem. However, you can't go around like a crazy person all the time. Develop within you the capacity for aggression; you should be able to bring this out when required. Controlled aggression is closely related to the will to win and determination; it doesn't necessarily mean 'going crazy' but that may be occasionally useful. Think of it as a slow burning anger and determination to triumph against the odds.

False motivation and all that 'hooaah' stuff is really a bit silly; you can't get all hyped up like you might before a game. False motivation and hooting and hollering will not get you far. You don't know when or where you will experience enemy contact. Yes, it may be more obvious if you have pre-sighted the enemy, and you can think about mental preparation in the lead up to initiating contact. But what if you are on a long tiring convoy move, perhaps a group of a few families heading out to a safer location? What about after hours of being wet cold and hungry? What if suddenly something happens and you have to react?

This is where the inner strength becomes apparent, the determination and will to win; turning it on. Getting together around the vehicles for a good old butt slapping pre-game hoot won't do you any good eight mind-numbing hours on the road later. The quiet determined professional approach is far more effective.

For both unarmed self-defense type training and weapons training you should work at drills which are simple and concentrate on action and the right kind of action when fear is all you know at that moment. Concentrate on the correct initial reaction and then the action that follows will get you over the potential for paralyzing fear and you will fall into the drills that you have trained, until it comes time to be able to think again and make the next plan or exit strategy.

For unarmed self-defense, it's not necessary to become a black belt at some martial art. Rather, train at something that is designed for practical self-defense and concentrate not so much on specific moves, but rather on reaction and response. Often some methods of training will have drills that teach this kind of instinctive response. The purpose of this is to allow you, when beset by the fear response, to instinctively take the right action.

An example would be learning Filipino Kali or similar. This is used as an example because it allows you to train in defense against attack with stick, knife and empty hand. Now, what is important about this, or what to take away, is not for example those super-sexy moves that you learned the other night to defend against such and such angle knife attack. You forgot those already. The purpose is not to turn you into a snake-fast knife fighter! No, the important thing is that it teaches you muscle memory and an instinctive reaction. So, the result is that when someone comes at you, you will instinctively react by doing something useful, such as putting out a block to stop or redirect the strike.

Something as simple as that will prevent you initially getting injured or concussed, allowing you the space to counter (disable them if possible) and then probably create space and get away. It is true that many people do not know what to do if assaulted. Fear overrides and they may freeze or crouch/cower, thus allowing the assailant to take advantage.

Don't feel the need to become a black belt, but train to react instinctively in defense. Learn some simple but violent counters. Strike at the eyes and groin. Learn how to punch, elbow, knee and kick so that you can deliver a violent counter assault on the assailant that will either incapacitate them, allow you to run, or get you the space for someone to help you or for you to draw a firearm. Try and not go to the ground, where you will be kicked and beaten to death by the assailant's buddies, but consider learning how to get out of it if you do go there. No-one really wins a fight; expect to get injured and don't be surprised if you do. Deal with the pain. Suck it up and drive on with the aim of getting your family or team out of there.

If you are attacked with a knife, and you have to defend yourself empty handed, you are likely to be cut. Run away. Throw a chair and run away. Think about stand-off distances, cover and concealment in any kind of encounter. Statistically, if someone runs at you with a knife from anywhere within 20 feet, you will not be able to draw your handgun and engage them before they are on you. This leads to the need for situational awareness (more later). Be suspicious. A little bit of paranoia will go a long way.

Post-event, question what the intent of others is. You may be in a barter situation, but is there anything suspicious about their behavior? Do they seem untrustworthy? Has one of their group begun circling? Think about posture (more later) and security (more later). If you are alert to your surroundings, mindful, then you will detect threats early and have a chance of avoiding them. If you are confident and alert, you will also deter potential assailants from choosing you as their victim. If you operate a buddy system, then you will never move around in groups of less than two, which will be a greater deterrent. Trust your intuition, don't suppress what it is telling you, and act on the warning signs.

Extract from a Blog Entry @ Maxvelocitytactical.blogspot.com

On Fighting:

The first thing you want to do with a fight is avoid it. This applies equally well both now, and in any post-collapse type scenario.

To help you with that avoidance plan, you need to work on being alert and aware. Not only will that awareness help you spot and avoid potential threats, but it will also help deter those predators that are observing you, weighing up their chances.

Being alert, carrying yourself confidently, and looking like you have a chance of handling yourself will go a long way to avoid the fight. Don't look like a victim.

'Mindset' is a bit of a 'tacticool' expression, but it means well. If you are not in the business of getting into fights, you have to worry about it coming to you. If you are suddenly attacked by a blitz attacker, perhaps some kind of psycho, bent on your destruction, then it will be a big surprise and they will have a good chance of overwhelming you. So you have to be ready to go if surprised.

The advantage of a psycho blitz attacker is that they are prepared to go all the way. You are not only taken by surprise, but you are weighed down by all the baggage of not wanting to be in a fight, conditioned by society, worried about self-defense laws etc. It is not a time for denial. If he does not take you out immediately, then you have to fight back. It's not a time for "Wait, try that again, I wasn't ready."

As for fighting styles, there are lots of options. I haven't been in a fight in a long minute, but growing up in the UK it is true that without guns in society, there is a readiness to go to hand to hand fighting: No chance of the other guy carrying concealed or having one in his truck - but he may have a claw hammer or knife under his jacket. Chuck out time at closing from the pubs was basically street fight time. As morals in society have crumbled, it is increasingly mob violence.

In the UK, most fighting is boxing based. On the streets, if you go to the ground you are most likely to be kicked into unconsciousness by his mates standing around. It's a bit of a mob thing. But there is more and more MMA in the UK, and thus grappling.

I don't truck with this advice about not punching people. Punch them in the head. If you can elbow or knee them, fine, but in the absence of that hit hard and fast as many times as you can until they go down and you can get away. That's the next point. If you can't avoid, defend aggressively, hit them with everything you have. Then, don't hang around for 'awards', get away.

If you do get in a fight, however cool your martial arts training is, expect to get hurt. Chin down, eyes up, prepare to take it and wade in to hand it back to him. It's not pretty and no-one will really win. If you can walk or run away from it, you have succeeded.

If you do get taken to the ground - and most people in the US train in Jiu-Jitsu/MMA so it is likely that they will at least try, know what to do to get out of it. You can't just be a 'stand-up' fighter and expect to get away with it.

That leads on to escalation of force. In this article I have not really been discussing weapons, but if you have them be prepared to escalate in proportion to the level of force being used against you. And it is not a medieval jousting tournament, so be prepared to over-match them. There is no chivalry in a street fight. Use force proportionate and 'reasonable' in the circumstances.

As for styles, whatever floats your boat. Just train in something that will allow you to damage the bad guy. I trained at school in Judo. I was on the team. I remember taking punches in school yard type fights while I closed, threw and clinched them. Seeing stars as punches come flying in is not cool; once I was forced to my knees by a flurry of punches before I managed to get in and finish it.

I decided that I needed to learn how to punch, so when I got to College I started Thai Boxing. That really does teach you how to inflict punishment, but you have to be able to take it too. In more recent years, when I get a moment, I do a bit of Filipino Kali. What I like about that is the reaction training to at least do something to avoid an incoming punch, stick, knife. As I get older, I like the idea more and more of not taking a whack to the head.

Granted, I'm no black belt, and when the fight starts, the adrenalin pumps and it all goes a little crazy. That's the time when you go back to what you know, which usually involves trying to punch the living crap out of the other guy. Whoever really has their mind in the fight, will usually overwhelm the opponent.

So, you have to be able to get a little crazy. 'Controlled aggression'. If you are actually crazy, then in the words of Miranda Lambert at the excellent concert I took my wife to not so long ago: "Hide your crazy (girl)."

If you are surprised by a blitz attacker, then you have to instantly turn on the crazy, not freezing or living in denial.

But remember, there is always a 'badder' dude in the valley, always someone tougher than yourself. Or maybe you are sick, exhausted and/or hungry, not on your top game.

Physical Preparation for Tactical Operations

"If you can fill the unforgiving minute
With sixty seconds' worth of distance run -
Yours is the Earth and everything that's in it,
And - which is more - you'll be a Man my son!"

KIPLING

This is a tactical manual and therefore there is a requirement for a certain amount of physical ability and activity to accomplish drills. However, it goes beyond that. You have a responsibility to yourself and your family to be in shape NOW. Illness and disease excepted, if you have your health you have no excuse to let things go. Post-event, it will be too late.

Take a long hard look at yourself; are you in shape and can you do better? The more physically fit you are the better you will perform overall in a survival or combat situation. You will tire less easily. There will be a lot to do that you may not be accustomed to; lifting, carrying, digging, loading, unloading, hiking etc. To be physically prepared, you don't need to be a super-person or a triathlete. You should be able to carry weight both on your back and in your arms. You should be able to dig and lift. Ideally, you should be able to carry a heavy rucksack uphill and fight. It is about being robust.

Try to do some basic fitness, some kind of aerobic activity like running, biking or rowing. Throw in some push-ups, sit-ups and pull-ups. Be the sort of person who will go out and dig that hole or lay that paving in the garden. Laboring would be good preparation for a post-event situation; if you work in an office, landscape the yard at the weekends. Go hiking. A certain amount of aerobic ability is needed, so that you can at least hike with a pack and carry your weapons. Train by running, walking or similar. There is no utility in being overweight and your mobility will be severely hindered in a survival situation.

On the tactical side, you can't be fit enough. Movement under fire is an extremely tiring activity. You may be running, crawling or 'fire and maneuvering', which is short sprints or rushes, followed by hitting the ground, firing and repeat. A lot of this is anaerobic activity, which means you can't get enough oxygen in however hard you breathe: 'sucking it in from China'. You can train for that with sprints and shuttles but really you just need to make sure that you have a good overall level of fitness and that your weight is controlled. You will have adrenalin to aid you and a lot of the ability to achieve this kind of physical activity is rooted in the will to win and determination of the individual.

Bear in mind that if you have a 'man down' situation and take a casualty, you will have to have the physical ability to move them. Casualty movement is a physical challenge. The stronger and more robust you are the better able you will be to add value to your team. Conversely, if your team members or yourself are overweight and unfit, not only will they find it hard to help the casualty or physically perform because they have let themselves go, it is also a lot harder to move a grossly overweight casualty.

You are likely to have to be some sort of hybrid between an infantryman and a farmer/laborer. Think the original citizen soldier. Conventional infantry work itself can be a lot like laboring; a lot of digging, such as trenches (foxholes), latrines, filling sandbags and making bunkers. Conventionally, if you are a line infantry soldier facing a threat of indirect fire, you have to start digging a 'shell-scrape' if you are going to be static in a location for more than fifteen minutes.

Patrol bases will have shell scrapes dug around the perimeter, in or behind which the infantry soldiers will live. Digging a 'stage 3' fire trench with overhead protection can mean constant digging as a fire team for thirty six hours. An ambush position in conventional warfare should be dug in, with shell scrapes dug for each firing position. This is to protect from both direct enemy fire and also against incoming artillery fire.

This is a far cry from the recent wars over the last 10 years, where some infantry have been engaged in this kind of work but many of the coalition forces involved have been conducting vehicle mounted mobile operations from secure FOBs, protected by HESCO bastions (HESCOs are large volume stackable wire mesh and cloth 'boxes' that are filled with earth or sand, like very large sandbags). Be prepared for a life of physical activity, from carrying weight to laboring and occasionally engaging in a firefight.

This is not a physical training manual and it will not presume to recommend various fitness regimes for you to follow. The point, as laid out above, is that you should take sensible measures to physically prepare and be ready for the demands that a post-event situation could put on you.

If you are the head of your family, then you need to be able to physically protect your family WTSHTF. Now, there are other aspects to this including age and illness. You only have to spend some time on a shooting range or even at the Mall for that matter, to see the various shapes and sizes that come through. Many of the range user types definitely rely on the old joke that, "You may be able to outrun me, but you won't be able to outrun this 5.56 / 9mm /substitute caliber here."

Being in such poor physical shape is only doing them and those they will need to protect a disservice. On the other side of this are those that are genuinely disabled or old, despite a healthy lifestyle. Many of the shooters on a range will be sensible law abiding older folk with CCW permits. They are determined to be able to defend themselves in a self-defense situation or home invasion. And they will, no doubt. But they will be less likely to be able to deal with the rigors of the overall post-event scenario and the physical demands. Even your combat veteran from Vietnam era is slowing down now.

So, beyond keeping yourself fit and healthy as best you can, there are limits to this created by age, infirmity, disease and disability. However, such characters can bring a huge wealth of knowledge and experience to the party and therefore the best approach would be specialization to allow best use of resources. Thus, the message here is not so much that everyone needs to be super-fit, more that there is no room for self-inflicted laziness and lard-asses: get out and keep physically prepared to the extent that you are able. Step away from the cookie jar!

Don't take supplements to artificially enhance muscle mass, and don't take recreational drugs. None of this will stand you in good stead post-event. Don't obsess about having 'six-pack abs'; this is neither important nor natural. Consider the utility of having a little 'reserve' around your waist, so long as it is not excessive.

On the long strenuous marches across the Falklands Islands by British Forces in 1982, carrying heavy weight advancing on the Argentinian positions, it was notably the PT instructors that suffered and fell out. The 'Gym Queens' never do well: they are often either on supplements or have too little body fat to sustain themselves. So, don't try and 'get massive' for its own sake and on the other hand, take a good look at you: for example, are you really a big boned guy, a big strong tough guy, or are you just overweight? Would you be better served reducing your body fat and being able to maneuver yourself better?

Weapons

"Opinions are like assholes, everyone has one."

Weapons are freely available in the United States. Therefore, there are plenty of weapons for people to use against you. Therefore it follows that to defend yourself you need to have weapons, and the right ones. Post-event, there is no room for moralizing about whether weapons ownership is right or not. Weapons are a necessary tool of self-defense. For a soldier, weapons are a tool of the job; you get what you are issued. There is little room for being a 'gun nerd'; save that for a hobby if you enjoy it.

At the basic level you just have to make sure you have the right tool for the job. There is no room for lengthy debate about this and that, and this widget, that caliber and this velocity and so on; some of that simply comes from being spoiled for choice. Make sure you have the right weapons for the job. Preppers will talk ad nauseam about the arsenal of weapons they need for this job and that job and all that, there is also a lot of nonsense out there about the capability of various firearms and ammunition. For example, the 5.56 (.223) is the US and NATO standard assault weapon combat round. It is highly effective in combat. For hunting use, it is considered a 'varmint round' and sometimes not authorized for bigger game hunting. This does not make it ineffective. If you are struck center mass with a 5.56 round, you are not going to walk it off.

This is really the point here – there is a tendency to disappear down a rabbit-hole of debate about what weapons you need. For tactical use, you are best served by tactical combat weapons, but at a pinch anything you have will have to serve. There is an additional prepper debate as to the other uses that you will require weapons for, which can lead to a whole armory full of niche weapons. You need to buy what you can afford and can comfortably train yourself to use for the worst case situation, which is you being targeted and hunted by fellow humans. In a survival situation, you can always use those tactical weapons for other uses, which would be an imperfect solution in an imperfect world.

For self-defense, you preferably need to have handguns, tactical rifles and shotguns. Get a decent handgun in something like 9mm, .40 or .45, something like a Glock or whatever you are happy with. Get a tactical rifle, something like an AR-15 or an AK in 5.56, 7.62 x 39 (short, AK type) or 7.62 x 51 (NATO = .308 civilian). If you are a sharpshooter or expert hunting shooter, then get a sniper rifle (long range hunting rifle). Have shotguns such as the Remington 870 pump-action available for close in home-defense type work, using 00 buck, slugs or similar self-defense shells, or perhaps to arm those less handy with a rifle with as a last ditch defense weapon.

Don't worry if the law only allows you to have tactical rifles, such as the M4/AR15, in semi-auto mode i.e. single shot: this is really all you need for the vast majority of situations, full auto being a waste of ammunition except in situations at close range facing overwhelming numbers of enemy. Rapid or deliberate fire from well-aimed single shots is much more effective, and your trigger finger can move pretty fast if it needs to.

Make sure your weapons are zeroed – 'sighted in'. Make sure that you have enough spare magazines and some sort of rig to carry it in. A minimum of six 30 round magazines would be acceptable, with more if possible. You can never have too much ammunition. Have body armor if possible.

Forget the message of all the TV shows and movies that you see where the actors grab weapons and run around with them as if they were some sort of accessory, with no more ammunition available or carried than what is in the weapon itself. You need to have a means of ammunition carriage and make sure it is on your body any time you go anywhere with the weapon.

Your weapon itself should always be handy. In any kind of field situation it should never be out of your arms reach, as a golden rule. Slings can be utilized so that you can keep the weapon on your body even when doing some other task. Don't get irritated and leave it leaning on a tree while you go off and do something else, because you won't be able to get to it in time. In your home or retreat, or trailer or cabin, make sure that the weapon is readily accessible but out of the reach of children; a post-event suggestion would be to put a shotgun or rifle up on nails or hooks above your bed, and have similar in each room so when you are downstairs you can have the weapon right there on the wall, out of reach of the kids but ready to grab if a warning is given (or if the door is blown off the hinges with shotgun slugs and a raiding team comes boiling through your front door because you never had a person on watch. Maybe get a barking guard dog if there are too few of you to mount a 24 hour watch rotation).

Carrying a weapon along with ammunition, trauma kit and ancillaries is heavy, hot and sweaty. More so if you have body armor and it is all set up as a single armor carrier with the ammunition pouches attached to the armor carrier, using the MOLLE system, just like you see soldiers doing on deployment. (MOLLE = **MO**dular **L**ightweight **L**oad-carrying **E**quipment: The system's modularity is derived from the use of PALS webbing, rows of heavy-duty nylon stitched onto the vest as to allow for attachment of various MOLLE-compatible pouches and accessories).

You have to suck it up and drive on. It is heavy and you will be sweaty, but if the tactical situation warrants the carriage of long weapons, ammunition and body armor, then you need to get on with it. You could consider multiple 'rigs' for different postures and situations, such as having a 'full battle rattle' rig set up based on a set of body armor with ballistic plates for defending against attacks on your location and maybe for going out on forage and patrol missions. Maybe a battle belt rig with ammo pouches and no body armor for when you are working in the yard. You can always combine the two and up/down-grade as necessary.

These are just suggestions but the idea is that you can modify your equipment to the situation, activity and threat while still carrying weapons and spare ammunition. More about this is covered in the profile and training sections.

Leadership

This is a complex topic. To touch on it: Post-event, we are concerned with operating as groups of friends or families and mixes of such. We may or may not have established leaders. These leaders may also be the natural leaders pre-event, such as parents, but they may not be the right people post-event, depending on their innate skills and qualities: i.e. their character. The skills of people vary widely, and some are better at things than others. It is also true that in times of crisis leaders will emerge, and they may not be the expected or established people. There is a strong argument that in a crisis there should be one leader, in the same way that there is 'only one captain on a ship'. The idea is to allow decisions to be made and acted upon without the paralysis of argument, debate and dissent.

However, remember that we are talking about a group of civilians, not bound by the Uniform Code of Military Justice, and therefore anyone who is to be a leader of such a group must hold the trust and respect of the people in that group, at least in the big things, not necessarily in all small things. There are three components to getting the job done: they consist of the needs of the mission, the team and the individuals. These can be conflicting and need to be managed in whatever way is determined to be the priority.

A group will be made up of people with multiple different needs and qualities. Ideally, whenever there is time for it, a leader will act in an inclusive way in making decisions for the group. At times of emergency, decisions may have to be made instantly and the group needs to understand that and at those times act cohesively to do whatever needs to be done, such as act to escape danger.

At other times, asking for opinions and including the thoughts of the other team members will be useful; they will feel that they are included and have contributed. The job of the leader is then to take all the advice and sift it to come up with a decision and plan, which the leader can then run by the group for final approval and then implement, with the willing cooperation of the team.

Certain types of individuals are not suited to working in a team; something that may be prevalent in our selfish, self-centered, lazy, modern society. If possible, do not have these types in your group. If you can't avoid it because they may be family or similar, then you just have to suck it up and drive on, minimizing their selfish morbidity as much as possible!

Post-event, we are not only interested in security and tactical capabilities. We are interested in living and rebuilding. Therefore we are living in a small community that has multiple needs. We are not simply a military unit on a mission, and therefore it is not that simple. Utilize the personnel assets that you have by allowing people to specialize in what their talents are. Delegate areas of responsibility to certain people, allow them to develop teams, and let them run with it and 'command in their own sphere'.

In military terms, this is called 'mission command' and basically mandates that you give a subordinate a mission and let them know your overall intent and allow them to get on and do it, asking for support as they need it. Here is an example why:

> If a commander tells unit A to "Capture that hill," and does not give them mission command or tell them the reason why, unit A will go off and capture the hill. If, now on top of the hill, they see that below them the bridge over the river is briefly undefended, they will sit on top of the hill and probably just report it in. The opportunity is missed.
>
> If the commander tells unit A, "Capture that hill, so that I can have you support unit B as they move up and capture the bridge."

and he tells them that his overall intent is to capture the river crossing, then we are in a different game. Unit A, on top of the hill and seeing the bridge undefended, but with the enemy massing to counter attack and re-capture it, could take the initiative and rapidly assault down, capture the bridge, and save unit B from having to attack a defended bridge. Unit A will have fulfilled the commander's intent.

We should also not forget that with the different characteristics and skills that people have, comes a diverse amount of talents, an example being inherent emotional intelligence. In a group in a survival situation, don't let the testosterone take over. Make a place for sensible, mature, maternal type females to input; they will be concerned for the good of the group, the children and the weaker members. Listen to their counsel; it may help stop the males from going off and making a hash of it all!

This is not intended to be a sexist statement, we all know that as many females as males can be selfish and useless in today's world, but there are inherent differences in strengths between individuals and sexes and bringing the female opinion in and respecting it could add a level of balance to decision making. It's not even really about the sexes at all, rather more about respecting the opinion of the sensible ones and giving it due consideration, and learning to deal with (manage) members of the group who are not ideal and perhaps more concerned about themselves, or perhaps given over to panic or irrational fears.

As a leader, you will need to be unselfish and concerned primarily for the group rather than yourself. This is similar to being a parent, and you may in fact be a parent in charge of your family group. A position of leadership will give you 'leader's legs', which is a way of describing how leadership gives you greater energy because you are concentrating on the planning and implementation and you are determined to get the mission achieved, so you get additional energy and drive from that. Don't forget that others will perhaps not have that.

A civilian group will also be comprised of all different ages, ability and physical health, and thus this needs to be considered. Push the team when necessary, but try not to drive them into the ground. Your team will gain respect for you if they see you as unselfish, competent and fair. It's not about being nice. Nice is great, but being a friend is separate from being respected as a leader. Put the needs of your team first: let them eat first, eat last yourself. Being a leader is not about being some kind of warlord or tyrant, taking all the spoils. First your troops, then yourself. 'Serve to Lead' as the motto of the Royal Military Academy Sandhurst goes.

Make reasoned competent decisions and treat all members of the team fairly. At the same time, do not neglect yourself: make sure you do get enough to eat and get some sleep. You are no good to your team if you drive yourself into the ground, and simply working long hours is not in itself a virtue.

Having a good command team will help you in this: have a strong supporting 'number two' (as in a good Platoon Sergeant, not a Dr. Evil henchman) and make sure that you have delegated to the right 'department heads' so that you have a leadership structure that takes some of the duties away.

However, remember that as the leader you are always ultimately responsible.

CHAPTER TWO

TO STAY OR GO

Stay in Place

This is commonly known as 'bugging-in', as opposed to 'bugging-out' to a 'Bug out Location' (BOL). Following the event, it would mean staying at your place of residence, or home, house, apartment. Where your home is will have an impact on how feasible this plan is. For those who live in remote locations, or who have deliberately built and maintained a remote, stocked, 'retreat', then the best course of action may be to stay put. For those who live in high population density areas, you will have to assess the dangers versus the advantages of staying at home.

Many people do not have the jobs, careers or financial means to buy or sustain a retreat, or to live there all the time. Some preppers have considered this and decided that they will stay at home. Others have the ability to maintain a separate retreat of varying sophistication and plan on driving there once the event happens. Others have joined groups to pool resources and create a joint retreat where members can go and help sustain and defend post-event; they will also have to travel. They may live in or near the cities for lifestyle and work. Some factors to consider about your home (enemy, ground & friendlies):

- Location: urban/rural. Remote?
- Defensive potential of your home itself.
- Defensive potential of your home location.
- Population density.
- Ability to move your family and equipment.
- Young children, elderly, sick and ill.
- Resources in the local area: food, water etc.
- Your preparations and food/water stocks.

- Numbers of defenders available.
- What would I have to do to make it more defendable?
- Likely threat from looters, mobs, civil disorder in your neighborhood.

There are numerous advantages and disadvantages for staying put:

Advantages:

- Does not require the financial cost of maintaining another location to establish a retreat.
- Does not risk movement (transit) in a hostile environment.
- Home comforts: all your stuff and supplies.
- Does not risk heading out to nowhere, unless you have a location you can go to, and ending up a homeless refugee.
- Network of friends, family, neighbors.
- Familiarity with terrain, local resources and features incl. water sources etc.

Disadvantages:

- Is your home defendable? Most homes are architecturally weak places to defend.
- Do you have the weapons and enough trained personnel to defend your home?
- What supplies have you stored and will you be able to get food and water once the gird goes down?
- Storage: Is your home big enough to store the essentials for long term survival?
- Being a target of looters, fire or other threat that could make your home untenable.
- Can you remain low profile enough to not be targeted by looters?

One of the main questions that will be considered when you are deciding whether to stay put or bug out is simply: Where will you go? Unless you have a specific location where you can be assured of a welcome, safety and supplies, then you may well be taking a great risk by bugging out. This is particularly true if you become part of a wave of refugees fleeing the cities into the countryside, where you imagine there will be safety.

But unless you have a specific place to go to, you are just a problem to the people who live there – you are an 'outsider' and potential trouble. Therefore, it may be a given that it is risky to stay where you are, but unless you have a specific place to go to you may be at more risk by leaving. Even if you do have somewhere to go to, depending on how far you have to go, the situation and if you are part of a wave of refugees, you may never make it, or find it very hard to get there, perhaps encountering violence and maybe even losing possessions or even sustaining wounds or fatalities in the process.

Now, it is a given that if you are in an area that is hit by an event that means that you have to evacuate, for example a biological attack, or a tsunami, or a dirty bomb or similar geographically targeted event, then you are going to have to get out. You may find yourself in a nightmare, and you may well want to consider how to get out of the metropolis under those circumstances. Even those with retreats may be forced out by such an event, depending on what and where it is. Being forced out of your retreat by an event could leave you no better than the mass of refugees.

You may well be living in a less than ideal location, such as a city or suburb or perhaps simply a location within an area of mass population density, such as the Eastern Seaboard, but unless you have somewhere to go and you are forced out by a specific event, you may well consider staying in place. This may be a better alternative to getting gridlocked on the roads or ending up camping in the woods among thousands of others.

If you decide on this strategy, then you will be able to store supplies in quantities based on what space you have available and you may face challenges such as looters perhaps earlier than those further from the cities. However, you will be in the familiarity and comfort of your home, albeit with the utilities either cut of or intermittent, and this will be advantageous to the mental health of those you are surviving with, in particular children and the elderly, and also those who have little experience of camping out and/or were in denial of the prepper philosophy and the need for it pre-event.

You will be subject to all the disadvantages elaborated on by those who advocate the isolated rural retreat and you will have to be ingenuous in responding to the challenges of supplies, such as finding water and other such needs.

If you do decide, or are forced, to stay put under such circumstances, then you would be best served by a covert approach and plan to try and sit it out in secret for a period of time. This may in fact be a hybrid plan where you consider an immediate evacuation to be unwise and you sit tight for maybe a week or two and then bug out. This would have the advantage of giving you time to sort your possessions and prioritize your supplies prior to loading and moving. It would also assume that you are able to remain covert and un-looted during that time, including retaining possession of your bug out vehicle and fuel supply.

Extract from a Blog Entry @ Maxvelocitytactical.blogspot.com

Long Term Security and Defense of your Retreat Location:

(This article is a summary from the blog and is covered in more detail in the chapter on Defense)

In this article I will discuss long term security and defense of your retreat location. We cannot predict now exactly what conditions will look like after a collapse and as such I urge you not to make too many assumptions based on your particular idea of what such a post-SHTF situation will look like. The purpose will be to give you the general principles and techniques of defending a location, which you can tailor and apply as necessary and appropriate.

It is best to adopt a mindset of flexibility and gather mental and physical knowledge and 'tools' in order to be able to develop your response and put some of these measures in place as you find them necessary and appropriate. For the article I will assume a broad post-SHTF situation of societal collapse with a general absence of law and order.

What is the threat? As a prepper hunkered down at your home, with food stores, the most likely threat will be from looters and marauders. These could take many forms from a simple beggar, through starving neighbors, mobs, tricks and deceptions, to a tactically organized group with weapons and equipment. The worst case is some sort of organized paramilitary style force with heavy equipment bent on forced redistribution.

Therefore, remain flexible and have an emergency rally point and extraction route should you be overmatched. Know when you have no alternative but to bug out. You can make this decision if you have the information before the threat arrives and conduct the bug out in good order. Alternatively, you may be forced to make the decision as the attack progresses and have to 'break contact' and withdraw under enemy fire; this is one of the most difficult tactical maneuvers.

Work on your leadership, decision making and decision points so that your response under the pressure of both time and enemy is optimal. Tied in with this is the need for clear rules of engagement and for the use of force appropriate to the threat.

This article is mainly concerned with defense of a single location and as such will not go into techniques such as mobile and area defense, which could be useful for a larger community. Remember, the best form of defense is to avoid the fight. But that may not be possible and you have to always plan and prepare for that fight. You can better avoid the fight by adopting a lower profile at your location, attempting to conceal your supplies and capabilities.

The opposite of this is to have a high profile and try to use threat of force as a deterrent. But remember that a good rifleman could sit out at long range and simply shoot your defenders in their sentry positions. In my opinion, the best approach for a small survivor group is to adopt a lower profile while maintaining the capability to defeat threats as they are encountered. The following are some principles of defense that you should consider and apply to your location and plan:

- *All Round Defense, in order to anticipate a threat from any direction.*
- *Depth, in order to prevent penetration of your defended position.*
- *Mutually Supporting Sectors of Fire, in order to increase the strength and flexibility of a defense.*
- *Concealment and Deception, in order to deny the adversary the advantages of understanding.*
- *Maintenance of a Reserve.*
- *Offensive Action (where appropriate), in order to seize or regain the initiative.*
- *Administration, to include:*
    - *Appropriate numbers of trained personnel*
    - *Appropriate weapons, ammunition and equipment*
    - *A watch system for early warning.*

Most modern family homes do not lend themselves to defense. The structure is vulnerable to high velocity rounds which will pass through multiple frame, wood and plasterboard walls, and also simple mechanical breaches are possible with tools and even vehicles used as rams. They are also very vulnerable to fire. If you try and defend your house from the windows, then you will not be protected by the walls framing those windows and the room can be filled full of high velocity rounds by an attacking group.

There is a real danger of being suppressed by superior firepower. If you stay back from the windows as you should, then you limit your fields of fire and unless there are enough of you defending then the enemy will be able to take advantage of blind spots to close with and then breach the house. You need a basement or other ballistic protected safe room for your noncombatant personnel (kids etc.) to shelter in; otherwise they will not be protected from the violence and from the high velocity rounds ripping through the walls.

One of the key things for a prepper defense of a location is to have an appropriate number of trained personnel with appropriate firearms, ammunition and equipment. You will also have to take measures to harden the building to slow down attempts to breach. You need to consider whether or not you want your property to look derelict; this could be good or bad in the circumstances. It would be worthwhile to consider boarding up or shuttering at least the ground floor windows and think about putting up door bars or even board up some of the doors. This will also help with light discipline.

External boards can make the place look derelict, but looking derelict could also encourage approach by potential squatters. You could put up the boards internally, or something similar, in order to maintain a low profile and slow any breaches. There a lots of pros and cons each way. When boarding up doors, ensure that you have at least two independent exits that can be used both for routine tasks but also for egress if you have to escape. Boarding up your windows and doors does not make them ballistically hardened. You could have sandbags ready to go, and you will need to consider a big pile of dirt to fill them from.

Consider the benefits of simple mass of soil in protecting you from high velocity rounds, and for the construction of fighting positions. Sandbags need to be at least two deep to protect against high velocity rounds. If you try stacking enough of these on a modern upper floor, or even a ground level floor with a basement beneath, then the weight of a constructed fighting position may cause a collapse. You could stack sandbags externally around designated window fighting positions on the ground floor, but you will need a lot of them. Other alternatives would include filling a chest of drawers with soil to create firing positions, or maybe even material such as steel plate that will weigh less but will provide ballistic protection.

From the principles of defense it is clear that we need to establish a plan which provides early warning, all round defense and mutually supporting sectors of fire. We also need to create depth, which is best utilized outside the building rather than with fall back positions inside the house. We can create depth using external fighting positions to keep attackers away from the house, which will also aid mutual support.

A key thing that will really help defense of a house is to have a second or more positions outside of the main building that can provide fire support, thus these positions support each other by keeping enemy away from the house and each other. This position(s) could also be another house or cooperating neighbor if it works out that way. This creates a 'cross-fire' so you must enforce fire discipline and allocate sectors of fire to ensure you do not cause 'friendly fire'.

A very important concept is that of 'stand-off'. This can be created with a combination of fighting positions in depth and cleared fields of fire with obstacles. If you have an obstacle, such as wire, it must be covered by fire to be effective. Utilize stand-off distances to keep enemy away from the property, combined with obstacles to slow vehicle and dismounted approach. Examples like wire are good for dismounted personnel and *also vehicles if it is correctly laid concertina wire. Obstacles such as steel cabling, concrete bollards or planter boxes and felled trees will work well against vehicles. This will also have the effect of reducing the risk of attackers getting close to set the place on fire, which they are likely to try if they can't get in to get your stuff.*

If we expand this concept we can see how a mutually supporting neighborhood with checkpoints/roadblocks and observation/fighting positions will provide a great advantage. Stand-off is also important in terms of engaging the enemy with accurate effective fire at the longest range that is physically and legally possible. If you are competent and have the equipment for long range effective suppressive fire, this can have the effect of keeping the enemy at arm's length and reducing the accuracy and hence effectiveness of their fire, which will prevent them successfully suppressing you and subsequently maneuvering onto your position to breach or burn the property.

In addition, consider the presence, placement and potential hard protection of any flammable sources on your property and close to your buildings, such as propane tanks and fuel supplies. Ensure they cannot be repeatedly fired upon by the enemy to cause a fire or explosion. The ability to generate accurate effective long range defensive fire depends on skill, equipment, positioning of fighting positions, your policy for the use of force and also the way the terrain affects weapons killing areas and ranges.

To engage at long range you have to reasonably fear that the enemy presents a threat of lethal force against your defended location. However, if you are in a closer urban or wooded environment you may find some of your fields of fire are limited and you will have to plan and position accordingly.

Administration is a key factor. While you are maintaining your defense you need to look after the welfare of the team, equipment and the site itself. Administration is what preppers usually concentrate on. This is your "beans, bullets and band-aids". This is an area where those that are non-combatants can really pull their weight and make a difference. You must maintain a watch system which will be tied in to 'stand to' positions and maybe some form of 'Quick Reaction Force' or reserve, depending on the resources and numbers available to you.

Your watch system can be augmented by other early warning sensors such as dogs and mechanical or electronic systems. Day to day you will need to keep the machine running and this will be the biggest challenge as time goes on. Complacency Kills! Depending on the extent of your preparations, stores and the resources within your property, this will have a knock-on effect to your ability to remain covert and the requirement to send out foraging patrols. People will also start to get cabin fever, particularly kids, and you will need to consider how to entertain them.

Consider that while mundane tasks are being completed, there is always someone on watch. People that are not on watch need to have weapons and ammunition carrying equipment close or on their person while doing other things. Consider carrying long rifles slung as well as handguns everywhere you go on the property, with at least a light bit of web gear with some additional magazines in pouches. Rifles should never be out of your arms reach if there is any kind of threat of attack. You should put rifle racks or hooks/nails on walls in key rooms, out of reach of kids, so that rifles can be grabbed quickly if the alarm is sounded.

Regarding your noncombatants or protected personnel; what you do with them depends on who they are. The younger kids will need to be protected in the safest location you have. Others will be useful to do tasks such as re-load magazines, distribute water and act as firefighting crews. Note that you need to have fire-extinguishers and buckets of water and /or sand available at hand during a defense to put out any fires.

The more tasks you give people during a crisis, the more the activity will take their minds off the stress of the situation and the team will be strengthened. Ammunition replenishment, water distribution, casualty collection point, first aid, watching the rear and looking after the younger kids are all examples of tasks that can be allocated to make people a useful part of the team when personnel resources are tight.

For this kind of defensive situation you will be well served by the ability to detect, observe and accurately engage enemy at the longest range possible by day and night. This is easily said, but would take throwing money at it to get all the equipment you need to best do it. In terms of firearms, I would recommend tactical type high capacity magazine rifles for the main work, backed up by handguns and pump action 12 gauge shotguns. The shotguns are good for close work and if the enemy gets in to the building, last ditch stuff. Long range hunting type rifles are good for observation (scope) and longer distance engagement.

You would be best served with good optics for your weapons and also observation devices such as binoculars. Think about night vision and even thermal imaging if you can afford it. You will also have to consider that even if you can afford a night vision device, it will only work for whoever has it so how will the rest engage? What type and configuration of these night vision devices, on weapons as sights or not? Without night sights you can fire at muzzle flash or use whatever illumination is available, white light or whatever. A good option is to have parachute illumination flares.

Loose barking dogs on your property are perhaps the best low budget early warning system; however consider that they may give away your position if you are trying to be totally covert. Decide on your priorities and strategy and tie that in with what money you have to spend on equipment. You can get expensive systems such as ground sensors, lights and alarms, but these cost money and you have to consider their use in a long term grid down situation. I would prefer to spend money on optics and night observation devices which will last without grid power (but will require batteries) and can also be taken with you if you have to move locations. Here are some basic suggestions for equipment to augment such a defense:

- *Appropriate tactical firearms & ammunition*

- *Web gear and magazines*
- *Ear and eye protection*
- *Body armor and helmets, NIJ level IIIa or Level IV*
- *Barbed wire, coiled (concertina) and for low wire entanglements*
- *Sandbags or other ballistic protection options*
- *Night vision devices*
- *Binoculars plus optical rifle sights*
- *Black out curtain and pre-cut plywood for windows*
- *Parachute illumination flares*
- *Trip-flares*
- *Trauma medical kit incl. CAT tourniquets*
- *Range cards*
- *Two way radios and/or field telephones*

If you have put a group together for such a defense, they need to be trained on not only tactical shooting and basic small unit tactics and movement, but also briefed and rehearsed on the defensive plan including fighting positions and sectors of fire. Consider that depending on your circumstances and the terrain, you may be benefited by running periodic clearance patrols around the property to mitigate against surprise attack, and to do this your team need to be able to patrol and move tactically, as well as respond to any enemy contact.

You will preferably have a medic with a trauma bag.

You do not want to ever run out of ammunition, so make sure you have as much as you can reasonably purchase. Like tactics, ammunition quantities are a subjective argument with many solutions. I recommend a personal load of six to eight thirty round magazines on the person, with at least as many full magazines for resupply. And once you have used that, you need another resupply! In a real life contact you will likely use less ammunition than you may during training and you must concentrate on effective accurate fire rather than simple quantity.

Train your team to engage positively identified enemy, or suppress known enemy positions. A rapid rate of fire is 30 rounds per minute; a deliberate rate is 10 rounds per minute.

Practice and rehearse the command and fire control procedures at your location, including the communication of enemy locations and actions. Use range cards to tie in sectors for mutual support and to prevent 'friendly fire'. Run 'stand to' drills like a fire drill by day and by night and be able to call out which direction the enemy threat comes from. Be aware of diversions and demonstrations intended to distract you from the main direction of attack. Always cover all sectors, even with just one observer looking to the flanks and rear in a manpower crisis. Keep unnecessary noise and shouting down, allowing orders and target indications to be passed around the position. Every team member is a sensor and a 'link man' to pass on information.

Having said all that, you are not going to open fire on just anyone coming to your location. Any actions that you take should be justifiable as self-defense. Do be mindful of tricks and the potential for snipers. However, don't give up on morality and charity and don't illegally open fire on anyone that comes near your defended location. You need to agree on rules of engagement for your sentries and you should apply escalation of force protocols to meet a threat with the proportionate and appropriate force necessary to stop that threat.

Have the ability to warn anyone approaching, whether you have permanent warning signs or something like a bullhorn that you use as part of your escalation procedures through warning to non-lethal then lethal force as you begin to identify them as posing a threat. Remember that escalation of force is a continuum and you can bypass the early stages and go directly to lethal force if taken by surprise and faced with a lethal threat that must be stopped.

Versus: Bugging Out

Unless you have no choice but to move to escape a threat, such as the reason for the event i.e. a virus, dirty bomb attack, or civil disorder, then you should only move if you have a safe place to go to, or your home is untenable. Getting out for getting outs sake, perhaps with nothing but a camper or a tent and heading to a National Forest like all the other millions, will simply leave you out there at great threat. You will likely not have enough stores, unless you planned for it, had maintained a store or cache, and packed up a trailer to take it all with you. You won't be able to live off the land and your security measures, unless you really can find a hole to hide in, may be worse out there in a tent than they would have been in your house.

It all depends on the situation. Remember that all the desperate people with no preparations will be evacuating too, as far as their fuel tank will take them, along the obvious lines of drift. They will become a mobile threat. The threat will not just be in your old neighborhood, but in all the neighborhoods and campsites that people are evacuating to. So there is a risk of looters and raiders in your old neighborhood, to be balanced against the possible network of all your neighbors who have an interest in defending it. On the evacuation routes, there will be a risk of banditry, ambush, robbery, rape and murder.

Timing

Consider when you are going to move, if you decide to move. If you live in a year round survival retreat, then you already bugged out, job done. If your plan is to get out early and beat the rush, then you need to have an eye on the situation to be able to make that judgment. Depending on the nature of the event you will get varying degrees of notice. For a slide down to a financial collapse, you may give yourself a trigger point at which you will move out and set up at your alternate location. If it is a sudden event, then given that you have gear to pack up versus the panicked mob that just gets in the car and goes, you may not beat the rush.

The problem with not beating the rush is that in a mass evacuation situation the main routes, and the alternates, will be blocked with traffic in gridlock. Once the vehicles run out of fuel, the roads will be blocked with broken down vehicles, probably with the occupants still camped at the roadside. That is a civil disorder situation waiting to happen. So there is a decision about timing and when to move. If you don't get out ahead of the crowds, you may be better off waiting. To be trapped in gridlock obviously prepared with desperate people around you, many of them armed, is to put your team at too much risk.

Route Selection

This has a close relation to timing. If you have an alternative location to go to post-event, then you should carefully map out and plan a route to that place that takes side and back roads, as well as alternatives. Remember that many people trapped by gridlock will also try and take those back roads, but if they have not looked into it so well then they may not be on the smaller roads that you can take away from the main lines of drift (Interstates) that will take you to your secondary location.

Your secondary location should of course be somewhere remote that hopefully not many other people will be headed in the direction of. If you decide to wait until the rush is over, then you may find that routes have cleared more, but they are likely to be blocked by broken down and damaged cars, and there will likely be much desperation and criminality along these main routes and pushing off to the side routes that parallel them. Choose routes carefully to 'cross-grain' the main lines of drift.

Location

There is an implication here that a secondary location must not be too far away to make it unrealistic to get there in an emergency. Don't try to cross multiple states, keep it preferably close, maybe within 50 miles or as close as feasible. You don't want to be going to obvious locations, such as the main national parks and forests. A secondary location would hopefully be one that you have planned and prepared for, but worst case if you had to get out, get out to somewhere remote but non-obvious and defensible, with anticipated low population density <u>after</u> the event. Areas of forgotten or bypassed wilderness or forest are ideal.

Conduct an area map assessment followed by reconnaissance and look for areas such as smaller parks or forest areas that will likely be bypassed by the mob as they head out. Look for these little non-obvious pockets that are away from the natural 'grain' of the land and the lines of drift as people travel out. If you are planning on bugging out, preferably buy some land in advance to turn into a BOL and put a structure and cache some stores on it. Worst case is having to bug out to another location and simply camp there, but if you have done some recon and are familiar with the area, perhaps as a camping or hiking spot, then you stand a better chance.

Access & Concealment

If you do have to bug out to a secondary location, try and conceal this location from others. Make it look non-inviting or simply not there. Preferably you will have stand-off distance from the nearest road and concealment from view/observation and preferably cover from enemy fire as well, along with observation of the approaches to your position. Unless you are a large capable group, you don't want to present an obvious defended location to potential raiders. Make sure that any defenses you have around the property are well back (stand-off) and concealed from the road.

Think about making it look derelict and non-inviting, but in a way that does not make it look like an idyllic deserted retreat for occupation by any group that comes past. Use your imagination. If you are bugging out simply to a campsite somewhere else, because your home location became untenable for some reason, then you want to be as covert as possible. Find somewhere such as a wooded area that is not an obvious national park or forest. Find a little used access road and camouflage your exit from the trail. Move all vehicles off the road and have the campsite somewhere back in the woods concealed by vegetation or ground.

Remember that everywhere has locals, even (or especially) the backwoods and make sure you are not moving into an area where your presence will be viewed with hostility, and don't move into someone's backyard. Beware of the boondocks if they are populated by the sort that will want to take your stuff and infringe on your liberty and property, particularly if they are the sort that may be 'partying in' the apocalypse on meth and PCP. There is a detailed instruction on defense below.

Numbers

For any kind of location that you wish to remain in, whether it be your neighborhood, your retreat, holiday home, cabin or camper/tent in the woods, there is an advantage in numbers balanced against available resources. However, getting together with others post-event can be risky (who do you trust/include/exclude and how to go about it) and you don't want to be a part of the problem, the great refugee mass. Conversely, a single family will have trouble subsisting while providing adequate watch and defense and would be vulnerable to fatigue followed by surprise and being overwhelmed.

This leads us back to preparation: it makes sense to organize with a group prior to the event, of a decent workable size of trustworthy people who can collectively look after each other. That's what prepping is all about. There may also be ancillary problems to this that you need to consider: who stays at the retreat or moves to the retreat with you? Who will want to bring their girl/boyfriend, lay-about best buddies, grandma etc.? Where do you draw the line? Have a plan and have an inner group of people who are part of it. Draw the line somewhere.

Does your teenage child have a girl/boyfriend who they are very close to and will they want to leave them when the SHTF? Will you want to include them, also because they could form a useful part of the group? But what about their parents – will they let their 'almost adult' child go, will they want to be included, and are they suitable people to have as part of the team? All these outcomes need to be considered in advance, to make those hard decisions easier.

Vehicles

This is not a detailed discussion about the best or ideal type of bug-out vehicle. Many people will simply have whatever they own at the time. It would be useful to have a vehicle that is powerful to be able to haul loads and potentially push other broken down vehicles out of the way and large enough for carrying the people and equipment that you need. Give consideration to a trailer that you can haul your stores in. A trailer will reduce the mobility of the vehicle but it may be necessary to carry all your equipment and stores if you have not already pre-placed these items at a secondary location. A trailer makes reversing in an emergency not a practical proposition.

A way to mitigate this would be to take more vehicles, if you had the drivers and access to more vehicles, so that you have more vehicles to carry stores inside of. This will also give you redundancy if one vehicle breaks down. Pick-up trucks are great for carrying stores. Mini-vans are maybe even better! Reason: if you stow all the seats in the back you have a huge cargo space that is not only covered but is low profile, so if you have to transit it is not so obvious that you have a whole bunch of gear with you. You can only use a mini-van in this way if you have other vehicles to carry the personnel, but of course a mini-van is not 4-wheel drive.

The number of vehicles and personnel in your convoy will also have a knock on effect to tactical potential, which will be discussed in more detail below. However, to introduce the concept here: one vehicle gives you limited load carrying ability and no redundancy. If you are a standard type family you likely have a couple of cars. Take both. If you have the ability to take three cars and have a driver and security in each, then take them because you will:

1) Spread out your personnel so that there is less risk with the destruction of one vehicle.

2) Increase redundancy if one vehicle breaks down or is immobilized.

3) Increased your tactical options.

4) Greatly increase your load carrying ability, perhaps without having to use a trailer which will benefit mobility.

Equipment

Full prepping equipment (i.e. 'list of lists') for a post-event scenario is beyond the scope of this book and is covered in detail in many other publications. Best case you will have acquired the necessary gear and food to survive in your location of choice in a post-event scenario. If you have not, or your preparations are in the early stages, then you should at least concentrate on the following basics to allow you to survive initially before taking whatever measures you deem appropriate to secure longer term security, shelter, food and water. Effectively, you need to be prepared for an extended, armed, camping trip with bad guys added:

- Suitable weapons for tactical self-defense.
- Ammunition. You can never have enough.
- Combat load carrying equipment for weapons, ammo and equipment.
- Appropriate clothing and footwear for the outdoors.
- Rucksack & daypack.
- Camping equipment: shelter, cooking, sleeping.
- Vehicles, spare fuel (treated with Sta-bil), spare wheels (be able to change a flat!).
- Food: as much as you can store and move if necessary.
- Water: as much as you can store and move if necessary.
- Water purification chemicals and equipment.
- Medical kit and prescription drugs.
- Trauma kit.
- Health & Hygiene items: baby wipes to hit the hotspots when you can't wash. Hand sanitizer. Lip balm. Pink Eye (Conjunctivitis) eye drops. Female items.
- Gear plus chemicals to keep the bugs away.

- Antibiotics if you can get a supply, or get them post-event.
- Navigation equipment and maps / compass.
- N95 masks/respirators. Non-latex gloves.
- Legal documents: passports, IDs, birth certificates, mortgage type documents etc.
- Cash/credit cards.
- Tools: machete, axe, knives, shovel, pick-axe, saw (chainsaw if possible as well) etc. Handyman tool kit. 'Break and enter' tools for 'foraging'.
- 550 cord plus duct tape!
- Flashlights
- Batteries
- Candles
- Disposable lighters
- Items to barter.
- Morale stuff, such as music, books, games, DVDS. An in-car DVD system can be used as a treat for kids, assuming you have the fuel/battery power, because you can play a DVD and they can sit in the comfort of the vehicle. Works while travelling and while static.
- Anything else you think you will need and either can have at home, at your retreat, or take with you.
- Any equipment for skills that will be useful for post-event, such as building or repairing stuff.

Extract from a Blog Entry @ Maxvelocitytactical.blogspot.com

'Camping after the SHTF':

This is an extract of some comments I made on a forum and the follow up. The background is that the envisaged scenario is more family survival in a WROL SHTF situation, rather than resistance operations against enemies 'foreign or domestic'. See my other post on 'tactical overnighting in the woods' for a more operational point of view:

Just a few thoughts on how you may have to adapt your camping once the S has HTF.

Assuming you have bugged out somewhere and are camping, because we are talking civil breakdown and all that, we have to assume that there are potential bad guys out there. This will mean that your camping will have to take on a more tactical form. Without going into too great a detail, here are a few factors you may want to think about:

1. Location: pick a concealed location preferably without an obvious access route, allowing you observation of the approaches to your campsite. Try to not be with others, unless they are part of your group i.e. don't be at a National Park campsite. Try to conceal your location. Avoiding trouble by using concealment is the best policy.

2. Light and noise discipline. No lights at night, keep the noise and goofing off down. This means no campfire at night, lamps etc. You are not camping; you are surviving in the woods. If they see your campfire, they are coming.

3. Cooking: tied in with the light thing, you should consider getting all your cooking done in daylight and eating earlier.

4. Security: make sure you have sentries out, even if this is just a roving guard. Also, use buddies to go do tasks, such as hunting or collecting water or wood.

5. Have a 'stand to' plan for if you are bumped by bad guys. Initially the sentry will be engaging them, but the rest need to roll out, grab weapons and move to defensive positions.

6. 'Bug Out": as part of the 'stand to" plan individuals should be designated to pack stuff up, organize kids, and get ready to move, whether you are camping by foot or with vehicles. You will likely need to move locations after a contact with bad guys, even if you get the upper hand. Either way, pack up, provide covering fire, and bug out to an established emergency rendezvous (ERV) location. Rally, check status and move off.

A question received:

'How often would you recommend moving the site? Would that help at all? Or is it best to remain in one spot till you are found (suspect someone is on to you) then move?'

Answer: That is a very interesting question and will depend on the circumstances. If you do suspect that someone is 'on to you' then you should move immediately before they get a chance to attack you in place, and keep moving until the threat passes. That could also lead into other types of response: if you are genuinely in a situation where someone is after you or following you then you should consider some type of ambush (offense being best form of defense) if you have the capability in order to take the initiative away from them.

When I wrote the original post, it was more security procedures in general, not specific. If you are out there and you don't suspect you have been noticed, then there is no real limit to how long you could stay in a place. You may be really well hidden so don't move just for the sake of it. Also, the more you move, whether by foot or vehicle, the more chance that you will be picked up on someone's 'radar' and perhaps followed, or walk into someone else's defensive perimeter. If you are well hunkered down, you could stay there so long as you have sentries and keep the security measures sup. Getting sloppy/complacent will get you found.

If you are not in such a backwoods situation and you suspect you may have been noticed, then you should keep moving; maybe only one night in each place until you get to a real well hidden place. If it is sort of high risk, you are moving, you can consider stopping late afternoon at a location to cook and eat, administrate, before moving to another location prior to nightfall to establish a camp and sleep. This is a dismounted jungle warfare technique designed to throw off anyone tracking you.

And further:

Re: leaving less sign at your campsite: *It can be hard, particularly if you are a family group with children rather than a small 'spec ops' team!*

You have to change the idea in your mind from 'camping' to being in a 'patrol base'. This will need to take account, again, of children etc. You won't be sitting round the fire drinking a cold one. There will be no fire sometimes, if you have to go 'hard routine'; cook during the day and if you can use propane camp stoves or similar which will not leave sign. Don't cut anything at your campsite. Dig latrines and fill them in. Pick up all trash and carry it out, sweep the area before departure and try to cover up any sign. Anyone with skill will realize that you have been there, but you can reduce signature. If you are in vehicle you may leave tracks anyway etc.

Think about rather than trying to eliminate all sign that you were there, reduce it as much as possible and then use deception, such as moving off in another direction then switching course. On the offensive side you can stop on your route and put in a 'hasty ambush', breaking track to cover the trail you just walked to catch any trackers. You should do this if you are on foot and before you stop and establish a patrol base anyway.

If you are less of a family group and more of a patrol, then you should be operating under stronger battle discipline. This would entail overnighting in a concealed location with all round defense and sentries. You would only put up rain tarps after dark, after evening 'stand to' and take them down before first light and morning 'stand to'. You would do clearance patrols of the area once you had moved into it and after morning stand to. *You would put in a snap ambush and use deception before moving into your night location. No fires, lights or noise. Consider the cooking and eating at a different location thing before moving into your overnight position.*

Re: Being Random: *I totally agree with that for any normal activities. Consider however that if you are in a camping area in the woods etc. you will want to reduce noise and sign. In a patrol position this would entail clearing a 'track plan' around the position and stringing commo string around it, moving leaves and sticks off the path etc. This allows silent movement around the perimeter and to each sleeping area at night. It also reduces the signature of tracks and can be covered up again prior to leaving; pushing leaves and sticks back over the track plan. Rather than denuding a wide area if you are moving a short distance to collect water, you may be better off with a single track plan to do this, reducing signature in grasses and reeds etc. Obviously, if this goes beyond a short walk to a water source, to a patrol, then you will change that and avoid all pattern setting, going back to the random model.*

Surveillance Equipment

A separate note on this subject: The ability to conduct surveillance, whether it is from a security post or an observation post or maybe during a recce patrol or even on a convoy move, will confer considerable advantage over the enemy. This will usually involve optics of some sort and having a good set of binoculars is invaluable. It is also useful to have magnification optics on your weapons for both observation and target engagement. This all adds to your stand-off capability. It is always an advantage to see the enemy as early as possible and to engage at the maximum effective range of your weapon systems. Kill the enemy as far away as you can to prevent him touching you, and if he is intent on doing so he will have to close the distance while all the time you are able to bring effective accurate fire down onto him.

Night vision equipment will allow you to 'own the night'. It is expensive and you have to think about what configuration you will have. You also need to have a lot of spare batteries, so perhaps it will not be a long term capability, but it may get you through the worst of it. In a grid down situation, it will be very dark out there; this can be mitigated to a certain extent by allowing your night vision to develop by not using white light and with various moon states, but you may simply not be able to see much out there.

If you mount night sights on a weapon, then you can't share that equipment unless you are swapping weapons around, but you can engage the enemy with that weapon in darkness. If you are doing security at a static location it may be all you can financially afford to have one or two sets of NODs (night observation devices) that can be used by sentries, perhaps hung round their necks and passed from sentry to sentry and used for periodic surveillance.

However, you can't translate a target seen with this type of NOD to an engagement with your weapons easily, unless you mount IR laser pointers on your weapons. These are activated by your hand on the front hand guard and zeroed to your weapon: you see the pointer through the

NVG (Nigh Vision Goggles) and can engage that way (you don't use your sights, you just look through the NVG, binocular or monocular type, for the laser pointer and place that on the target). So, although night vision equipment confers a great advantage at night, you have to give some thought to the expense and how you will tie that in with a plan to be able to both observe and engage the enemy using these systems.

You can always go 'old school': use of white light. This could be searchlights, perhaps with a lit perimeter, and maybe even the use of trip flares on the perimeter. That is not so low profile. What is really useful is to have a stock of parachute illumination flares. These can be sent up if enemy is suspected on the perimeter or seen with NVGs, and will allow engagement of the enemy by all those defenders with weapons, not just those with night vision. Remember that if the enemy is firing you will be able to return fire at their muzzle flashes in the darkness.

A good stock of parachute flares can be invaluable. They will burn for around a minute and you can keep putting them up as long as you need them; you can also be clever and use them to aid you in other ways, such as ordering a break and conducting movement in the dark, before lighting up with flares again. Someone should be designated to fire the flares and because the flares make a large signature when they are fired, a lot of smoke, then they should do so from behind hard cover. The flares will drift with the wind and some skill is needed when using them.

Also, remember that we are not a Tom Clancy-esque black ops team and creeping about with NVGs may be either a little expensive or a little too covert and tactical for the skills of your group. It may be better, whether defending or conducting an attack or raid; to just go old school and 'go noisy' putting up flares and engaging with noise, light and aggression.

Profile

This is an interesting topic and links in to the discussion of weapons (above) and law enforcement (below). Profile refers to how you appear as you are conducting yourself post-event, whether it is how your house appears, how your vehicle's look, or how you yourself appear. This mainly refers to the visibility (high profile) or concealed (low profile) carriage of weapons and defenses. This may be more relevant in a 'slide' situation where the crisis worsens over time until we finally reach collapse; you will need to make judgments about how to adjust your profile and when to do so.

Pre-collapse, you should have given thought to obtaining concealed carry permits (CCW) and own weapons so that if you feel the need to, you can carry a concealed handgun in a legal manner. There will be some point in the slide, whether it happens gradually or overnight, when you will feel threatened enough by the situation and the changes to your environment where you will want to break out your tactical equipment. For a post-societal situation you should have tactical gear available as discussed under the weapons section above: handguns, tactical rifles and shotguns with some form of vest, rig or carry-bag that will allow you to carry sufficient spare ammunition. Body armor is ideal.

Extract from a Blog Entry @ Maxvelocitytactical.blogspot.com

Body Armor:

I was asked a question about body armor, what type to get. It seemed like a good topic for a post:

I am a fan of body armor. In any kind of 'kinetic' situation when receiving incoming small arms fire, it will significantly reduce the chances of sustaining a penetrating wound to the torso. Such wounds are often not survivable. Refer to the chapter on Casualties or more discussion on wounds and treatment, plus extremity bleeding etc.

One thing you need to do is research the 'NIJ' levels for protection, and decide what you want to get.

In basic terms, you have the 'soft armor' portion and the 'plates" that insert front and rear. If you have a plate carrier, you only use the plates. This gives you less protection than if you include the soft armor, but the soft armor does not protect against high velocity (rifle) rounds.

So it's a balance, between levels of protection, weight, bulk and heat retention. The NIJ levels of protection are:

Soft Armor:

Type IIA (9 mm; .40 S&W)
Type II (9 mm; .357 Magnum)
Type IIIA (.357 SIG; .44 Magnum)

Plates:

Type III (Rifles)
Type IV (Armor Piercing Rifle)

The calibers listed are the rounds that this level will protect up to, inclusive of lesser calibers.

Personally, I have a set that I had for working in the Middle East. It was a 'low profile' set that still had front and rear plates. The soft armor portion is level IIIA and the plates are level III. You don't actually need level IV plates, unless you feel the need to protect against armor piercing rounds. Military armor has level IV plates. This set of body armor simply came in a soft cover, no pouches attached. It meant that I could wear it under a shirt, or more operationally I used to wear my gear over the top of it, depending on the low or high profile nature of the mission. So that is a useful way to go, lots of flexibility.

What I have now, on the civilian side, is a battle belt, an assortment of 'low profile' 'man bags' that can carry magazines, and I have taken the soft armor and plates out of the cover and put them into a plate carrier that I bought online. It mirrors the military gear I used to wear. So it is no longer low profile, unless I replace the armor in the original soft cover. I have a full tactical vest set up.

If I wanted to go low profile, I can replace the armor in the soft cover, wear it under a shirt, and carry a 'man bag' with spare magazines in. With the tactical vest, you can get ones that take soft armor (level IIIA stops powerful handgun/shrapnel) and/or plates. So you can get a plate carrier, or a full set with soft armor. A simple plate carrier will be lighter and cooler, but offers less protection. The soft armor gives you greater protection, just not against high velocity rounds.

So what? Decide what sort of rig you are looking to set up. Research the NIJ levels that you want. You can buy the stuff in a civilian style soft cover and put it into a tactical vest if you want. You definitely want the plates, and you need to decide if you also want the soft armor too. You can buy plates on their own, and the plate carrier s can be found on amazon and multiple other sources (Links on the blog).

Body armor can be heavy, hot and sweaty. If you have a 'MOLLE' style tactical cover you can set up a full tactical vest by attaching ammo pouches and the like to the body armor cover. This makes it heavier, but it allows you to carry your gear. If you are contemplating being involved in any kind of tactical kinetic situations, you need to get over the whole hot, heavy and sweaty thing. Suck it up and drive on. Do more PT/drink more water. You will benefit from the protection and you need to carry your ammo and IFAK anyway, plus ancillary gear.

If you are working in the heat, and you want to compromise, use a plate carrier. This gives you the same high velocity rifle round protection but without the greater soft armor torso coverage that will protect against handgun rounds and shrapnel.

Don't go the other way and simply wear the soft armor, like cops do under their shirts. This provides protection against handgun rounds and some can be anti-stab vests also. But there is no protection from high velocity rifle rounds. You can still wear a set with plates under a shirt if you need to be a little more low profile, for instance if driving through a hostile environment trying to remain low key.

For a situation where you expect full breakdown and tactical challenges, it would be ideal to have some sort of armor-carrying vest with the MOLLE style attachments for magazine pouches and ancillaries, very similar to the way the military or SWAT teams carry gear – 'full battle rattle'. You can utilize a vest like this, or chest rig, even if you don't have body armor. You can also wear it over the top of less-tactical body armor, such as the lower profile police type vests that can go under clothing. A high profile approach will be useful post-event when you feel that a tactical event is likely and where it does not really matter that you are carrying weapons openly. Such a profile (or posture) can also act as a display to make it obvious that you are a hard target and best not to bother you.

You should consider the overall impression that you give: whether you are simply wearing outdoor clothing and your gear, or whether you are wearing some form of camouflage (military or hunting) or military uniform, and whether this is perhaps a standardized uniform approach with your group. You may appear more like a militia if you wear all the same uniform, which may be good or bad depending on your assessment of the situation.

If you are actually military or police, serving or retired/reserves, you could utilize elements of your uniform. This will have a follow on effect with other survivors and could be good or bad depending. If they really think you are military, then they may mob you expecting some form of aid. If there is martial law, then looking like military may be a bad thing (this does not refer to 'impersonating' military or police, just the wearing of uniforms that may cause you to be mistaken for military or police). Looking smart and uniformed with your gear professionally set up could also gain trust and respect from other groups. You may well be retired military, and looking like such could work for you. However, if you deserted to look after your family, then you may want to adopt a lower profile!

A high profile approach would mean the open display of weapons and military style load carrying gear. This could apply to your person or also to your home or retreat: are you trying to hide or are you presenting a strong front with obvious defenses and fighting positions? A lot will depend on the situation, your adopted strategy, and your defensive capabilities. Post-event it may simply not matter anymore that you are adopting a high profile and it may simply be better to have the weapons and equipment immediately to hand.

A low profile approach does not mean that you have to necessarily be less well armed. Low profile is a sliding scale from simply carrying a concealed handgun to carrying the full tactical weapon and ammunition scale but doing it in a lower profile manner. You could wear your body armor and full rig, and then cover it with a large shirt. This will work only when you are in your vehicle, but that may be sufficient. The body armor and ammo pouches under the shirt will make you look fat.

You could wear low profile body armor under normal clothing, have your assault rifle on the floor of the vehicle or in a sports bag, and carry spare ammunition in some form of tote or 'grab' bag. Many types of these are sold on the web, in various stages of profile from tactically obvious to looking like a 'man-bag'. If the situation warrants it, you may want to give consideration to how to adopt a low profile, the equipment required, and how to best throw off the cover and bring your weapons to bear on the enemy in the event that the situation goes kinetic.

Practically, if you are operating from vehicles you will want to set up your gear to work for you in these situations. If you are low profile in the early stages of a slide, then just wear your normal jeans and a loose shirt over your handgun in an appropriate concealment holster. You can have a grab bag ready to go, whether this is a day pack or satchel like man-bag that you can sling over your shoulder with additional gear in it. Keep your long rifle somewhere concealed but accessible, maybe in a gym bag in the foot well.

If you are not wearing body armor, then you may well be served better by utilizing a belt rig rather than wearing a load carrying vest. Load carrying vests work well when you are wearing them in conjunction with body armor because with the armor on, sweating underneath and having your torso covered is no longer an issue. If you only have lightweight police type armor without ballistic plates (which will only stop handgun and not high velocity rounds) you may again find that a belt rig, almost like a police duty belt, will serve you well.

Because you will be in a vehicle, you don't want any pouches or bulky items around your back. Choose a decent web belt and attach your handgun holster to one side and two or three triple magazine pouches for your long weapon, as well as pouches for handgun magazines, to the other side. Put your trauma first aid pouch (IFAK) on the other side. You could put additional items such as flashlights, knives, multi-tools, mace or maybe even an extendable baton (ASP type, for escalation of force situations) on the belt also.

Don't worry about making this like military web gear: you don't have enough weight to necessarily need the yoke (suspenders) and you don't want items like canteen pouches in the way. You can wear a hydration bladder in a vehicle and your grab bag (backpack or satchel type) will hold additional gear for when you have to get out of the vehicle. This sort of set up will give you a versatile lightweight rig that still carries the ammunition you need. Have both a rig like this set up as well as a ballistic armor carrying vest 'full battle rattle' which will allow you to adjust your protection and posture to the threat/environment.

Law Enforcement Issues

Closely related to issues of which profile to adopt are the issues of law enforcement and martial law. Depending on the event, and the speed of the slide, we may find ourselves in a gray area where some law enforcement is operating, but the situation is out of control and civil disorder and violence poses a real threat. It may also be that some law enforcement personnel are in denial and continue to operate despite the relevance of what they are doing having been negated by events.

What if you are transiting to your BOL and are driving down back roads and you come across, or are pulled over by, a zealous local sheriff's deputy? Is he still operating under the pre-event standards? Will he take exception to the fact that you look like armed soldiers driving through his area, even though it is obvious that you are a group of families heading to safety? It all depends on his assessment of the situation. You could be low profile but he may decide to search the vehicle, or your low profile may be easily unmasked by a quick scan of the inside of the vehicle during the traffic stop.

As law abiding citizens the officer should be on your side, but what if he does not like what he sees? What if you are a single family transiting 'out of dodge' and he decides that he wants to take your weapons or perhaps take the husband into custody for his carriage of loaded assault weapons (and for generally looking like a badass – never underestimate the potential for a 'pissing contest' if you are on an Alpha Male's turf!)

Does that threat from the officer put the family under lethal threat by disarming them in the collapse environment? What would you do? The hope would be that the officer understands that you are law abiding citizens acting in the interests of the safety of your family in a dangerous environment. Hopefully he sees the team as being on the right, not wrong, side of the law. Does he see you as a crazy 'survivalist' or someone on the same side as the law?

Martial law may also be a problem, particularly when transiting to a BOL or generally moving around if you have to. The military may consider that they are 'the only sheriff in town' and they may take exception to the carriage of weapons. It all really depends on the nature of the event, the threat, and how obvious it all is. It is to be expected that as the event continues, military units such as National Guard deployed in home defense will probably dissolve as increasing numbers of individual's desert to look after themselves or their families. This situation will also put more armed and dangerous personnel out there, looking to survive.

It is to be hoped that in the aftermath, units such as National Guard do not produce local 'warlords' who realize that the situation is lost and set themselves up to maximize their position in the post-event disorder.

In situations where military discipline remains, the same issues as described under law enforcement apply, and therefore you should consider your profile. If you are actually a deserting or 'failing to report for duty' military member, then be aware that you may be captured if stopped and inspected at military traffic control points. If you are simply retired or non-activated and you look like a military person, then hopefully they will see you as being a professional and all on the same side. It all depends on the individuals encountered and their command culture.

A note on military & law enforcement personnel: It should not necessarily be assumed that just because someone is, or has been, in the military that they are therefore a 'good egg' or in fact useful to your team. The military is a vast force with personal in a huge array of military operating specialties (MOS). The military has suffered from problems of recruitment and standards of personnel, and also its own struggle with obesity and standards of training. This is in no way intended as a disparaging comment on those who have sacrificed for their country, so don't take it as such. As one who has served, the comment goes to the reality at the heart of the situation.

Be careful who these veterans are: it is possible to deploy and never leave the base (Forward Operating Base or FOB, hence 'Fobbits'), which is not necessarily in itself a negative mark against these individual's, it is simply that they were doing the job assigned to 'meet the needs of the army'. Conversely, they may have spent all their time outside the wire, but still not be a good person or good soldier. Also, they may have had very limited or no combat training/experience and depending on the individual it is possible that they absorbed very little of use.

It is possible to get through current basic training by doing very little and meeting hardly any of the standards: there is a reluctance to fail people and basic training is conducted at the standard and speed of the weakest trainees.

Conversely, there are also individuals, units and MOS within the military that are very 'high speed' and produce a high quality of trained and experienced individuals. Therefore, simply have your eyes open when considering the utility of a former military person to your group.

Similarly, everyone is an individual with their own qualities and potential. You may have someone who has never deployed, but who is an excellent soldier, or who was never in the army but did a bit of some sort of relevant training, is a quick study, and makes an excellent soldier. Other types can be really useful, again depending on the specifics: woodsmen and hunters are an example. They come in various guises, from overweight blustering 'oxygen thieves' to real outdoors types who may make excellent scouts or snipers. It all depends on the individual and a lot has to do with attitude and receptiveness to learning.

Sometimes veterans are not ideal because of that factor: they may be set in their ways and not necessarily as good as they think. Just because they did something a certain way, and got away with it, does not mean they are skilled soldiers or that their way is right. Sometimes experience is just getting away with the wrong stuff for long enough. Beware of arrogant blustering types or super-tough guys. Look for people who mix confidence with humility: we are back to the quiet professional again.

Think about the origins of today's special operations forces. 'Back in the day' the selections to get into these groups may have been either non-existent or very different from today's well-choreographed 'Olympic' endurance events. Often, it was inspired 'geeky' types who started these things off, or provided the expertise. Look at the origins of the British SAS in the Second World War: the original SAS was a pretty aggressive bunch of daring tough guys who did not necessarily get it right all the time in North Africa. Their target was German airfields behind enemy lines and they had all sorts of problems, such as parachuting in high winds, tactical mobility, getting lost in the desert etc.

The Long Range Desert Group (LRDG) was operating as a recce group at around the same time in North Africa and had been set up by an initially amateurish bunch of 'jolly good chaps' who had spent the years between the wars, based in Egypt, going on expeditions in vehicles in the desert and perfecting desert driving and navigation. They had even driven from India to Egypt. It came to be that the SAS got with the LRDG and had them taxi them to some of their raids deep in the desert behind enemy lines, leading to the SAS developing their own mobility capability, which is the historical precedent behind todays SAS mobility troops and the 'pink panthers' (pink was discovered to be the color that provided the best camouflage in the North African desert).

Imagine a post-event scenario. There is no Special Forces selection event: the situation is the selection event. We don't really want Neanderthal tough guy's, we want thinkers who are men of action; such as the ham radio guy who figures out how to communicate to other survivor groups, or the mechanic who manages to fix your vehicles after an EMP attack, or build an electricity generating system from scrap materials.

Be wary of the description of someone as a 'sniper'. For a sniper, the shooting is the smaller side of their role. A sniper team is trained in skills such as covert movement, concealment, observation and communications. A sniper can be better considered a battlefield sensor. A sharpshooter or perhaps 'designated marksman' is perhaps a better term for the team member you have who is an expert shot and has an accurate long-range weapons system. Such a sharpshooter will be invaluable as a force-multiplier and will be able to bring accurate fire down on the enemy in both offensive and defensive operations.

Situational Awareness

A key trait to be developed is situational awareness. This will take the form of a general awareness of threat and will be strengthened by specific ground knowledge in your area of operations (AO). Training, followed by the experience developed as the situation progresses, are key to this sense of awareness. For your specific AO, the time spent learning ground truth is invaluable to building this awareness of the local environment. Some key indicators:

'Indicator': a sign that is noticed when something is not right in the environment. This could be a sign of impending attack.

'Presence of the Abnormal': Indicators that something is amiss. Examples could include: Presence of unusual objects at the side of the road, perhaps with no explanation and not usually present, such as trash bags, disturbed earth or even animal carcasses - indicators for an IED.

'Absence of the Normal': This could take many forms, but again is a key indicator for an attack. Examples could include: (1) a usually busy market day, main street of a small town, market stalls are out and stocked, as you move through you notice that the area is suspiciously quiet and absent people. Odds are, something is about to happen. (2) No traffic on a road that usually is fairly busy at that time of day. - Indicator for a potential ambush, perhaps an IED or a complex ambush.

Observers: 'Dickers': The term dicker refers to enemy personnel or sympathizers who loiter in areas in which you are operating in order to pass on information. There may be multiple of these observers hanging about in your AO. Sometimes they may be obvious, sometimes they may go unnoticed. The purpose may simply be to observe friendly forces procedures in order to gather information for an attack. They may also be there to observe reactions to an attack or to pass on information on movement in order to facilitate an attempted attack. They may be in possession of cell phones, ICOM radio 'walkie-talkies' or video cameras.

One of the key things with situational awareness is learning to trust your intuition, your gut. Experience will help you with this but it is all too easy to rationalize away that nagging feeling of doubt, and you must listen to it.

Mitigation

There are a number of ways that a threat can be mitigated:

Avoidance: Simply put, avoid the threat. Given that you will be operating in an area where there will be, by the nature of the situation, a general threat, then the threat as a whole cannot be avoided. However, given judicious use of quality information and ground truth it is possible to mold operations to attempt to avoid specific threats while at the same time facilitating necessary movement.

Judgment: Closely tied in with avoidance and the use of intelligence is judgment. Judgment is an intellectual and experience based asset and should be used to make decisions on which missions to run based on an assessment of available information.

Routine: Routine must be avoided, however tempting and comfortable it feels. NEVER SET PATTERNS. Patrols, security patrols, supply and logistics movement; it must be ensured that these movements do not set routine patterns. The enemy will observe patterns and plan attacks based on routines. Vary times, routes and patterns.

Routes: Closely tied in with routine is the need to avoid setting route patterns. A useful tool is the 'honesty' trace where returning team leaders mark a map board in the Operations Center (if you have one) with routes taken; this can be used as a basis to see historical patterns and plan future missions. Team leaders must be cognizant of what they are doing and what routes they are taking. If patterns are being set, the enemy will observe it and lay a trap. If possible, team leaders should be inventive with routes taken, and vary them as much as possible within the terrain available. There will always be limitations and choke points.

Deception: Leaders should give thought to how they can conceal their intentions from the enemy even for routine moves. Any way that can shake up the norm will create uncertainty with the enemy. For example, it may be that a leader is scheduled to take his team on a foraging trip. There is potential for operational security (OPSEC) to be compromised and potentially there will be an attack. What can the leader do other than drive out to the site on a standard route? Conjecture: Can they move out the day before and overnight, arriving at the site from a different direction the next day?

Observation: Closely tied in with awareness, observation is a function of all members of the team. It is tied in with training and professionalism. Team members cannot be lazy or complacent. They must be observant for threats and indicators; sectors must be covered while moving and static.

Complacency Kills: There is a temptation to become complacent as the post-event situation progresses. Success can lead to complacency. Tied to this is the danger of being in the wrong mental state when an incident happens. There is a danger of denial, leading to ineffective response to contact. This is particularly a risk if the team is inexperienced and has not previously been in contact. Example: a team returning from routine forage. They are looking forward to chow and a DVD and are joking with each other in the cab of the vehicle. Suddenly, unexpectedly, there is a harsh concussion followed by the road being torn up by automatic fire, with rounds striking through the side of the vehicle. The sudden noise and violence of such a contact on its own has the potential of being paralyzing - if the team members are not in the right mental state, this can result in mental denial of the true situation and a reaction of freezing. It is the responsibility of all to train, rehearse (muscle memory) and constantly visualize (mental preparation) potential outcomes and situations while on patrol to ensure that if an incident happens you are in the right mental state to react without delay. You have to be able to mentally adjust to their situation having 'taken a left turn'. Such situations, where you may experience this 'dislocation of expectations' can result, without proper training and preparation, in a flight or freeze response, rather than the desired fight response.

Training & Preparation: Thorough training in the designated Tactics, Techniques and Procedures (TTPs) and Standard Operating Procedures (SOPs) is essential to success on the ground. Team members must be exposed to training and conduct as much rehearsal and tactical exercises as possible. This will also aid in team building and cohesion, which will benefit performance once post-event. Thorough training will also inculcate the necessary mitigation methods, mind-set and procedures in order to allow effective performance on mission.

Communication: Communication is not only essential for coordination of units while on mission. It is also essential to mitigation in the sense that all team members must be aware and functioning to detect threat and any suspicious activity must be communicated to commanders so that necessary avoidance measures must take place. Also, effective After Action Reviews in the form of debriefings of all team members following missions will be essential to build the ground truth picture, and develop trends in order to predict enemy activity. This can be fed back in to future missions as a cycle. Threat and intelligence must also be effectively briefed down to team members in order to keep them updated and develop their observation skills and effectiveness.

CHAPTER THREE

DECISION MAKING

"If you can keep your head when all about you
Are losing theirs and blaming it on you;
If you can trust yourself when all men doubt you,
But make allowance for their doubting too;"

KIPLING

Introduction

Inherent to any collapse or survival situation, as well as your current everyday life, is the need to make decisions. This is starkly illustrated by the previous chapter and the example of the 'stay or go' decisions that are discussed. Post-event, such decisions can literally be life or death matters and it is helpful to have a logical approach to this process. Such a logical approach, where you will go through a series of steps in order to make a decision, has utility in several ways.

Firstly, the logical process will ensure that you thoroughly consider the situation without missing out key considerations. Secondly, the process will help your mind work in a crisis where you can cling to the 'life-raft' of a logical step by step process that will help you think through the situation where panic may be a potential issue, and perhaps where you are in an environment where others are panicking and there is a danger of you being swept up in it. Thirdly, familiarity with such a process will help your thinking process so that even without the tools or written materials for such a process, you will train to have the mental tools to work logically through a problem and make a decision.

A key thing to do in a crisis is to make a decision. Often, right or wrong, simply so that you take some action. Hopefully, you will take the right action but being paralyzed by the enormity of the situation will not help and you need to do something. In a tactical kinetic environment, you need to make decisions. Go left, go right, but make a decision. Don't sit on the 'X'. This is where the mental discipline of a decision making process is so helpful, because in a time crisis such as a kinetic tactical situation you will not have the time to go through a formal decision making process, but hopefully your training in these processes will enable you to think rapidly and logically to make a decision and MOVE.

Now, there are several things to consider here. Below, we will go through a series of examples or process that you can use. One of these is the Military Decision Making Process (MDMP). This is a tool used by the planning Staff to offer courses of action (COA) to the commander that they work for. It is usually a time limited process that may be ongoing but also may be an isolated process. The problem with it occurs when courses of action are created, and decisions are made, based on simply the information that the Staff has at the time. This may be imperfect information and may need to be developed or further information gained, perhaps as reconnaissance is continued or the operation progresses.

To make such decisions and carry them out without recourse to review is a significant problem and can lack the ability to develop the situation as the plan progresses. It is sometimes stated that a commander must have the ability to make a decision and stick with it, follow it through to the conclusion. This will have utility in some circumstances, such as where you 'went left' but on reflection should have 'gone right' but your team is now deep in the poop and the only way out is to fight through to the conclusion.

But otherwise, when you are not so deeply committed, you must try and avoid inflexibility of thought and develop the ability to process new information and amend the plan accordingly. You were going to stay in place, but new information appears that makes that unwise or untenable. The 'stick in the mud' part of you does not want to leave your carefully prepared home and supply dump, but you must have the mental flexibility to do so if it is in the best interests of protecting your people.

The Military Decision Making Process

This is a planning tool that will develop courses of action; once you decide on what you consider to be the best course of action it will become your plan. Be careful of making decisions in isolation and trying to follow them through without considering the new information that you gather, perhaps as you move from your home to a designated hide or retreat location. The level of detail of the planning is dependent on the amount of information available and the time that you have to plan.

MDMP is a seven step process consisting of:

- Receipt of Mission
- Mission Analysis
- Course of Action (COA) Development
- COA Analysis
- COA Comparison
- COA Approval
- Orders Production.

Receipt of Mission: You will not be given a mission, but as a prepper you will decide on what that mission is. This will be decided by circumstances and information feeds that are available to you. As a side note, intelligence is defined as information that is analyzed and processed, so you will likely not have intelligence, but you will have available information that you can process to become your own intelligence. You will have your overall mission, which is likely to be the survival of you and your group, but to move towards that you will have to decide on the smaller mission, which is what you are using MDMP for.

You may be making the stay or go decision, or be running out of water and looking for a way to collect some more, or perhaps someone you care for did not make it to the retreat, cut off by the event and subsequent chaos, and you are considering the viability of a recovery operation. These are just examples of the sub-mission that you will encounter as part of the overall survival process.

The MDMP has utility for these missions. It is helpful for you to state this mission, usually in the form of a task to achieve with an 'in order to' second part which achieves the requirement for mission command. It may be that you are giving this mission to a tactical team that you send out so use mission command to give them the mission and purpose: "Forage team will conduct a recce in the vicinity of Devastation Avenue in order to (iot) find a source of water for re-supply."

Mission Analysis: This is where you, or the group you gave the mission to, will analyze that mission and pull relevant considerations and actions from it. The mission consists of the tasks given to you (the mission) together with the unifying purpose, which is the part after the IOT phrase, against which all factors falling out of the MDMP process will be considered. There are four questions to mission analysis, which will result in considerations that will be incorporated into the following MDMP process:

- INTENT: Commanders intent. What is his/your desired end state? Where is the main effort? How must my action directly support my commander's intent?
- TASKS:
  - Specified: What tasks must I complete to fulfill my mission?
  - Implied: what tasks fallout from the specified tasks that I must complete to fulfill my mission?
  - Examples: I have to defend my retreat; therefore I must have suitable weapons and training. Or, I must get to

objective Alpha, which is across a river and the bridge is down; therefore the implied task is that I need to conduct a river crossing.

- CONSTRAINTS & FREEDOMS OF ACTION: What limitations are there on my freedom of action? Time, space, resources, control measures, rules of engagement, assets, logistics, legal and law and order. By when do I need to make my decision? Use the 1/3 : 2/3 rule where you only take a third of the available time for your planning process, allowing subordinates 2/3 of the time for their battle preparation. Issue a warning order to set battle procedure in place.
- CHANGED SITUATION: Has the situation changed since the mission was received or the estimate completed (constantly review your mission analysis)?
    - Nothing changed: No change, mission confirmed.
    - Minor change: Same mission, same plan.
    - Significant change: Same mission, amend plan.
    - Major change: Possible new mission and new plan. Refer to superior commander, or if not possible, act in support of his main effort, taking into account his intent.

WARNING ORDER: This is not strictly a part of the MDMP but it is a part of battle procedure. You will issue as much relevant information as you can to allow battle procedure to start, amending and issuing further warning orders as required. The mnemonic for the principles of battle procedure is: **CAKE**

    Concurrent Activity
    Anticipation at all levels
    Knowledge of the grouping system
    Efficient drills

The purpose of which is to ensure that your machine is ready to go once you are ready to issue specific mission orders. It should not be the first they are hearing of the plan!

Course of Action Development: Develop at least two Courses of Action (COAs), three is better, but more than three is probably too many. In this step the staff Analyzes Relative Combat Power (friendly assets vs. the enemy's assets), Generates Options, Arrays Initial Forces (where friendly forces are arrayed as well as the best information on the enemy is arrayed), Develop the Scheme of Maneuver, and prepare COA statements and sketches. The COA sketch is a one page (usually PowerPoint) diagram that shows a map of the plan with all the critical tasks listed along one side. COAs need to pass the suitability, feasibility, acceptability, distinguishability, and completeness tests. This means that the plans each need to be realistic given the assets, restraints, constraints, and assumptions listed in the previous step. The two to three COAs need to be distinct from each other, not just minor variations of the same plan.

Course of Action Analysis: This step is known as war-gaming. The staff will have gathered all the information available, determined assets available and the assets the enemy has, identified facts and assumptions, and developed a couple of plans. Now the plan is put to the test in a table top exercise.

There are rules to war-gaming. At all times, remain unbiased towards a COA; approach war-gaming as an honest assessment of the plans in order to determine their strengths and weakness. Next, list the advantages and disadvantages of each. Continually assess the COA feasibility, acceptability, and suitability. If, while war-gaming, it is determined a COA just won't work, then stop war-gaming it. Next, avoid drawing premature conclusions and gathering facts to support such conclusions. Finally, compare the COAs in the next step, not during war-gaming. When war-gaming, focus on one COA at a time, from start to finish, without discussing how this COA has an advantage over the other. Finally, war game the COA from start to finish; go through friendly action, enemy reaction, friendly counteraction for each event (or enemy action, friendly action, enemy counter action if the enemy strikes first). One person is dedicated as the enemy side; they will fight to win for the enemy, which could even be representative of a natural disaster.

Course of Action Comparison: Now is the time that the various COAs are compared to determine which one is the best option, and therefore which to go with. The actual comparison of the COAs is critical. Use any technique that facilitates reaching the best decision. Start by evaluating each COA from different perspectives, using the evaluation criteria that were already established. Now, compare the COAs to determine the one with the highest likelihood of success against the most likely enemy threat and the most dangerous enemy threat. This is done through a simple matrix with COAs listed across the top and the evaluation criteria listed down the side. The criteria can be weighted in order to give more strength to those criteria which is most important. After each COA is graded and weighted, they are totaled and the one with the lowest score wins. You now have your COA.

Course of Action Approval: Within the military, this is a formalized brief to the commander by the staff with detailing the results of the war-gaming process and their recommended COA. At the end of the briefing, the commander decides on a COA and then issues final planning guidance.

Orders Production: Now that the COA has been approved, the staff gets to work finalizing the plan that will result in an order to subordinate units.

Summary: The MDMP has a lot of utility; however its greatest utility outside of a staff planning room is a simplified version of the war-gaming process, the course of action development and comparison. The full MDMP is a resource and time consuming process that requires practice and training in the war-gaming. There is simpler tool that is known as the 'Combat Estimate' and will be covered next.

The Combat Estimate

The combat estimate, or simply estimate, is an excellent tool that utilizes the MDMP. It used to be called an 'appreciation' and this was changed to 'combat estimate'. The estimate is a process very similar to the MDMP but it is more designed for use by an individual commander making decisions on the ground and without a large staff to war-game for him. You can still bring in others to help you but it is not such a complex process to complete.

Combat estimates form part of leader training and are initially practiced very formally to ensure that the process is sound within the trainees mind. For a combat leader, practice of the estimate process will be trained from formal written through oral to dynamic estimates during live combat training and will result in an embedded decision making process in that individuals mind that at its basic level will enable sound decisions of the 'go left, go right, or go up the middle type'.

Estimates can be completed off a written scenario. They are then practiced during 'TEWTS', which are 'Tactical Exercises without Troops': where leaders will be looking at the ground over which they are expected to conduct the estimate, whether that is an attack, defense of other scenario. Estimates will then be completed dynamically during field training exercises, such as a platoon advance to contact, where the estimate will be typed out in a small plastic folder and the leader will take a few minutes to fill it out with sharpie before briefing the plan and carrying it out. By the time this process of training is complete, the leader will have the estimate as a tool for written planning, or simply in his head when out on the ground and where decisions need to be made. Here is a version of the estimate:

COMBAT ESTIMATE

Mission: The tasks given to you and the unifying purpose, against which all factors are considered.

STAGE 1 – MISSION ANALYSIS	
QUESTION	**CONSIDERATION**
1. **INTENT (Why?)** 2 up, 1 up, my role	2 Up: Superiors role in his commanders plan Desired end state? Where is his main effort? 1 Up: Commanders intent? Concept of operations? How must my action directly support my Commanders intent?
2. **TASKS (What?)** - **Specified** - **Implied**	What tasks must I complete to fulfill my mission? What are my implied tasks?
3. **CONTRAINTS** **(What not?)** **(When?)**	What limitations are there on my freedom of action? Control measures? Time? Space? Resources? Rules of engagement? Assets? Timelines? Logistics? Political? Strategic? Legal? Law Enforcement? Martial Law?
4. **CHANGED SITUATION** (Continuous process throughout operation)	Has the situation changed since orders were received or the estimate completed? **Nothing changed**: no change, mission confirmed **Minor change**: same mission,

	same plan **Significant Change**: same mission, amend plan **Major change**: possible new mission and new plan. (Refer to superior commander, or if not possible, act in support of his main effort, taking into account his intent).
5. **CONFIRMATORY CHECK**	Clarification Up, if required
ISSUE INITIAL WARNING ORDER	

STAGE 2 – EVALUATE FACTORS		
FACTOR	DEDUCTIONS	TASKS/ CONTRAINTS
GROUND/ENEMY (Consider Ground and Enemy together – use Intelligence Preparation of the Battlefield (IPB)) * Note see below. **GROUND / ENVIRONMENT** Routes/Axes (Enemy and Own) Mobility Corridors (Enemy and Own) Dominating Ground	*What is deduced from this? Ask 'So What?'*	*What tasks or constraints fall out that need to be incorporated into the Courses of Action (COA)?*

Key Terrain/Vital Ground Killing Areas Objectives Going Obstacles Choke Points Visibility Distances Wind (NBC Considerations)		
ENEMY Center of Gravity Decisive Points Enemy Intentions Air/Helicopter Threat Known Dispositions and Organizations Weapons and Equipment NBC Capability/Likelihood of use Key Vulnerabilities Morale Strengths and Weaknesses Logistics and Supply situation	*What is deduced from this? Ask 'So What?'* *Need for Reconnaissance?*	
Likely Enemy Course of Action	*Can you counter it?*	*What is the effect in you and what counter-action do you need to take?*
Worst Enemy Course of Action	*Can you counter it?*	*Stay or Go?*

FRIENDLY FORCES Air & Flanking Forces Own Forces Capability - Organization and Equipment - Dispositions and Availability - Training - Readiness - Motivation - Strengths and Weaknesses Combat Service Support (CSS) - Demand - Current state of combat supplies Replenishment Requirements - Distance - Duration - Availability / Scarcity	*What is deduced from this? Ask 'So What?'*	
SURPRISE and SECURITY Deception: how can I deceive the enemy? Surprise: how can I seize and maintain the initiative? OPSEC (Operational Security): how can I prevent	*What is deduced from this? Ask 'So What?'*	

the enemy discovering my plan? Protection: how can I protect my own forces and plans? Security: Tactics techniques and procedures giveaway? Big picture security?		
TIME (identify constraints) Fixed Timings Enemy Timings Time required for tasks (e.g. orders, movement etc.) Additional time required due to degradation Earliest and latest time for H hour	*What is deduced from this? Ask 'So What?'* *'H-Hour' is the time that an attack or operation will begin.*	
OTHER RELEVANT FACTORS e.g. Political, Strategic, Event Type, Law and Order, Martial Law, Rules of Engagement, Legal etc.	*What is deduced from this? Ask 'So What?'*	

SUMMARY OF POSSIBLE TASKS		
Essential Tasks? Optional Tasks?		
TASK	COMBAT POWER REQUIRED	DEDUCTIONS

* Note: IPB (Intelligence Preparation of the Battlefield) is a systematic process which requires the production of a series of graphic overlays depicting basic data on weather, terrain and enemy deployment; the latter may be based on no more than an assessment of his doctrine. It is also a dynamic process in that data can be added or adjusted at any time before or during combat. The integration of these graphs will show; possible enemy options, own information gaps and decision points.

STAGE 3 - CONSIDER COURSES OF ACTION		
FORMULATION/CONSIDERATION OF COA		
COA	ADVANTAGES	DISADVANTAGES
1		
2		
3		

STAGE 4 – COMMANDERS DECISON

SELECTION OF COA

WHO?	**CONCEPT OF OPERATIONS**
WHY?	Sub Units Involved
WHAT?	
WHERE?	**COMMANDERS INTENT** – including vision of the desired end state
WHEN?	Outline of the intended operation including **MAIN EFFORT**

UPDATE WARNING ORDER

DEVELOPMENT OF THE PLAN AND ORDERS

PLAN:
1. Task Organization: who does what, roles
2. Mission
3. Execution: Concept of Operations:
   Intent: overall idea of what the commander is trying to achieve
   Scheme of Maneuver: Who, what, where, when
   Main Effort: most critical part of the execution, where commander will concentrate effort
4. Sub-Unit Missions or Tasks: their role within the plan
5. Coordinating Instructions: Times, locations etc.
6. Service Support: logistics & supply
7. Command & Signal: incl. position of commander during the operation

REVIEW

The above process for the combat estimate can be utilized for your prepper decision making post-event. It may be that not all the factors for consideration are relevant at all times and others can be added. Remember that once you get to COA consideration you need to be brutally honest in comparing them and selecting the best plan. One of the biggest decision making mistakes is to 'situate the estimate' in advance and try and make the end product, the decision, fit with what you wanted going in to the process.

When you have covered tactical operations as covered in the following chapters, on topics such as Defense and Offensive operations, you will find that the estimate fits very well into decision making for these operations. In addition, you can utilize the fooling principles to compare your COA against to determine their validity and advantages/disadvantages:

Principles of War	Functions in Combat
Selection and maintenance of the aim	Command
Maintenance of Morale	Firepower
Offensive Action	Maneuver
Surprise	Protection
Concentration of Force	Intelligence & Information
Economy of Effort	Combat Service Support
Security	
Flexibility	
Cooperation	
Administration	

CHAPTER FOUR

TRAINING

Training Processes

The importance of training cannot be underestimated, both for the preparation of specific TTPs (tactics, techniques and procedures), and also for the development of skills, confidence and the right mindset. This includes conditioning for combat. It would not be enough to simply read this book and store away the information contained; the content should be drilled and practiced. There could be some utility in having simply read it and then look to train individuals in a secure location post-event, but you still have to be able to master the contents yourself.

It is a useful point that it is unlikely that you will be able to maintain indefinitely a trained team ready to go. Some of those that you plan to survive with will be of the wrong age or physical ability to do much training (although there will be tasks that can be allocated to them to help, even such as reloading magazines, which has the benefit of giving them something to do to keep their minds off the emergency); also your team will evolve and post-event after some have not made it and others have joined you, it is likely that you will have a fairly new group of people.

You can't just tell people what to do, because they are civilians and they have no concept or experience of what you really mean; conceptually in their minds they will not be able to relate to what it is that you want. So it is more than likely that once you are in a secure location you will have the task to train up whatever team you have in the basics of weapons, shooting, security and basic tactics. Even if you have a group of veterans, who you perhaps want to use as a tactical team, you will want to draw up a series of TTPs (based on your knowledge plus input from their various experiences) and then train and run through the drills prior to going on mission.

There are a couple of mnemonics that will help with this: KISS & EDIP:

KISS:

- Keep
- It
- Simple
- Stupid*

(*Note: you can't fix stupid, just work with it!)

(*Note 2: one of the problems with stupid, is that when people are, they are often too stupid to realize it.)

EDIP:

- Explain
- Demonstrate
- Imitate
- Practice

KISS works for all tactics and military operations. EDIP helps to remember the best method of instruction. Explain the concept; demonstrate it to them, either yourself or have a demo team; have them imitate the technique or skill; then once it is understood have them practice it.

As a general outline, if you have a group of people that you need to train up you will adapt the training to the overall standard and experience of the group and you will 'crawl, walk, run' through the training. For example, if you want to train up a unit in some basic security and perhaps patrolling duties, then you should start with the basics and work up.

Start with the basics of shooting and then move on to the various positions. If the situation allows, throw in some strength and conditioning training. Once they have the basics of shooting them move them on to movement and communication. Start at the individual level and work up to buddy pairs, fire teams and squads. You will practice drills dry, first as explanations, then demonstrations then walk and run through, and then you will move on to doing it as a live firing exercise. You could have the trainees on the range and have them fire and move towards the targets (enemy), then they can learn to withdraw by fire and maneuvering away, and then peel to the left and right.

Once they have these basics down, you can then move on to teaching them field-craft, formations, patrolling and battle drills. You start at the basics and work up. If you have the ability, you should conduct live firing exercises. If you have the land and you are far away from prying eyes or ears, you can construct enemy positions and add realistic targets. You can conduct maneuver against these positions, utilizing safety personnel moving behind the firers to ensure that they do not engage when friendlies are too close within their arcs of fire ahead of them.

At a basic level, you can construct individual 'jungle lanes' by using a draw or stream bed and either placing targets out that will be seen as they progress down the lane, or even better have cabling so that the targets can be pulled up by safety personnel walking behind the firer. So, in essence, start at the basics and then work up to create realistic imaginative and interesting training that is tactically relevant. Once you have covered the basics the more and better 'battle exercises' that you create whether dry, blank or live, the better.

Battle exercises should have a scenario and use 'role players' to set the scene i.e. you have the squad in a preparation holding area and the role player comes out, gives the squad leader a brief, and leads them to an area to observe a target. The scenario is perhaps squad attack, recovery of items, or hostage rescue. The role player leaves them and the squad leader makes a quick plan and conducts the mission. This is all then debriefed (AAR – more later) and the lessons learned and assimilated.

Prior to conducting any sort of operation, it is necessary to conduct rehearsals. These are a form of training where whatever drills you have are practiced specifically for the upcoming mission. The various actions that you expect to conduct during the mission will be run through, as well as a run through of standard 'actions on'. Rehearsals will be done in the specific teams and vehicles that you will be utilizing for the upcoming mission, with equipment configured accordingly. Rehearsals normally follow an 'O Group' (orders group), where the operations order, or plan, is briefed to the team, using a standard format and usually either a map, a sand table or a model of the ground.

Rehearsals are usually termed 'day & night' or 'noisy & silent'; the first is more of a walk-through talk-through and the second is done in silence, dressed and equipped for the mission, preferably on ground similar to the mission ground. Usually the second rehearsal happens just prior to going out, and will also include pre-mission inspections and if it is a covert type mission such as a recon patrol where there is a need for silence, the team members will be made to get up and down from the ground to check for equipment noises (note: the old school way was to have them jump up and down to check for noise, but it makes more sense to have them do things that they will be doing on mission, such as get up and down and walk around). There will be more about orders in the tactical portion of this manual. If possible and the tactical situation allows it, test fire your weapons prior to going out.

Training is important because it generates inside you the knowledge and skills. Having the skills is more important than having the equipment. Having the right equipment is ideal and will make life a lot easier, hence our preparations. However, with the right equipment and without the skill is a bad situation. Without the right equipment and with the trained skills is better – you will be able to acquire the equipment and improve your situation.

Being a gear nerd is great; getting a new piece of 'Gucci' web gear is just as good retail therapy as a woman going out and getting new shoes and handbags. It's important to be prepared and you can make your life a lot easier if you do have the right equipment. And then the event happens just when you flew to the opposite end of the country on a business trip – now you have to get back to your family with no gear: Standby, Go! Don't be a faker – 'all the gear, no idea'. If you are getting the gear, then get the training. Be honest with yourself about your abilities, fitness and level of training. Take a long hard look at yourself and ask yourself if you are ready.

Extract from a Blog Entry @ Maxvelocitytactical.blogspot.com

Good Solid Training:

Many of you will have heard of the phrase 'crawl, walk, run' where it concerns training. It is very true, and it is important to get the solid building blocks of your training in place, whether as an individual and then as a team, before you try and move on to more complex drills.

I write this because I have been thinking about a lot of what I see out there, the 'tacticool' stuff. I also use as an example those movies where the heroes always seem to have perfect information and perfect technology, movies such as 'Mission Impossible'. Very seductive images, but imagine if they were trying to do that stuff for real: how do they have such perfect knowledge?! In the real world, 'Murphy's Law' says that if it can go wrong, it will. As such, using technology can be very helpful and very useful, but when you begin your training you should do so without the gadgets. This will also mean that when the gadgets fail, you will still be able to continue, overcome the inconvenience, and succeed.

So, what are some basic examples of this?

1) Map reading: make sure you are proficient at navigation with map and compass. You will utilize GPS when it is available, but if for whatever reason it is not, you have a reliable back-up. Have the paper maps and

compass. You may run out of batteries, your GPS device may fail, or the GPS grid may be shut down.

2) Basic Tactics: when you train your drills, whether it be squad level break contact drills, foot or vehicle mounted or whatever, make sure you start off just using voice commands and hand signals. You should be able to do all these things with technology, without radios. Add the radios later to enhance communications, but expect and anticipate communications failure.

Don't be seduced by all the cool technology. Use it as a tool to enhance your operations when you can, but don't be reliant on it. You won't have perfect information and your gear is likely to fail at some point, particularly in a post-collapse situation.

Plan for the worst and hope for the best.

Also consider that the more low-tech you go, the less detectable you are by modern technology.

A last word on 'the basics': It is my experience that what is considered 'the basics' in terms of tactics is really all there is. These 'basics' don't really get any more complicated than they are. As an example, fire and movement: from individual up to Company or Battalion level, fire and movement is what it is. There are variations on how to do it, and some ways work better than others, but there is no super-secret 'secret squirrel' technique to it. As an example some of the break contact drills that I lay out as options in 'Contact!' and 'Rapid Fire!': These are 'simple drills' in the tradition of using in combat drills that are simple enough to work under stress: KISS – Keep it Simple Stupid. These are the same drills that are used by the British SAS and SOF.

The key point here is that it is not making a drill complicated on paper that makes it 'high speed'. It is making the drill simple and logical enough that can be successfully carried out by trained operators when under enemy contact. The real skill to all this is to train good solid drills but be able to bear up under the stress, pressure and fatigue of being out there for long periods of time; being hot and dehydrated or wet and cold, without adequate sleep and food. That is when it counts. Intestinal fortitude and backbone. That is what separates the more 'high speed' operators from the 'tacticool' mall ninjas.

Weapons Safety

Tied in closely with training is weapons safety training. It is very important to concentrate on safety issues when training those in the group, both new and more experienced shooters. It always important to be 'mindful' when around weapons – to not be mindful is to invite an 'unthinking moment'. An unthinking moment can result in a negligent discharge simply because you were distracted or were not fully concentrating on what you were doing. A common mistake, when unloading the weapon at the end of a mission or perhaps for cleaning, is to check the chamber without removing the magazine. The bolt will ride forward, chambering a round, and when the trigger is squeezed a round will fire. You should consider building an unloading barrel or bay (a round catcher) at your defended location for this reason.

If unloading is taking place unsupervised, then the weapons should at the very least be pointed in a safe direction before loading or unloading them. Don't load and unload weapons in vehicles. A negligent discharge may well kill someone around you, and if you are at your base or home, it may even go through a wall or walls and hit, maybe, a child.

The basic safety rules for weapons are as follows:

1. Treat every weapon as if it were loaded.
2. Keep your finger straight and off the trigger until you intend to fire.
3. Never point your weapon at anything you don't intend to shoot.
4. Keep your weapon on safe until you intend to fire.

Don't let kids play with weapons, but familiarize them with them and teach weapons safety and respect. Teach them the right thing to do around weapons, this will be particularly important in a post-event situation, when weapons are very much in evidence, and should be taught now.

Weapons should generally be pointed in a safe direction, unless at the enemy when you want to engage them. Don't play, mess around, or goof off with or around weapons. Always utilize the safety catch – even when training in fire and movement, make sure it is applied when moving between positions.

Avoid 'flagging' friendlies with your muzzle i.e. pointing the weapon at them. This is an important point but can be taken to ridiculous degrees, with people getting all feisty and threatening others over unintentional and brief 'flagging'. What is more important is being professional and making sure your safety catch is applied. In some, very professional, armies and teams there is not such a focus on the whole flagging issue, which means you don't have to go to extreme lengths, when perhaps turning around, to avoid flagging anyone in your patrol. Just be professional and in control of your weapon.

To be clear, this is not to say that "Max Velocity condones flagging." Not at all. For example, the British army carries its weapons differently, not in the extreme low ready that the US Army has adopted which can be uncomfortable and 'wrist-twisting' on long patrols. For example, the British Paras use a more horizontal carry, which means that a muzzle may pass over another soldier when turning around. Deliberate pointing of weapons is to be avoided, but operationally you will notice that weapons carriage is often amended to a more horizontal method for practicality on long missions.

When conducting 'cross-decking' drills (more later) there will be a number of professional operators cramming into vehicles with weapons: everyone will be doing their best to make sure their weapon points in a safe direction and they will ensure that their safety catch is applied. That's just reality among professional operators.

So to state it again: Make sure that unless you are imminently about to engage the enemy your trigger finger is outside of the trigger housing, along the side of the weapon. Don't play around or mess with your trigger or safety catch in any way.

Shooting & Weapons Training

You need to get to the range and practice shooting. Once you have learned how to shoot and get a decent group on the range, you have to figure out some way to learn different shooting positions and how to combat shoot. Once you can do this, you need to learn how to fire and maneuver (shoot, move and communicate as a member of a team).

It may be hard to find a range where you can do this, but there are alternatives: do paintballing or airsoft, or just get out and run about in the woods practicing the drills in this manual. Be wary of commercial paintball/airsoft places: it is not the same as a situation with real weapons and bad habits can form. Better to consider the use of paintball or airsoft weapons on your own terms, as part of your own training away in the woods somewhere, to allow you to practice the correct drills. Consider shooting training in the following:

- Prone (lying) position
- Kneeling or squatting
- Standing
- Prone, firing around cover
- Kneeling, firing around cover
- Standing, firing around cover
- Firing from inside buildings: stay back from the windows, preferably on the other side of the room in the shadows. If you have time to prepare a defense, fire from behind a vision screen such as a torn curtain or blind. Additionally, be behind hard cover in the room, such that the cover is on the far side of the room from

the window i.e. chest of drawers filled with dirt or sandbagged position. Being back from the window will limit your fields of fire, but your sector of fire should be tied in with others covering their sectors to prevent a gap in the defense.
- Moving targets: make sure you practice 'leading' the target so that your shots don't pass behind the mover.
- Firing from inside vehicles: fire through open windows, through the glass of closed windows, or through the body of the vehicle if necessary. Don't drive around with weapons hanging out of car windows unless you want to look like an Iraqi police team.
- Changing magazines on the move: you can drop the empty magazine, but in a post-event situation you don't want to be throwing your mags away like that, you want them available for reloading. Consider the use of a dump pouch if you are wearing a plate carrier style rig. If you are old school and are wearing a web belt, then empties can go down your shirt or jacket front, where the belt will stop them falling to the ground.
- 'Slicing the Pie' on a corner: this is used when operating in buildings. If you have to look around a corner, don't just stick you head around or poke your weapon around (it could be gabbed by an enemy waiting just there). Step back from the corner and raise your weapon to the ready position, then slowly move to circle out so more and more of the area around the corner comes into view, all the while your weapon is pointing where you are looking so that you are not surprised and you can immediately engage any threat that comes into view. It is called slicing the pie (you could call it's called slicing the pizza if you wanted) because you are moving around the corner in little segments, like pieces of the pie.

Figure out which is your dominant eye and learn to shoot primarily with that hand; controversial yes. If you are right eye dominant, then shoot right handed and patrol right handed; in a crisis, all this changing of weapons to the other side, for instance to fire round cover or patrol on a certain side of the trail, will only result in a cluster.

When firing around cover, the idea is to keep as much of your body mass behind cover as possible; exposing as little as possible to the enemy. For a right handed shooter, this is easier from the right side of the cover than the left. When looking around something like a corner, get down and peer around low, where the enemy will not expect to see your head. Rather than 'other handed' shooting practice, what actually can be more useful is learning to handle the weapon, shoot, and change magazines if one of your hands/arms is injured.

The Marksmanship Principles are as follows:

1. The position and hold must be firm enough to support the weapon.
2. The weapon must point naturally at the target without any undue physical effort.
3. Sight alignment (i.e. aiming) must be correct.
4. The shot must be released and followed through without disturbance to the position.

Saying the same thing, the U.S. Army Fundamentals of Marksmanship are **STAB**:

1. **S**teady Position
2. **T**rigger Squeeze
3. **A**iming
4. **B**reath Control

Note: details of the U.S. Army Fundamentals can be found easily online.

When shooting, the body should be viewed as a tripod. In the prone position the tripod is formed from your chest and both elbows. As you breathe in, your chest rises and the muzzle of the weapon dips. As you breathe out your chest falls and the muzzle rises. To adjust sight alignment with the target, don't just pull the barrel over – adjust your body by scooting back or forwards or left and right with your whole lower body/hips.

Place the front sight on the target and focus on the front sight. As you breathe, the front sight will go up and down on the target. As you breathe out, the muzzle will rise; when it is on the correct point of aim, briefly hold your breath and squeeze (don't snatch) the trigger. Once the shot has gone, gently release the trigger and continue to breathe. To check sight alignment, try closing your eyes and continue to breathe steadily, then open your eyes and see where your sights are: on target or not?

Adherence to these principles will establish a basic standard and allow you to achieve better group sizes (i.e. smaller, because your shots are more consistent and strike closely together). Once you have done this, you need to move to combat shooting where there is a physical element (you will be out of breath) and many shots will be 'snap shots'. For this, there is not so much of a steady breathing method as outlined above, it is more about gaining experience and judging the 'wobble' to briefly hold the weapon steady and squeeze off the shot. Between shots, make sure you open both eyes and look over the sights to prevent tunnel vision and aid target acquisition. When learning to shoot: 'crawl, walk, run'.

In a contact situation, the danger is that people will not correctly aim their weapons, or they will shoot while looking over the sights and not really concentrate on killing the enemy. When in contact, the aim is to kill or suppress (neutralize) the enemy so that your team can move without being shot. Rounds cracking over the top of the enemy in their general vicinity will not make them take cover. Rounds striking close to or actually hitting the enemy will distract them from their aim and increase your survivability.

Take a moment to visualize this and practice it. When training for contact situations, take a moment to actually aim and fire the weapon at the target. When you are doing training where you have a live 'enemy' whether it be with airsoft or blanks or some other training method, practice actually laying your sights onto them and pulling the trigger; unless you are prepared to take another human life you are no good on a tactical team.

With the advent of good body armor with front and rear ballistic plates, training of soldiers in standing shooting positions has changed from the 'old school' way of turning your body off to the side with one leg forward, to the new way of standing straight on to the enemy. The reason for this 'straight on' approach is to present the front armor plate to the enemy; when standing side on you are presenting your side, less protected, ribcage to enemy fire. So the change is related to protection from enemy fire. Standing straight on is not as natural a shooting position and is not as relevant if you don't have body armor plates. Therefore, make your own decision on how best to train for standing positions.

Some of the techniques you see out there are positive developments; some of it is 'tacticool' stuff.

Practice some short range instinctive shooting with rifle, shotgun and handgun. Learn how to instinctively point the weapon at the enemy at close range and rapidly 'unload' on them until they go down (i.e. until the threat is stopped). At very short range this method does not actually use the sights and relies on instinctive, practiced, pointing of the weapons at the target at closer ranges. This can be taught with rifle, shotgun and pistol.

What is also useful is to practice drawing your weapon and aligning the sights on the target. This can be done 'dry' at home. When drawing a handgun practice getting the weapon up and aligned; you may be surprised that the weapon may be crooked in your hand. With an assault rifle, you can practice 'ready ups' from the low ready position to the standing firing position.

As opposed to the close range instinctive 'shotgun method' shooting outlined in the previous paragraph, for anything a little further away (perhaps beyond 10 yards, see how it works for you) then you need to take a short tactical pause between bringing the weapon up, aligning the sights and returning fire. Firing without doing this will get rounds down the range, but they may be wasted. This is a fine line: returning fire quickly will distract the enemy, but returning accurate fire that strikes them after a very short pause to align sights, will be far more effective.

For those that have not been in combat, it would be useful to have an understanding of what it feels like to be under fire. 'Small Arms Fire' (SAF) is considered to be incoming high velocity rounds from assault type rifles and machine guns. Post-event, that is any incoming fire from hostile firearms. Incoming effective SAF is a violent experience. There is a difference between effective and ineffective fire. Effective fire can be defined as fire that has already caused casualties, or would do so if you continued on without taking cover.

Incoming rounds can make various sounds. Mainly, when a high velocity round passes close to you it breaks the sound barrier and makes a loud violent cracking noise like a bullwhip being cracked by your ear. If rounds ricochet they can spin off making that distinctive whining or buzzing sound. Rounds striking near or around you will be loud and violent; they will tear stuff up, rip things apart, take branches down out of trees, smack into the asphalt tearing it up, kick up dirt and dust where they strike. Rounds at extreme range may make more of a buzzing noise. The old type army ranges where they had people in a trench down-range putting the targets up and down were a useful battle inoculation method because this gave the soldiers the experience of rounds cracking by a couple of feet above them; don't go and have someone fire rounds past you in substitute, that would not be clever – "Don't try this at home!"

So, SAF can be a strange experience. It can either be very obviously close, violent and dangerous, or if not directed effectively at you can seem like an innocuous curiosity. It's making the connection between seeing it at a distance and realizing how dangerous that will be when it is directed at you that is important. Night time tracer fire is an example. It looks slow and graceful as the tracer from the machineguns arcs across. The tracer rounds are only every one in five rounds and the 'laser light' effect is deceiving of the true violence. For newbies, often making the connection and understanding the true danger of the situation is an initial problem.

However, it's a fine balancing act between being in denial of the reality of the situation, versus being paralyzed by fear. Sometimes it is a better strategy to compartmentalize to deal with the situation NOW and worry about it later. Seeing the strike of incoming rounds, once you are battle inoculated, can be a simple event to which you have to respond appropriately: communicate, locate the enemy, return fire and move as appropriate to the threat.

You don't want to find yourself in a situation of overwhelming fear. Make fear your friend; respond appropriately and with the necessary urgency to the situation. Try not to panic.

In a survival or combat situation your job is to survive and endure. You have to act appropriately, adjust your thinking to the reality of the situation, and get the right stuff done. Have a positive mental attitude. However, don't be one of those positive thinking crazies: be a realist, plan for the worst and hope for the best. If the situation is crappy, have a laugh and a joke about it, a bit of black humor. Be aware of the ludicrous nature of situations and see the humor in them.

Compartmentalizing is a useful tactic; try not to eat the whole post-event elephant at once, rather deal with the elephant a little at a time: i.e. deal with the immediate stuff, with a view to the strategic situation in the background. Don't try and 'drain the whole lake' at once, but deal with the 'crocodile closest to the boat'. It is almost useful to have two minds: have the overall reality ticking away in the back there, but concentrate on the immediate and be a little in denial of the overall situation while you are doing so, even though you know it is there and will need to be confronted eventually.

If you compartmentalize effectively, you can shelve away the stress of the immediate situation and deal with it in the short term, perhaps even to the point that you don't realize the effect that the stress is creating somewhere in your mind. That is why you are able to operate in a hostile environment without becoming incapacitated by the fear of 'what if'; knowing what the enemy can do and has done to others. Build a mental fort, become a little 'OCD' about stuff so that you can create some rituals that keep your mind working. Later, when you are safe at home, you may find yourself crying quietly for apparently no reason, because some of that stress popped out from somewhere.

If you are in a dangerous environment, such as combat or a post-event situation, you can't dwell too much on the what-ifs. You also can't dwell too much on the fortune or misfortune of chance – the *if he had been two seconds quicker such and such would not have happened* thought process. This kind of thinking can lead to denial because, for instance, when the roadside bomb goes off and you are wounded, you can't be thinking *why me, why did this happen to me, if we had left on time we would not have been hit* etc.

In such environments you have to create a mental fort based on whatever you can to justify the non-craziness of what you are doing (even if it is a little crazy, when you step back from it). If you are out on convoys in Afghanistan, take strength from feeling good about having your gear on all set up right and ready to go, the armor of the vehicle, the drills your team just practiced, the fact that you did some good route planning; justify it to yourself and build a little mental confidence.

A fearful nature will dwell on the possibilities too much and yes, your perfectly set up gear rig will not stop that IED from tearing through the vehicle, but let's be a little in denial of that so we can get our job done.

Navigation

The ability to navigate on land is an important skill. If you are not competent at navigating then you will be unable to move around with any real confidence or purpose. If you are working in teams and relaying information to each other then you will need to record and relay the map coordinates of that location; if you can't do it with any accuracy then it simply won't happen.

There are various aids to navigation, the most important being GPS receivers. They are wonderful, buy them and use them. Have an in-car system that you use for normal day-to day navigation – there is no reason why this same system could not have your BOL registered in it for your evacuation (but recorded under an innocuous name, so anyone acquiring it can't put two and two together and find your BOL).

Have a hand held GPS for dismounted movement and for in and around your BOL. Use it regularly for hiking and buy and download the mapping software so you can actually see, and view your position, on an electronic map on your handheld GPS. Be intelligent when using routes suggested by your GPS, particularly road selections made on your vehicle GPS. Don't be a slave to the machine. Consult the paper map beforehand and apply some reason to the process – make sure that the GPS selected route is sensible and practical and where you actually want to go.

However, be prepared to operate without your GPS. Batteries could run out, you could lose it, forget it or have it stolen. EMP attack could wipe out the geospatial satellites that allow you to fix your position. The system can be turned off. Cyber-attack could destroy the system. How long would it operate for post-event?

Be prepared to get back to basics. Always carry a map and compass. In your car, have paper road maps or atlas for your state. For your home/BOL/likely foraging areas have suitable paper maps. Either get the waterproof ones or use a good map case. Get used to map reading by going hiking using the maps – have the GPS as a back-up, but simply have it running in a pocket to record the track, but use the map to navigate.

You ideally want maps somewhere in the scale 1:25,000, 1:50,000, 1:75,000 and worst case 1:100,000. Learn and understand the basic map symbols and features and how contour lines work. You should train yourself so that when you look at a map the features pop out at you and you can relate map to ground. Understand what contour shapes on the map will look like on the ground.

You should purchase the 'Silva' type combination compass/protractor type compass that allows you to instantly take a bearing straight off the map. The military prismatic type compasses are ideal for taking azimuth/bearing of objects but to interface them to the map you need a protractor. The Silva type compass allows you to do away with this step; they are the type of compasses used for orienteering. Detailed instruction on map reading is a topic that is out of the scope of this manual. A theoretical followed by a practical course of instruction would be ideal. Learn to do the following:

- Know your map symbols
- Know your main map features: hill, valley, spur, draw, saddle, and ridge. Cut, Embankment, cliff.
- Know contour lines and the interval. Contour lines are lines of continuous height drawn to represent the shape of the terrain on a map. The build-up of contour lines of various heights shows the shape of the ground and the terrain features mentioned above.
- Use water features such as streams to help the terrain 'pop' out of the map – streams will be running in low ground and in draws rather than on spurs and high ground, so the network of streams will highlight the lie of the terrain.
- Know how to use grid references: 4, 6 and 8 figure. Read the horizontal scale then the vertical scale 'along the corridor and then up the stairs'. Grid squares are usually 1 km across. This is the same as the military MGRS system.

- Know how to take an azimuth or bearing from the map from a point to a point so that you can walk it on the ground.
- Know how to use your compass.
- Know how to compensate for magnetic variation and where to find it on the map key.
- Know how to measure distance.
- Know your pacing over various terrain for 100 meter distances.

Basic military map reading teaches taking an azimuth between two points, measuring the distance between the two, and then walking on that bearing while pacing for distance until you reach that second point. If you reach an obstacle, box around it by pacing out, beyond and back in to resume your original line. This technique is not what is primarily used for more advanced map reading, such as orienteering. It is too easy to deviate from the azimuth and miss the end point. This should be used when there is no alternative.

To make following an azimuth easier, you should sight your azimuth, sight along your compass, and pick a terrain feature on the horizon to head to, while pacing. Once you reach that point, take your azimuth again. In poor visibility, send out one of your team to the limit of visibility, talk them on to the right azimuth, then walk to them and repeat.

More advanced techniques focus on a better understanding of terrain association i.e. what is the shape of the ground and how does that relate to me. Am I walking up or down hill? How can I orient the map to the ground by locating that saddle feature on the map, identify it on the ground, and relate the two? Some techniques to use in addition to the basics of azimuth & distance:

> Hand railing: use a linear terrain feature to lead you to your destination. This also has a tactical application: you would handrail a feature such as a road by not being on it, in case of ambush, but by following it to a flank.

Check off features: know that as you head on an azimuth you will, for example, cross a stream, then a ridge, another stream and then a trail. Check these features off as you move.

Aim off. If you are forced to follow an azimuth across country to a point on a linear feature, when you arrive at the linear feature unless you arrive exactly, you won't know which way to turn. Aim off to one side deliberately so that once you hit the linear feature you can turn and walk in to the point.

Contouring: following a specific height around a feature. This is also a useful method of travel, saving energy by minimizing altitude gain and loss.

Terrain features: follow terrain features, such as ridges or valleys. This makes navigation easier, but if you are following natural lines then you may be making yourself more prone to ambush. Think hand railing and maybe follow a ridge or valley by contouring somewhere half-way up or down the slope, not in or on the actual feature itself.

Cross-graining: this is a physically hard way of crossing country. Often used in a jungle setting, you simply take an azimuth towards your destination cutting across the grain of the land. Very good for avoiding ambush, but lots of altitude gained and lost = tiring.

CHAPTER FIVE

BASIC PRINCIPLES

Introduction

"It's not the critic that counts, but the man in the arena with blood on his face."

The following forms the beginning of the main tactical instructional part of this manual that will cover basic principles through dismounted and vehicle mounted movement, tactics, offensive and defensive operations.

Some of this will be in the form of generic instruction that can be taken and applied to whatever operations you may be conducting post-event, and is more geared to a team of individuals of military age and capability conducting operations as a tactical team. Some of it is more specific, such as to moving your family to the BOL, and will therefore be more concerned with the protection of children and non-combatants.

The idea behind the more generic stuff, which is closer to infantry and close protection tactics, is not only to provide the principles, but also allow you the freedom to train for operations that we may not envisage now, but may be necessary some time post-event. For example, once the initial survival event is over, in time we may see a restoration of normality. Or we may not, or normality may come after several or many years of chaos. We must therefore survive during these times and adapt to the circumstances.

It is under these sorts of conditions that we can envisage conducting operations closer to infantry soldiering, such as patrolling, raids, ambush, which may be necessary if your secure location is threatened by hostile forces.

Thus, the inclusion of offensive operations is not intended to pave the way for a family group to head off and conduct a camp attack, but to allow a formed tactical group of survivors to conduct such operations. It is important to note that tactics, beyond the basic principles, are a matter of opinion and should be tailored to your situation, capabilities and the threat. There is no right or wrong answer to a tactical decision, beyond what works and what does not, so long as you adhere to the basic principles. In after action reviews during tactical field training, you cannot tell someone that going left, or right, was wrong, you can simply point out the pros and cons of that decision balanced against the combat estimate and the factors present.

Basic Fieldcraft

In any kind of tactical environment you need to constantly remain alert and consider security and the protection of your team. You will always remain mindful of where you may be positioned relative to potential threats. You will be concerned about ground, the positioning of weapon systems and the tactical formation and positioning of your team. If you stop somewhere to rest, you will establish security and always maintain a watch.

It is only possible to rest in a tactical environment, which includes sleeping, cooking, washing, cleaning weapons and any number of other tasks, when there is security in place and a watch rotation established. Try and position yourselves well so that wherever you are, you use the ground to conceal and protect you.

When moving in a tactical environment, do so in a tactical way. Keep appropriate spacing, perhaps five to ten meters depending on the cover, and don't bunch up. Don't stand about in a gaggle. Think about being a tactical bound from other groups in your formation. Individuals should spread out appropriate to the ground and cover. If you stop, take a fire position. This is one of the areas where personal discipline is very apparent and should be hit hard in training.

If you have to do some form of administration, do it as buddies with one facing out and providing security while the other tactically does his thing. If you are stopped, take a fire position on a knee or in the prone position, whatever is appropriate to the ground. Don't just stand there. Cover your sectors of fire, which should add up as a group to a full 360 degrees around the team. Watch out, not in. Practice discipline: noise and light at night – stop talking. Don't drop trash. Don't smoke in a tactical environment.

Make sure that your attire and carriage of equipment is professional. This is not about looks, partially so, but mainly about functionality. So long as you are not on a covert mission masquerading as a homeless bum, don't appear like one. This does not imply the need for barrack room style disciplines of shaving etc. – such may not be practical anyway and it is also a feature of a professional infantry soldier's life to go on 'dirty patrol' in the jungle where shaving is not done because open facial wounds could result in infection. So, don't shave if you don't want to. Don't have a haircut if you don't want to, but make sure that your equipment is secured and that your weapon is clean and functional.

The point is that soldiering is not about uniformity, it's about professionalism and attention to doing things the tactically right way. If on patrol and not on some other task where you may sling your weapon, make sure that it is kept at the low ready and held in both hands. Exceptions to this are examples such as the 'Bosnia Carry' where the weapon is held in one hand slung by the side of the body so as to show a more friendly profile and not alarm the locals. Something like this may be applicable to your situation.

In a tactical patrol type environment you will want to move about with the weapon held correctly in both hands; as you move about, the weapon moves and points with you, ready to be brought up into the firing position as necessary.

Make sure that when you are moving about your posture expresses confidence, professionalism and determination. Be observant and actively observe your sectors as you move. If the enemy is lying in wait ready to spring that ambush, you want him to look at you and hopefully see you as too hard a target, or at the least you will sow some doubt in the mind of the enemy that you may be able to exploit with a reaction to the ambush of speed and aggression that may get you out of there alive.

Battle Preparation

The following is a good mnemonic to remember the stages of tactical battle preparation:

- Security – ensure 360 security is maintained
- Ammunition – distribute, load in magazines.
- Weapons – clean. Function test. Test fire if possible.
- Personal Camouflage/clothing – appropriate to the operation
- Equipment – ensure you have it all and it's 'squared away'
- Radios – batteries, frequencies, call-signs, radio check
- Special Equipment – tailored to the operation i.e. breaking tools for foraging.
- Orders – Team Leader briefs on the operation.

'SAWPERSO'

Observation

As you patrol and observe your sectors, make sure that you are actively scanning and observing for the enemy or anything that is of significance. When scanning foliage, you should be looking 'through' the cover rather than at it. It takes some practice to do this, but you must make an effort to look through the foliage to what is beyond and behind it; this is actually very effective and you can see through and into woods and foliage with this technique.

At night, your eyes will adjust to the darkness. When your eyes are adjusted, don't expose them to any white light; use red or green light for tactical pin-light flashlights because this light will not ruin your night vision, which may take 30 minutes to return. Your eyes are made up of rods and cones and the rods are what your eye uses to see in low light conditions; the rods are located around the outside of the eyeball and for this reason if you want to see something better at night, don't stare at it but look slightly off to one side. At night, your hearing becomes very useful as a sense so it is important to make little noise and make stops (listening halts) to listen to your environment. Between sight and hearing it is important to be mindful of your surroundings and environment and in general be aware. There are specific reasons why things are seen, this helps when trying to spot the enemy and also while camouflaging yourself:

- Shape
- Shine
- Shadow
- Surface
- Silhouette
- Spacing
- Movement
- Muzzle Flash
- Aircraft
- Thermal Imaging

Nature does not create straight lines therefore manmade objects can often be spotted due to these factors. In addition, aircraft have a unique perspective on objects on the ground and can identify you relatively easily. Also, avoid the urge to look up at a hostile aircraft; your shiny faces turned upwards to look at it will make you obvious on the ground.

Camouflage

Views on camouflage have changed in modern Coalition armies over recent years. It used to be that a lot of time and effort was spent on utilizing foliage to enhance camouflage. Where recent wars have taken place in places often denuded of foliage, and at a high speed mobile pace, use of foliage as camouflage has taken a back seat in favor of reliance on 'universal' type camouflage patterns. A good set of camouflage or drab colored clothing and matching equipment suitable to the terrain is invaluable. If you are using natural foliage to enhance the concealment of individuals or positions then there are various factors you need to take account off:

- Lay leaves the right way up.
- Don't use too much i.e. you can break up the shape of a helmet with grass, but it's no good if the helmet then becomes a huge grass matt.
- Pay attention to foliage dying, very important on positions where it may be there for some time. Replace frequently.
- Change foliage as you move through different types of terrain.
- Use foliage to break up the pattern of head/shoulders/helmet.
- You will need to utilize elastic cord sewn into your equipment and hat/helmet straps to effectively use foliage.

Camouflage face cream has also fallen into disuse. If you are out in the woods and forests, you should consider it for your face, hands and wrists (exposed parts). The main problem with faces is that they shine with sweat; it's not all about the color of skin. So, all skin tones should consider the use of cam cream. It's actually made from the same stuff as make-up! There is a skill to applying cam cream: not too much, not too little, just right. It is not necessary to make a work of art out of it, tiger striping every inch of exposed skin – and it will sweat off anyway, so you will need to re-apply it as required.

Use of foliage as an addition to camouflage will most likely be used for pure tactical operations such as recce patrol, ambush etc. and will not be so likely utilized in normal post-event day to day movement. As a basis, along with considerations of profile, consider wearing decent quality outdoor/military or hiking/hunting type clothing that is either camouflaged in an appropriate pattern or just drab outdoor colors suitable to your environment.

If you are going to use military camouflage, use one that is appropriate to the terrain you are operating in. Don't just get a pattern that is cool, such as outfitting your team in urban camo when you will be operating in the woods. Use desert camo if you are going to be operating in a desert area or woodland if you are in the woods.

Be aware that the current (as of writing 2012) US Army ACU's, which are in the UCP (Universal Camouflage Pattern), are not a good idea. The idea was a good one, but the chosen colors do not provide good concealment. The competition is currently underway to replace the Army camo pattern for the uniform. You would be better with the old style woodland BDU or desert DCU uniforms, or even something like the British DPM (disruptive pattern material) which is similar to the woodland BDU. An excellent option is 'multi-cam' by Crye Precision which is currently in use as the operational uniform for Afghanistan. This is wonderful camouflage and would have fitted the bill as a much better universal camo pattern than the chosen UCP. Multi-cam is available commercially.

Also, remember that you don't have to be 'in uniform' either as a team or as an individual. If you are wearing a load carrying vest or body armor then you may do well to wear camo or drab (earth tone) colored pants and a drab t-shirt or shirt under your rig. The rig itself needs to be either a camo or drab color and this covers most of your torso so it will suffice: you don't have to wear full BDU uniforms, including the shirts, and these can be uncomfortable under a rig anyway. That is why the military issue the under-armor type combat-shirts with the long camo sleeves, specifically to go under body armor while troops are deployed and working in hot environments. When wearing body armor and equipment, you spend your whole day with a sweat soaked t-shirt under your armor anyway, so get used to it.

Countering Aerial Thermal Surveillance

Thermal Imaging is a different thing than normal image intensifying, which magnifies available light. FLIR (Forward Looking Infra-Red) or TI

(Thermal Imaging) picks up heat, and really it is about heat differentials, which allows it to create an image. It can be seen as white (hot) on a black (cooler) background, or the color view can be flipped. You can also be seen as a cooler spot on a hotter background. The thing about FLIR is that it can be blocked by some form of cover. In a similar way to cover from view and cover from fire, the best form of protection is hard cover, and things like foliage, if you have enough, will also protect your from view by the operator. That is why FLIR is so useful in places like the desert where there is not a lot of cover, and you get almost perfect images of people.

What you have to watch out for is your body heat starting to heat up the thing you are taking cover behind. So, if you want to hide from FLIR, you want to block the image of your body heat, and also the view of any non-environmental heat that you may generate into your cover. It has been talked about that you can use blankets to help with this, but eventually you will heat up the blanket so that can only be a short term fix.

 A good idea, if you were mobile and had no choice, would be to carry a combination of a space blanket sandwiched in something like a normal blanket or better a military camouflage poncho liner blanket. Be aware that you also have to be camouflaged against normal non-IR naked eye. A flip problem is appearing as a hole in the background, so you want to think about your cover being the same temperature as the background if possible.

Movement is always a problem, and will attract the eye of an operator. So, if you think you may be under observation, don't move. But unless you can disguise your human shape, you will be seen anyway. Best thing: get in a cave!

It's a big topic, but basically your night vision type goggles (NODS/NVGs) are image intensifiers, which simply help you to see via available light at light, such as moonlight. They can also use active infrared light in the near infrared spectrum, which is like a spotlight that you can't see with the naked eye. So, image intensifiers can be passive or active. Active is a problem if someone else has one, then they can see your light like daylight to them, even though it is dark to the naked eye. That is why US technology works well at night against low tech insurgents who don't have the gear.

Thermal imaging is the system where you see the heat differential, such as the clips you can find online or from a police tracking helicopter. That uses IR technology, but IR is a big spectrum so has a lot of uses. To simplify, the thermal/IR imaging cameras see the thermal signature.

Military BDUs are usually designed to be IR retardant, which reduces IR signature. Often, this comes with specific care and washing instructions, and you can ruin the capability. There are also issues of how a material matches the background in terms of emissivity/reflectivity, and I would beware use of a tarp due to the way the surface reflects. That is why something like a Mylar blanket could be used but to line something with less reflectivity, such as some kind of camouflage material or a blanket type thing. So, wearing IR retardant gear will help, you will be "less white" on the imager, but you will still be seen.

Thermal imaging is just that, it is not an x-ray machine, but it will see radiated heat and if you warm the object you are under or behind it will be able to see you. Bottom line is you need some way to block the heat signature but also have that material matching the background in a decent way. For instance, something like a 'ghillie' suit would probably work well. Maybe you could create a 'ghillie' blanket' with an inside Mylar space blanket that would be bulky but that you could pull over you, hopefully the 'ghillie' material side would match the background a bit better and would not reflect. Carried on the outside of a ruck you would hope that it would adapt to the background temperature and then be ready to deploy and get under as necessary; if you hear the chopper in time. If you don't hear it (i.e. Drone) you won't know it's up there.

The whole IR thing is a little confusing because 'IR' or infrared is basically a non-visible part of the light spectrum that has lots of uses (ask a science teacher....). The confusion comes in when we talk about Image Intensifiers and Thermal Imaging. They both actually use IR technology, but in different ways. Image intensifiers just amplify ambient light. Thermal images see the heat differentials, but they both use IR. I went on the net and found this on Wikipedia to help describe it:

"Active infrared night vision: the camera illuminates the scene at infrared wavelengths invisible to the human eye. Despite a dark back-lit scene, active-infrared night vision delivers identifying details, as seen on the display monitor. Infrared is used in night vision equipment when there is insufficient visible light to see. Night vision devices operate through a process involving the conversion of ambient light photons into electrons which are then amplified by a chemical and electrical process and then converted back into visible light. Infrared light sources can be used to augment the available ambient light for conversion by night vision devices, increasing in-the-dark visibility without actually using a visible light source. The use of infrared light and night vision devices should not be confused with thermal imaging which creates images based on differences in surface temperature by detecting infrared radiation (heat) that emanates from objects and their surrounding environment."

"Thermography: infrared radiation can be used to remotely determine the temperature of objects (if the emissivity is known). This is termed thermography, or in the case of very hot objects in the NIR or visible it is termed pyrometry. Thermography (thermal imaging) is mainly used in military and industrial applications but the technology is reaching the public market in the form of infrared cameras on cars due to the massively reduced production costs. Thermographic cameras detect radiation in the infrared range of the electromagnetic spectrum (roughly 900–14,000 nanometers or 0.9–14 μm) and produce images of that radiation. Since infrared radiation is emitted by all objects based on their temperatures, according to the black body radiation law, thermography makes it possible to "see" one's environment with or without visible illumination. The amount of radiation emitted by an object increases with

temperature, therefore thermography allows one to see variations in temperature (hence the name)."

Much as I would not like to contemplate our own assets being used against citizens, there are theoretical situations where knowledge about mitigating the threat could be useful. However, never assume an enemy has an all seeing ability and just give up. Friction, assets and battlefield clutter, plus human error, comes into play. We survive in those gaps.

For instance, often people do not give enough thought to the full scope of a collapse, beyond stocking up and having a couple of weapons. What if in a post collapse power vacuum another power moved in? What about China? Then, rather than a civil war you may be fighting as insurgents/partisans/freedom fighters, if you so choose. The foreign invader may not have, or perhaps be left with after some combat, full all seeing capability. Perhaps the main threat is Chinese FLIR equipped hunter killer helicopters?

For an interest discussion, this is something that may be considered and you may need emergency counter measures in case you are caught out. Also, you can amend your operating procedures to have camps in suitable defiles in densely forested areas, or even ratlines on urban areas, to counter the threat.

The key factors in mitigating the threat or aerial TI surveillance are good use of ground and vegetation cover, considered movement and the use of air sentries. Think about creating Mylar based 'thermal ponchos' similar to how they are described above. If you use them, string the poncho up from poles or trees to keep the material away from your body and avoid heating it up.

Basic Movement

There are many factors to movement; some will be covered in greater detail below. Generally, you will be in a formation, whether you are dismounted or vehicle mounted. The formation will be determined by the team leader and will be suited to the ground that you are crossing. The team will want to avoid obvious places where ambush can occur, so that will probably mean hand railing any trails or roads, staying out of sight in the cover to the flank. Some basic formations:

- Single File: 'one behind the other'.

- File: it's just a double file. If following a trail and it widens out to a track or road, individuals alternately step left or right to the edge of the trail all the way back down the line.

- Line: everyone 'gets on line' facing a direction, usually where the enemy are. Make sure you keep spread out tactically. This is a skirmish or assault line.

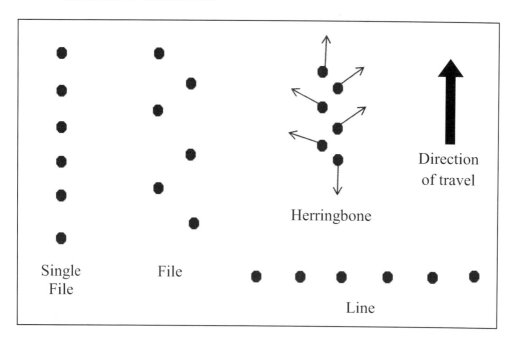

Figure 1 - Basic Formations

- Herringbone: This is a stop formation. Imagine a file or single file. Everyone stops and gets down, alternatively facing out either left or right. If it's close country legs will touch. It it's a trail then there will be the space of the trail up and down the middle. Looked at from above, the alternately prone individuals make up the impression of fish bones

Taking Cover

When the team comes under effective enemy fire the team leader should make the decision to take cover; this does not preclude individuals taking cover if they feel a pressing need, but the idea of the leader call is to prevent inexperienced troops taking cover if it is just stray ineffective rounds and not effective fire directed at the team. The command is "Take Cover!" and everyone will instantly get down. There are two ways to learn this.

Old School:

- Dash – quick dash that leads into a dive,
- Down – dive to the ground, protecting your weapon,
- Crawl – into available cover,
- Observe – for the enemy,
- Sights – set your range on your sights.
- Fire – fire at the enemy

'Dash, down, crawl, observe, sights, fire'

Modern:

- Return Fire
- Take Cover
- Return appropriate fire

'RTR'

This RTR technique advocates a quick return of fire at the enemy to disturb their aim, followed by getting down and then taking a more considered approach to continue to return fire. This is only effective if you see the enemy, or the cover they fire from is obvious, and you can fire at where the enemy is. Good for close ranges like Jungle Warfare or in the woods. If you are at longer ranges and have no idea where the enemy is, you are simply standing there (effectively freezing) while you take that instant to look for the enemy. Better to move and get straight down.

Basic Tactical Principles and Techniques:

Fire & Movement (F&M): This overriding principle states that when in contact and engaged with the enemy there is never movement without fire support. This is also known as 'bounding over-watch' and sometimes termed as 'having one foot on the ground'. F&M ties together the soldier requirements to be able to shoot, move and communicate; F&M combines all three. However, F&M is a principle that applies to any size of formation; thus F&M applies to movement of two soldiers, fighting together as a buddy pair, thru Fire Team and Platoon levels and upwards. For the purposes of this document, we are concerned with F&M between individuals up to three or four vehicles, or dismounted vehicle teams, working together. The principle of F&M is applied to dismounted and mounted vehicle operations, or combinations of the two.

F&M Technique: when fire and maneuvering, the whole idea is to make it as hard as possible for the enemy to hit you. When working with a buddy or larger team, you should keep the shouted commands to a minimum. The movement should be a flow that you get in to. Once you are in a fire position and engaging the enemy, shout "MOVE" and your buddy will move. He will also know that you are firing so he will know to move. He will then get down, shout "MOVE" and it's your turn. The procedure for moving is as follows:

- Identify your next piece of cover.
- Crawl out of your cover, to the side or rear.
- Get up and rapidly dash forward, randomly zigzagging about.
- No more than 5-10 yards, 3 to 5 seconds: "I'm up, he sees me, I'm down."

- Crawl into cover.
- Engage the enemy.

If you are static in a fire position for any period of time, beyond the time taken for a normal bound, then you should move your position every time you have fired a few rounds, just slightly, by crawling back and popping up again at a slightly new place. The main effort of all these procedures is to make it hard for the enemy to 'get a bead' on you. You are trying to foil his attempts. Don't get up, or keep popping up, where he expects your head to be. The main interruptions to F&M are the following:

- "STOPPAGE!" – go firm in cover and clear the stoppage, buddy keeps firing.
- "MAGAZINE!" – change magazines in cover. Buddy keeps firing.
- "MAN DOWN!" – Casualty. Maintain fire superiority.
- "BACK IN!" – To notify your buddies once you resume firing.

Depending on the volume of the effective enemy fire that you may be experiencing, which is directly related to the success of your attempts to gain fire superiority, will determine how you move. On open ground, there may be little utility to crawling, if you are in open view, and you may be better rapidly fire and maneuvering over it, perhaps even just taking a kneeling fire position. Speed and volume of fire may be your friend under those circumstances.

However, when there is heavy enemy fire you will likely end up crawling, unless you can get in some cover that will allow you to move, such as dead ground or a ditch. If you find yourself 'pinned down' then it is important that you locate the enemy and return fire. You need to return fire to allow movement, even if it is just crawling out of there. 'Winning the Fire Fight', which is gaining fire superiority, will take courage under effective enemy fire. On a first contact with green troops, heavy effective enemy fire may create a freeze response in the team and they may take cover and not return fire. Leadership will come into play, and the personal courage to get your head up and return fire. Try and train to drill a response that will break the freeze; more on that later.

Returning briefly to the studies showing that many people do not return fire in battle, because of the innate resistance to killing another person, this can reflect in many ways, some of which will help you. Volume of fire does not equate to effective fire. The enemy to be afraid of is the one who carefully lines you up in his rifle sights and takes your team down one round at a time. There may be none of these, or one of these, in the enemy force. Often, seen for example in Afghan tribal type engagements, the fire is mainly not accurate. In these sorts of fights it is often amazing how no-one, or at least not more people, get hit despite a huge noise and volume of fire. Many of them will be firing high, on automatic, and without correct aiming. These types of engagements are decided more on a psychological basis, a sort of moral supremacy, of which side felt it came of worse and makes the decision to withdraw. This does not mean that anyone caught will not be savagely mutilated and killed, it's just that these engagements can be decided more by posturing than actual effective fire and numbers killed. Some people are firing because the group is firing and they are not really making a great effort to kill anyone.

Think about a hunter shooting a deer. An accurate powerful round is used that will kill the deer, likely a similar caliber round that will be used when that same hunter becomes a post-event survivor, possibly if his shooting is actually good enough he will become a sharpshooter (sniper if his patience and field craft are good enough). Think about being against that guy with his rifle and scope? Terrifying. But a lot depends on him. A firefight is not target shooting. People are moving, taking cover, firing back.

The point is that often the expected potential effectiveness of the available weapon systems does not work out that way, with an enemy force wiped out by 'one round one kill'. It is a minority of people that are the cold blooded killers. Many will find other things to do in the battle, or fire in the general direction of the enemy, or not fire at all. None of it is cut and dried, which is why not as many are killed in combat as you would think.

How to put this concept into words? In a place like Afghanistan or Iraq, sometimes fire can be coming in around an element, and there can be a great deal of it, but it is mostly not effective and may even be at extreme range. It's almost like the weather. Sometimes someone will be hit, other times you get those stories about rounds passing through clothing and equipment; but the reason that coalition forces are able to operate in such environments without more casualties is due to the great ineffectiveness of much of the fire. This is also not just about the use of armored vehicles, although it helps survivability: many coalition forces have been cutting about in open vehicles, with minimal armor and surviving such 'lead rain' quite well. The other side of this is that when the enemy really knows what it is doing, and is composed of seasoned fighters, then expect effective fire that will kill.

Bounding Over-watch: This tactic is essentially the same as F&M, except that it applies when enemy contact is likely or imminent, but has not yet begun. Supporting elements are placed in an over-watch position to cover movement with **potential** fire support. This is sometimes termed 'dry fire and movement'. An element will 'go firm' in a location while another moves, then vice versa. This may be done at a running speed, or at patrolling pace, depending on the situation and the likelihood of enemy contact. It is normally conducted at a patrol pace, which is a steady walk, and unlike fire and movement can be conducted over longer distances, with much greater distances between bounds: you are simply making sure you have a covering group deployed while you move forwards.

Hard Targeting: this is a technique that a team can apply if they think that the threat is high enough (i.e. sniper etc.) when entering or exiting certain locations – which could be one of the gates of your defended location. Individuals burst out at a running pace, zigzagging about, for a certain distance and then resume a patrolling pace. If contact occurs, then they will go straight into fire and movement and seek cover. Hard

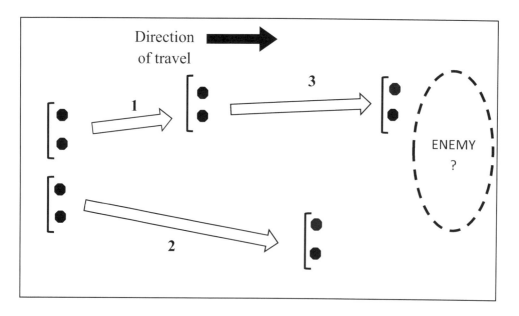

Figure 2 - Bounding Over-Watch

targeting can also be done when breaking cover on a patrol or advance to contact, perhaps when you have to leave the protection of a wood line to continue the movement. You can hard target out and then resume your patrol pace if no contact occurs.

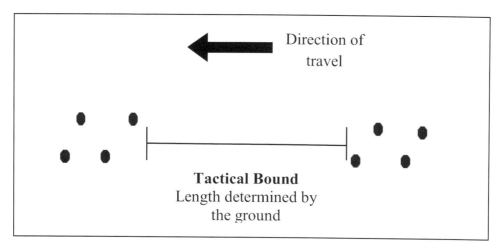

Figure 3 - Travelling Over-watch

Mobile (or Travelling) Over-watch: This is where covering elements do not go firm, but rather the whole formation is mobile. This can be with dismounted teams or while mounted in vehicles. A tactical bound is maintained between elements; with the idea being that one element will not be caught in the same effective fire as the other, but will be able to support the other element by fire.

Security: Due to the 360 degree nature of the threat, security sectors must protect all round the unit. It is easy for individuals to become focused (tunnel vision) on the direction of enemy fire. Complex attacks may involve firing points from multiple directions and attacks from the flank and rear. Difficult though it is, team leaders should counter this by assigning personnel to cover the flank and rear as part of their sectors of fire.

Accordingly, 360 degree security is an integral part of operations, while mobile and while halted. Sectors need to be assigned so that 'all round defense' is achieved, utilizing mutual support to tie in the arcs of fire of weapons systems. This applies to mounted and dismounted movement and halts. Mounted and dismounted formations are utilized in accordance with these principles and the particular configuration employed will depend on the ground and situation.

Maneuver Techniques

The following are some techniques that can be employed to conduct F&M and bounding over-watch. These techniques need to be practiced and adapted to the particular unit or team; the key point is the application of the principle of F&M – there are many ways to conduct the specifics. F&M is primarily thought of as a method to move forward and close with the enemy. However, F&M is used for any maneuver of elements on the battlefield while in contact; this means that it will also be used to maneuver to the flanks and rear. In the context of this instruction, F&M will most likely be used to move away from the enemy, either to the flanks, rear, or along an escape route

Successive Bounds: This is where elements are maneuvering; the first element makes a bound while the second element provides supporting fire to cover the movement. The first element 'goes firm' and provides supporting fire for the second element to move. With successive bounds, the second moving element moves up level with the first element. The second element never goes past the first, just moving up level.

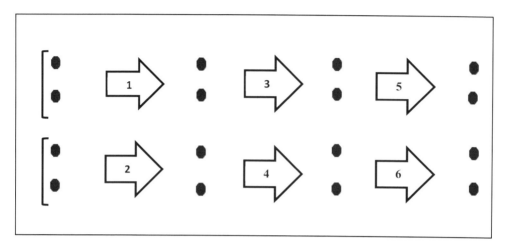

Figure 4 - Successive Bounds

Alternate Bounds: This technique varies from successive bounds because the second element moves up past the first element. The elements do not move in front of each other, this would mask fire and lead to fratricide; they remain side by side but 'leapfrog' past each other.

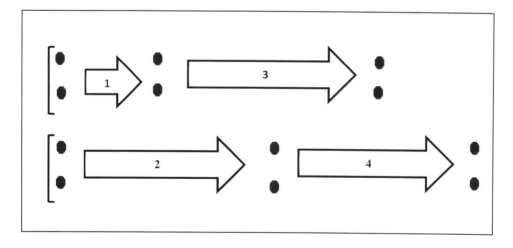

Figure 5 - Alternate Bounds

Note: Alternate Bounds contain the potential for bounds to get too long, but the technique covers the ground faster. Successive bounds are safer in close contact: "I'm up, he sees me, I'm down." Note also that these bounds may be completed at the crawl, not always up and running, depending on weight of enemy fire

Peeling: This simple but highly effective technique is mainly used to move to the flank; elements or individuals are in line facing the enemy threat and will 'peel out' to either the left or right. This is a good technique for moving along a linear feature, such as a road or ditch, while producing maximum suppressive fire. It can also be used as a method of moving to the rear (i.e. if the unit was contacted from the front while in a file formation), but in that case because the team will be in line (single or double file) the firepower generated to the front is limited. However, if there are enemy on both sides of the road, the technique can be used from the file with individuals peeling from one end of the formation, down the center ('down the tunnel'), to the other end, thus moving the formation out along the linear feature while generating maximum suppressive fire towards the enemy on both sides: this is known as a 'center peel'.

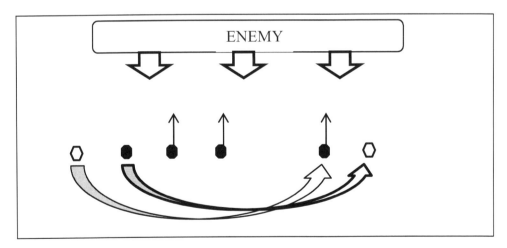

Figure 6 - Peeling to the Right

With the peel, when the formation needs to move right, individuals or elements will move from the left side, behind the formation, and peel back in on the right. The opposite for moving left. As each individual passes the next man, who will be providing suppressive fire, he shouts something along the lines of "Move!" or "Last man!" or kicks his foot etc., in order to ensure that the next man knows to move.

The technique is a flow of constant fire and movement. It can also be used, for example, as a way of moving to a flank out of an area of open ground to cover, when contacted by an enemy to the front.

Angles of Fire & Flanking

Never underestimate the power of moving to the enemies flank. When conducting F&M, you will be moving in an imaginary 'lane'. As you get closer to the enemy, you will start to obscure each other's fields of fire as one buddy moves forward of the other. If you are spaced correctly apart, this effect will be reduced. The best way to assault an enemy is with the fire support element at a 90 degree angle to the assaulting element. This will mean that the assaulting element does not get in the arcs of fire of the supporting element until they actually get onto the position, at which point the supporting fire element will simply switch their fire away to either the left or right depending on the side which the assault element is coming in from.

By maneuvering to the flank you can also gain tactical surprise, regain the initiative and gain psychological advantage over the enemy; doing this can gain you a psychological victory where you break the enemy's cohesion and will to fight, causing them to flee or withdraw. There will be more on the specific tactics of maneuvering to the flank later. Consider that if you are engaged and you leave a fire support element in place, then you take a concealed route to the enemies flank with an element of your group, you will allow your fire support element to continue to engage the enemy as you maneuver onto the position.

You will also tactically surprise the enemy and this is where the psychological element also comes in. The enemy will be unbalanced by your flanking move and will fear being cut off, 'rolled up' and overrun. If you continue to keep the pressure on and assault towards the enemy, you will either cause them to flee, surrender, or continue to fight on so that you have to fight through and clear the position, in which case you will at least have the benefit of the 90 degree assault/fire support angle to give you maximum protection as you close with the position.

Tactical Terrain Terms

It is important to develop an infantryman's eye for the ground. When you are driving about, you won't be thinking about how pretty it all looks, rather, you will be noticing the way the ground is shaped and how there are certain folds, dips and higher areas. You should think, for example, what if there were an enemy position on that spur, how would I approach it? How does the ground shape and what does it give me in terms of routes to the enemy position. Look at the ground in terms of how is a shaped and see the nuances of rises and hollows that will perhaps give cover from enemy fire.

Forward slope: this is the part of the hill that slopes down towards the direction of the enemy. It is very good for defender's fields of fire and observation and makes the enemy attack uphill, but it allows the defenders on the slope to be exposed to enemy direct fire and observed indirect fire.

> Direct fire is fire, such as rifle fire, that goes directly from A to B in a flat trajectory.

> Indirect fire is fire, such as mortar fire, that goes up and down: this means that it can be fired over terrain features. If fired over a terrain feature, such as from one valley to another, it requires an observer to be able to see the target and communicate adjustments to the firing line.

Reverse slope: this is the part of the hill that slopes down away the direction of the enemy. It would mean that the enemy has to come over the crest and then attack you. It limits defenders fields of fire and observation and allows the enemy to attack down towards you, but it puts the high ground in the way and thus shields you from direct fire, and indirect fire would need to be observed. Reverse slopes are often considered better than forward slopes for defensive positions in conventional warfare where the enemy is equipped with artillery and mortars.

Counter-Slope: This is a combination forward and reverse slope: you are on the reverse side of the hill, but the ground slopes back up again, giving you a mini-forward slope. Ideal.

Enfilade Fire: this is fire that strikes the enemy from the flank. Imagine the trenches in the First World War: a line of advancing enemy infantry. Imagine firing a machine gun along that line from the side (flank): the stream of rounds would be best positioned to hit multiple enemies along the line, with minor traverses of the weapon. Imagine that same line of enemies advancing straight on to you: coming right at you your rounds would pass through the line and beyond; you would have to traverse the weapon considerably to encompass the enemy within the stream of rounds. You will engage the enemy with enfilade fire from a defilade position.

Defilade: a position from which the enemy can only engage you with direct fire, and observed indirect fire, when they are in your killing area. This means that as you are set up to hit the enemy from the flank, you will be tucked in behind a fold of ground, maybe in the side of a draw, so the enemy can't see you before they appear in your killing area, when you hit them from the flank with enfilade fire. The idea is that they are advancing in a direction and you set up to hit them from the flank of their line of march, from defilade. This is the survival tactic for anti-armor troops in a general war scenario: the anti-tank weapons will be set up in defilade positions so that they engage the enemy from the flank (due to the weaker armor on the flank and rear of battle tanks and armored vehicles) and the enemy can't see them or return fire until they are in the killing area. Imagine you were set to take out the school bully. You know that in the playground he can take you down easy. So you get your baseball bat and wait round the corner of the alley. He can't see you until he is in view from the alley i.e. in your killing area, whereupon you whack him on the head with your baseball bat from the side (flank) i.e. with an enfilade bat strike.

Dead ground: This is positional related. From the position of the observer, whether you or the enemy, some ground will be unable to be seen. The ground on the other side of a ridge is an example. However, going back to the idea of having a soldiers eye for the ground, this can be very nuanced and slight slopes in the ground or shapes in fields, draws and small valleys can provide dead ground in which you or the enemy could move or hide. An example could be the way some road medians are shaped. They may be wide grassy expanses, devoid of any cover, but when viewed from the enemy who may be to the side of the road, the shape of the way the median slopes, often down to a central lower drainage, would put you in dead ground to an enemy ambush to the side of the road, perhaps in such a way that you would be able to crawl out if stuck there.

Killing area: Also known as a Kill Zone, this is an area that you or the enemy has designated as the kill zone. Depending on the circumstances, it may have been prepared, perhaps sown with mines and booby traps, IEDs and registered for indirect fire. The enemy will be covering the killing area with potential fire. The killing area is often known as 'the X'. It is always imperative to 'get off the X' as soon as possible.

Vital Ground: this is ground, the possession of which is vital to either the defender or attacker. Without this vital ground, you will fail. If you are defending your home or retreat, then the vital ground is probably the building itself.

Key terrain: ground that confers a marked advantage on whoever possesses it. It may be a little knoll next to your retreat building. You may decide to put a bunker on it to support your main position, but if the enemy destroys the bunker and gets their own machine-gun team up there, then they have an advantage conferred by this terrain feature.

Cover from view (Concealment): this is simply a type of cover where the enemy may not be able to see you, but the cover will not stop enemy fire. Examples are foliage, thin walls, and vehicles.

Cover from fire: this is 'hard cover'. It is usually formed by the shape of the ground and will provide cover from view and enemy fire. Being in a ditch or trench is an example of cover from fire.

Obstacles: these will only ever slow the enemy down. If you are building a perimeter, don't put out some wire/fencing and then go to sleep! All obstacles must be observed and covered by fire to be effective. Otherwise, the enemy will have the luxury to spend as much time as they need getting through or past the obstacle. Obstacles should be tied in with observation and early warning, for example it may be that you don't have the resources to observe the whole perimeter, but you could put out some kind of early warning devices such as trip-flares, noise or light devices, to alert you to enemy presence. But remember, if you are not observing, then the enemy always has the potential to detect and bypass or deactivate your early warning systems. Consider the use of night vision to enhance night observation capabilities, and don't forget the utility of low-tech methods such as guard dogs. It doesn't even have to be a scary kind of guard dog: if your family pet barks at intruders, then he is right for the job. You are taking him with you, aren't you? Geese are also noted as alarm animals. If you had little in the way of defenses, but you had a perimeter fence, a pack of dogs would go a long way to acting as early warning and defense devices within your perimeter.

Tactical Bound: this is a distance that is not specific, but which is determined by and depends on the ground. The idea of a tactical bound is that two formations will stay apart by a distance where, if one unit comes under effective enemy fire, the other unit will not be pinned down by that same fire. In close country the distance shrinks, in open country it expands.

Field of fire: this is the area that is covered by a direct fire weapon or weapon system. It will be determined by the range of the weapons and the shape of the ground and any obstacles to fire. A field of fire may be allocated by a leader and integrated with other fields of fire. It may be necessary to 'clear fields of fire' when you will cut vegetation growth back from your property or position to reduce concealment available to the enemy and provide clear fields of fire against anyone crossing that open ground.

Arcs of fire (sectors): this is where the left and right limits of a weapons firing sector are specified. This can be with actual physical 'arc sticks' which limit the traverse of the weapons or by designating features i.e.: "Your left of arc is the right side of the farm building, your right of arc is the left edge of the clump of trees."

Stand-off: this is a distance where the threat can be kept away from you. It can be tied in with fields of fire. If there is a fence or wall around the perimeter of your property, then you can consider the stand-off as the distance between that perimeter and your property. If there is no actual obstacle there, then you have no stand-off, unless you intend to simply keep an intruder back by weapons fire alone.

Momentum

This concept refers to the requirement to maintain pressure on the enemy force during an engagement: mainly in offense but it also applies to defense. This pressure will be applied through to use of firepower and maneuver. You do not always need to be moving in order to maintain momentum; you could be maintaining suppressive fire which will neutralize the enemy. Maneuvering will increase the effective angles of your fire and create enfilade, and will therefore unbalance the enemy, hopefully breaking cohesion and will.

When you think about maneuvering in a tactical environment, think less about speed and running about. Of course, sometimes you will have to run fast! If you watch a Hollywood movie, there is lots of running about and firing while running, often with competing mobs of henchmen running at each other firing. Attacks are portrayed as a running assault. This is historically true in some circumstances, such as attacks 'over the top' in the First World War, and Russian "Huraahh!" charges in the Second World War. But this is what you do if you have lots of people and you don't mind losing some (or lots) of them!

If you are a small professional force, or a small group of friends and family, then there is no such thing as an acceptable loss. If you are forced to do something tactical then you want to be thinking more along the lines of 'slow is smooth and smooth is fast'. Use ground and cover, move steadily using accurate fire and movement in dead ground to apply steady pressure on the enemy, making use of angles of fire and flanking movement to increase that pressure and psychological advantage.

Try to break the enemy's cohesion and will to fight. Maintain momentum and steadily move up to increase the pressure. If they think they are getting surrounded and you are closing with them, they will likely want to break and run, they will not want to be cut off and killed in place. Sometimes you want to give the enemy a route to withdraw on. If you are really serious you can let them withdraw on a route but have cut-off groups in place to ambush them as they do so.

A very useful skill to develop both in defense and offense is the ability to 'read the battle'. This takes training and experience. You should be able to tell by the information you receive, from reports from your sub-units, by direct observation and also hearing the direction and sounds of the battle, what is happening. If you have moved to the flank, even without radios you can hear when the fire support group has increased to rapid fire to cover your final assault. You can hear where the enemy fire is coming from and its intensity, and you can anticipate that they may try and flank you and roll you up, and you will hear once they begin to do so, but for instance you will have anticipated this and placed weapon systems to cover the relevant avenues of approach.

Operational Tempo

This again is not so much about speed, it is more about organizing your decisions, preparations and executions so that you can act faster than the enemy and get inside his decision cycle. So before he can react, you did something and dislocated his expectations. This is about getting inside his 'OODA' loop: Observation, Orientation, Decision, Action. If you maintain a high operational tempo then you are making your combat team operate at a higher rate than that of the enemy.

Historical note: We often talk about the best form of defense being offense. We also take about having an offensive mindset in defense (more in the chapter on defense). In the North African desert in the Second World War, the British Parachute Regiment fought for a period of time as ground infantry, not conducting airborne operations. This is where they gained the nickname 'The Red Devils'. The Germans named them such because they were often covered in the red North African dust and the tails of their parachute smocks would hang down behind them looking like devils tails.

The Para's developed a reputation for aggression and tenacity; they were an elite force. They had adopted a local shepherd's expression as a war cry: "Woahhh Mohammed!" and would shout this as they were assaulting the Germans. The Paras took the offensive spirit in defense to the extreme on many occasions: once they got wind that the Germans were forming up in an FUP (Forming Up Position) for an assault, they would leave their positions and charge the enemy in the FUP, completely dislocating and disrupting the enemy in their preparations and routing them from the position.

CHAPTER SIX

CASUALTIES

"When you're wounded and left on Afghanistan's plains,
And the women come out to cut up what remains,
Jest roll to your rifle and blow out your brains
An' go to your Gawd like a soldier."

KIPLING

Introduction

No discussion about surviving in a hostile environment and using weapons to defend against lethal threats would be complete without a discussion on wounding and trauma care. This is a very detailed subject and this instruction will concentrate on actions at the point of wounding and an introduction to some basic techniques as used by both Combat Lifesavers and Combat Medics in the US Army.

It is important to remember that both for civilian first responders and for lifesavers on the battlefield, there is an expectation that casualties will be evacuated promptly to definitive care, either at the local emergency room or at the combat hospital (CASH). Time to care is either the time for the first responder ambulance to retrieve the casualty to the hospital or for combat casualty evacuation to get the combat casualty to the CASH, which is hopefully less than one hour and no more than four; this will depend on the remoteness of the casualty and the availability of assets such as helicopters or vehicles to evacuate the casualty.

In a post event situation, you probably will not have access to an emergency room. You may have access to trained medical professionals and you may have access to some supplies and equipment. Some injuries will require surgical intervention to save life and this may or may not be available. Secondary infection will kill casualties, just like in the old days, so you need to have access to antibiotics. You may end up bartering for medical care, if you can find a doctor or surgeon. You need to prepare yourself as thoroughly as possible with medical training, resources and supplies. What follows is a summary mainly about trauma care and does not substitute for training and professional knowledge.

The U.S. Army trains soldiers as Combat Lifesavers (CLS) to a certain standard, which equates to providing battlefield first aid. Combat medics are trained on the civilian side as EMTs and on the military 'Whisky' side (from 68W –sixty-eight-whiskey - the MOS indictor) at a more detailed level to deal with primary care and battlefield trauma. What medics learn on the whisky side would be illegal for an EMT to do. EMTs are basic life support and often the role of an EMT comes down to being able to provide CPR and providing 'oxygen and rapid transport' to the emergency room. For a combat medic, for casualties 'on the X' only limited interventions are allowed, and even once 'off the X' but still in a tactical environment CPR is not considered appropriate on the battlefield.

Some procedures that are appropriate in a civilian ambulance situation are not appropriate on the battlefield. Ambulance crews may give fluids to casualties on the way to the hospital, where blood is available. They can keep putting the fluids in and get definitive care once they arrive at the emergency room. In a battlefield situation, fluids are not given except in specific circumstances. In simple terms, when you go into true shock by losing circulating body fluids (i.e. blood) your blood pressure will drop. As your body responds to the injury and the loss of blood, it will draw blood into the vital organs at the core of the body, at the expense of the limbs.

Thus, as blood pressure falls you begin to lose the distal pulses (i.e. in the wrist and foot), then closer and closer to the core until you have no pulses but the heart, and the heart will be the last to give out at the lowest blood pressure. In a combat situation, if you give too much fluid, there is a danger of 'blowing the clot' and effectively bleeding out while diluting the blood left in the body, reducing its ability to carry oxygen. Also, fluids frequently given such as Lactated Ringers are rapidly absorbed into tissue so over time they are not really effectively increasing the volume of the blood. Hence the giving of fluids in the ambulance, where in very simple terms you can keep putting it in until you reach the emergency room and blood/plasma products are available.

The fluid given for a traumatic wounding on the battlefield is not lactated ringers or similar, but Hextend, which is a starch product. Over roughly an hour, 500cc of Hextend will draw fluids out of surrounding tissue and bulk up to around 800cc. Guidelines state that you can use a maximum of two 500cc bags, 30 minutes apart. The protocol is only to give fluids if there are no radial (or pedal) pulses, which are the pulses in the wrist or foot. The reason is that you want to bring the blood pressure up enough to restore distal circulation to the extremities but no more, because you don't want to blow any clots or cause the casualty to bleed out. For other injuries such as dehydration other fluids are still given, but not for trauma.

The fact is that a large number of combat injuries are not survivable. Sometimes this will be obvious and the casualty has no chance of survival. Other times, survival will depend on appropriate interventions followed by rapid evacuation and definitive surgical care. There is a difference between being able to keep someone alive at the point of wounding and continuing to keep them alive due to the presence or absence of available definitive care.

Do what you can to initially prevent death and get them to someone who can help, or worst case read some books on battlefield surgery and do something yourself, even if it's just cleaning, debriding and suturing wounds and providing antibiotics, hoping that internal injuries and bleeding are not too severe and will heal in time.

Combat Medic protocols do mainly assume that body armor is worn, which will reduce the incidence of penetrating trauma sustained in combat to the torso and the damage and resulting internal bleeding.

Historically, 90% of combat deaths occur before the casualty reaches the treatment facility. The three major, potentially survivable causes of death on the battlefield are: extremity hemorrhage exsanguination (severe bleeding), tension pneumothorax (oxygen shortage and low blood pressure due to a collapsed lung, a condition that may progress to cardiac arrest if untreated) and airway obstruction. Historically, the most frequent and preventable of these causes of death is extremity bleeding. Thus, think about it: wear body armor if you can. Most wounds to the extremities will cause death by bleeding out, and this is preventable.

As with all things medical, in reality things can be very complicated and involve complications and reactions of individuals to treatment. Much more complicated than what is written here. The purpose of CLS training is to simplify diagnosis and treatment of certain injuries and conditions to allow procedures for certain interventions, in the hope of equipping CLS to save lives. It's not the whole answer, and medical professionals could give you the detail and the lists of possible complications of any of these interventions. For a wider view of medical care, extending beyond combat trauma, read useful books about it, and if you have the time available get some medical training.

Tactical Combat Casualty Care (TC3)

Casualty actions and procedures are comprehensively covered under Army Tactical Combat Casualty Care (TC3) Procedures. A summary will be given here. The summary involves techniques that involve training; this will give you an idea, but you need to collect the right equipment and train to be able to do it. Worst case, most of the 'Whisky' training videos can be found online, so you can at least see what is required and prepare yourself.

The three main preventable causes of death on the battlefield are: extremity bleeding, airway obstruction and 'sucking chest wounds' (pneumo or hemo-thorax, or combinations). Combat Lifesavers are trained and equipped to cope with these problems at a basic level. Casualties will need to be seen by the Team Medic and then rapidly evacuated for more complicated procedures. Some combat wounds are simply not survivable and will not respond to medical attention i.e. severe internal bleeding or visible brain matter etc.

Unlike the normal ABC medical protocol that you will have heard about, the combat protocol for trauma situations is H-A-B-C, which puts hemorrhage before Airway, if it is indicated, but still includes circulation for less serious bleeds and IVs. The other big difference is tourniquets: tourniquets used to be considered a tool of last resort. Now they are considered a tool of first resort in a combat environment. The following article does not presume to attempt to give all the answers, but it is a basic summary.

Combat lifesaver (CLS) training should be given a high priority to ensure that casualties who would have a chance of being saved at the point of wounding are given the immediate care that they require. Individual First Aid Kits (IFAK) should be maintained, stocked and carried as per your team SOP. The IFAK can be improved from how it would arrive as issued by the US Army and additional medical supplies should be placed in the pouch as per guidelines from the Team Medic. Additional tourniquets can be carried on the person as per agreed SOP, such as in the lower left ACU trouser pocket. The IFAK should be inspected prior to every mission as part of PCC/PCI procedures. The IFAK should be carried in standardized place on your gear and it will be the resource that the CLS will use to treat you when you are reached. CLS will **not** treat from their own IFAK. Suggestions for the IFAK:

- CAT Tourniquet x 2 (one carried in pants pocket).
- Needle decompression kit (pen case style).
- Occlusive dressing.
- Israeli pressure bandage.
- Kerlix or preferably:
- Combat Gauze (commercially available as Quick Clot brand)

- ACE bandage (for wrapping up Kerlix or combat gauze wound packing)
- Tape

CLS should not expose themselves to danger in order to recover a casualty. It is the job of the tactical commander to make and execute a rapid plan, including gaining fire superiority, to recover any casualties if the tactical situation allows it. It may not. The situation may not allow immediate casualty extraction and treatment. Consideration can be given to ways of reaching and treating a casualty that minimize risk i.e. use of vehicles as mentioned later etc.

Care Under Fire

In this phase the casualty is 'on the X' at the point of wounding. This is the point of greatest danger for the CLS. An assessment should be made for signs of life (i.e. is the casualty obviously dead). Cover fire should be given and fire superiority achieved. The casualty should be told, if conscious, to either return fire, apply self-aid, crawl to cover or lay still (don't tell them to "Play dead!"). Once it becomes possible to reach the casualty, the only treatment given in the care under fire phase, if required, is tourniquet 'high and tight' on a limb in order to prevent extremity bleeding. The casualty should be rapidly moved to cover (drag them). Be aware of crowding, secondary devices and 'come-on' type attacks.

Tourniquet application: 'high and tight' means right up at the top of the leg or arm, right in the groin (inguinal) or armpit (axial) region. The tourniquet needs to be cinched down tight to stop the bleeding.

When applying tourniquets, they need to be tight enough to stop the distal pulse i.e. the pulse in the foot or wrist, if the limb has not been traumatically amputated. You will not be able to check this pulse at this phase, so just get the tourniquet on tight and check the distal pulse as part of the next phase, tactical field care.

Traumatic amputation: get the tourniquet on high and tight and tighten it until the bleeding stops. Note: in some circumstances there will be pulsating arterial bleeding and severe venous bleeding, but other times it is possible that there may be less bleeding initially as the body reacts in shock and 'shuts down' the extremities, but bleeding will resume when the body relaxes. So get that tourniquet on tight.

Compartment Syndrome: you don't want to be feeling sorry for the casualty and trying to cinch the tourniquet down 'only just enough'. Tighten it to stop the distal pulse. If you don't, the continuing small amount of blood circulation into the limb can cause compartment syndrome, which is a build-up of toxins: when the tourniquet is removed, these toxins flood into the body and can seriously harm the casualty.

Tourniquets used to be considered a tool of last resort. Now they are considered a tool of first resort, and one can be on a limb for up to 6 hours without loss of that limb.

For an improvised tourniquet, make sure the strap is no less than 2 inches wide, to prevent it cutting into the flesh of the limb.

Tactical Field Care

Once the casualty is no longer 'on the X', CLS can move into the Tactical Field Care phase. This may be happening behind cover, or as the convoy speeds away from the killing area, possibly at a rally point, or subsequently as the convoy speeds back to a safe haven. On the battlefield, CPR is not appropriate: a casualty needs to have a pulse and be breathing for further treatment to occur (CPR may be appropriate, for example, if the injuries occur at a safe location, from some sort of accident). This is where the CLS conducts the assessment of the casualty and treats the wounds as best as possible according to the H-ABC mnemonic:

Hemorrhage: During the Tactical Field care phase, any serious extremity bleeding (arterial or serious venous) on a limb, including traumatic amputation, is treated with a tourniquet 2-3 inches above the wound. Axial (armpit), inguinal (groin) and neck wounds are treated by packing with Kerlix or combat gauze and wrapping up with ACE bandage.

Once you have dragged the casualty to cover, you will conduct a blood sweep of the neck, axial region, arms, inguinal region and legs. This can be done as a pat down, a 'feel' or 'claw', or simply ripping your hands down the limbs. Debate exists as to the best method. Conduct the blood sweep and look at your hands at each stage to see if you have found blood. Once a wound is found, check for exit wounds. Ignore minor bleeds at this stage: you are concerned about pulsating arterial bleeds and any kind of serious bleed where you can see the blood rapidly running out of the body.

Beware of deliberate tourniquet application to the lower limbs, below the knee and elbows. The two small bones there may cause problems, particularly with traumatic amputation, and the tourniquet may either not be effective or cause further harm to the casualty. Assess it. Also, if the injury is, for example, below the knee, then don't put the tourniquet over a joint (i.e. knee), put it above the joint.

Airway: CLS can aid the airway by positioning (i.e. head tilt/chin lift to open the airway) and use of the NPA. An NPA should be used for any casualty who is unconscious or who otherwise has an altered mental status.

- Consider use of an OPA/NPA and suction. Again, you need to be trained on these items.

- Combat medics are trained to carry out a crycothyroidotomy ('crike') to place a breathing tube though the front of the airway. This is an effective way of quickly opening the airway on the battlefield. If you are trained and have the equipment you can use patent airways that insert into the mouth and are of the types that paramedics are be trained to use: Combi-tubes and King Airways.

- A crike will save life but assumes that you are heading to a hospital for treatment and repair. The tube will go through the membrane and this will need to be repaired. However, if it is your option to save life, do it and figure out the details later.

Breathing: Occlusive dressings are used to close any open chest wounds. Check for exit wounds! Check the integrity of the chest: ribs and breast bone. You will have to open body armor to do this. If signs of a pneumo/hemo-thorax develop (progressive respiratory distress, late stages would be a deviated trachea (windpipe) in the neck as a result of the whole lung and heart being pushed to one side by the pressure of the air build up in the chest cavity) then needle chest decompression can be performed (NCD).

- If you don't have a specific occlusive dressing, use something like plastic (or the pressure dressing packet) and tape it down. The Old school method was to tape three sides to let air escape, current thinking is to tape all four sides down to seal the wound.

- NCD involves placing a 14 gauge needle, at least 3.25 inches long, into the second intercostal rib space (above the third rib) in the mid-clavicular line (nipple line). This is basically a little below the collar bone, in line above the nipple. The needle is withdrawn and the cannula is left open to air (tape it in place). An immediate rush of air out of the chest indicates the presence of a tension pneumothorax. The manoeuver effectively converts a tension pneumothorax into a simple pneumothorax.
  - The definitive treatment is to get a chest tube in, in the side of the chest (eighth intercostal space); to drain the blood and air that is filling the chest cavity.

Circulation 1: At this time, any high and tight tourniquets can be converted to either a tourniquet 2-3 inches above the wound, or if no longer necessary a pressure dressing or packed with kerlix/combat gauze.

Any other less serious wounds are dressed at this point with pressure dressings or gauze. Don't bother with minor cuts and wounds; they are not life threatening at this point.

Circulation 2: If no distal (wrist or foot) pulse is present (and the casualty in in an altered mental state) then give fluids: 500cc Hextend wide open. If a distal pulse is present, then administer a saline lock in case fluids or medications are required later. Check again 30 minutes later and if the radial pulse is not present, give the second 500cc Hextend bag.

Assessment: Once the H-ABC's are taken care of, consider pain medication if you have it. Be aware that pain medication such as morphine can suppress respiration and therefore may be dangerous depending on the type of injury. You also don't need to give pain medication to an unconscious or altered mental status casualty. If time and circumstances permit you will then go into a full head to toe assessment of the casualty, looking for further injury and treating as you come across them. This is where you would take a more considered look at the casualty, make sure you have found all the injuries, and treat other injuries such as breaks, non-life threatening bleeds and lacerations and burns.

Use splinting to reduce pain from injuries such as breaks, burns and other suitable wounds. Burns are treated with dry dressings, not wet. The reason for this is hypothermia: burns reduce the skins ability to regulate body heat and treating a wounded and shocked casualty with wet dressings can bring on hypothermia. Be aware that circumferential burns i.e. all the way around the limb can act as a tourniquet on the limb. Burns to the chest can interfere with breathing and an escharotomy is a procedure to cut around the skin on the chest to reduce the constriction of full thickness burns.

Once you have treated the H-ABCs you should cover the casualty with a thermal blanket to retain body heat and reduce the risk of hypothermia. You will continue to monitor the casualty and perform interventions as necessary both prior to and during the evacuation.

Casualty Movement

Casualty movement is one of the greatest challenges in the treatment and evacuation of wounded personnel. Manual drags and carries work over short distances but cannot be sustained. Suitable litters, such as the TALON II and the SKED, should be carried on vehicles for use on both vehicle and foot extractions from contact. The greatest aid to casualty movement and extraction will be the vehicles themselves.

A vehicle, particularly if up-armored, can be used to cover, conceal, extract and evacuate a casualty. Space will be tight inside vehicles, but it is possible to treat a casualty while evacuating them and thus lessening the time to definitive care at a treatment facility. For significant trauma that may be beyond the scope of the CLS, rapid evacuation with the best possible CLS/combat medic care on route will be the greatest lifesaver.

The classic Fireman's carry has largely gone out of favor, mainly due to the weight of casualties today: not only the body weight due to increasing obesity and also the weight disparities between soldiers, such as a small female and a large male, but also because these differences are increased when the weight of body armor and equipment is added to that of the individual. The most effective short distance movement is the drag.

The Hawes carry has replaced the Fireman's carry: the casualty is behind the rescuer, laying down the back of the rescuer with arms around the neck/shoulders. This carry is easiest with some level of consciousness from the casualty. The rescuer holds the arms around their chest and leans forward to take the casualties weight on their back. The casualty's feet will drag or scoot along the ground. The Hawes carry allows the rescuer one hand to operate a firearm as they are moving. If you have the fitness and a decent weight relative to the casualty, you can still do the Fireman's carry, which allows you to run.

CHAPTER SEVEN

POST EVENT VEHICLE MOVEMENT

"Tactics are like opinions, everyone has one."

Introduction

Mobile vehicle and dismounted tactics is what many soldiers and security operators do/did in Iraq and Afghanistan; either escorting convoys, doing administrative moves, or carrying the personnel that they are tasked to protect. Surviving and reacting to roadside and site ambush and attack were what it was all about.

In the early days, 2004, many operators had soft skinned vehicles. Rounds go through those like a knife through butter. The only protection is limited to the engine block and the metal part of the wheels. Thus, if forced to take cover behind a vehicle, take cover by the wheel wells. It was possible to add steel plate to vehicles to add protection, similar to 'hobo' Humvee's used by US military at the time. Remove the interior door panels and add steel plate, sloping up above the window base to provide cover for shoulders. Armored vehicles became the norm later, and really in an environment such as Iraq armored vehicles are required. They would be ideal post-event, but who has one?

There is a difference between a tactical mobile force that you may decide to organize post-event, perhaps utilized by a retreat to conduct operations such as mobile perimeter defense or foraging parties, versus a family traveling from A to B, perhaps from home to a BOL, or because they have to move again due to a necessity to relocate, for whatever reason. For the tactical force, TTPs will be covered in more detail later.

By way of introduction, such a force could consist of multiple vehicles manned by trained operators. To create 'technical' gun trucks you can use a pick-up truck. Put in a pintle mount in the truck bed for the weapon of choice, preferably a SAW or 240B/M60 type automatic machine gun type weapons. Then build up the sides of the truck bed to the preferred height with steel plate, to protect the gunner while standing at the pintle mount. Remember to armor the cab and to test the steel plate to stop NATO 7.62 (.308). You could also mount a steel plate to the front bumper to provide protection to the engine block / radiator from the front and perhaps therefore an increased ramming ability - which could also be used to 'ram raid' stores and other locations if foraging for food in a TEOTWAWKI situation, or to push aside a road block or vehicles used as a road block. If you wanted to get really serious, you could take out the windshield and replace it with two steel plates, fitted so as to leave a narrow gap for vision and to allow the passenger to shoot forwards.

For a family travelling in a post event situation, there are multiple risk factors. For now, the assumption will be travelling in vehicles, for which you have sufficient additional fuel stored and you are able to carry your required people and stores in the vehicle for movement to your destination. If you don't for any reason have vehicles, such as running out of fuel, EMP or whatever, then you should consider acquiring additional vehicles and/or fuel before you consider taking off on your feet.

If you do have to walk, then consider creating some sort of cart system, maybe using strollers if you have kids, both for child and equipment movement. You could also consider moving using bicycles with trailers and even horses. However, even in an EMP situation some vehicles will still work, even if yours don't, so if you have to bug out you should put serious consideration to obtaining vehicles and fuel so that you can drive rather than take on alternate means of travel. When on the roads, some hazards that you should consider:

- Jammed roadways
- Law enforcement/military traffic control points (TCPs)
- Illegal traffic control points (ITCPs)
- Manned roadblocks
- Unmanned roadblocks

- Ambush – static
- Ambush – mobile
- Urban areas
- Mob
- Trick or con

General Movement Considerations

The type of environment envisioned is a post-collapse situation where there has been a breakdown in law and order. This section is therefore not primarily concerned with the sort of 'bug-out' movement that families may conduct in response to a localized natural disaster, where you have to get in your car with some basic equipment and move out of the impacted area. Rather, this is directed at those who find they have to move locations after a significant societal collapse has happened.

The reality for many families is that is that they are not set up in a self-sustaining retreat right now. For whatever reason, they may be in an urban or suburban environment. They may have nowhere else to realistically 'bug out' to. They may have a goal to achieve the retreat, but not be there yet, or have bug out land that is fairly basic and requires them to move to it following a collapse. So there may be a reality gap between those that have achieved the gold standard of location and preparations, and those that are not there yet.

What we are really concerned about here is a collapse of society, the veritable 'TEOTWAWKI', where it all goes to chaos, the 'SHTF'. Most of us will be left to survive where we are, in our suburban homes or whatever applies to you. Now, it is true that some will be better set up than others. Reasons include location, such as an inner city one bedroom apartment versus a big house on several acres in a sub-division, or the amount of preps that you have: food supplies etc.

Everything depends on the situation and the threat that emerges, including your own personal and family situation and preparations. One key thing is not to make assumptions now, but to remain flexible. It is strongly advised to not to 'head for the hills' by reflex, because unless you have somewhere to go you will be out there with the rest of the refugees in the chaos. If you even have a minimal amount of preparations at home you should shelter in place and make do the best you can. This should be a low profile shelter in place where you set yourself up to draw minimum attention to yourself as the waves of chaos pass. You may be sheltering in a basement with your family, for example.

Of course, if the threat changes, then you will need to adapt to it. An organized gang of well-armed marauders going house to house in your neighborhood would be an example of when to make the decision to bug out. Be flexible and don't go the opposite of the 'head for the hills' mentality and die in your basement simply because you did not want to pack up and go. However, it is almost a given that for anyone sheltering with supplies in this way there will at some point come one or more challenges such as home invasion from outside groups. This will also probably apply to those in rural retreats at some point as the horde fans out looking to survive. Be ready to respond and defend yourself against these challenges as necessary. Think of how it will likely be after the event, not how things are right now. Those in the rural retreats will probably have a rude awakening when they realize that the horde has reached them and the demographics have changed!

There are two main things that you have to achieve, phases if you like, in order to survive in the long term:

1) Have enough stores, firearms, tactical ability and numbers if possible, as well as a covert location in order to survive the event and the initial chaos and disorder. This is a short to medium term goal.

2) Long term, you will need to be able to live in a protected sustainable community. All prepper's stores will run out in the end and the only solution to survive and thrive is to be able to produce food and protect your people and your resources.

So, unless you started in a sustainable protected retreat, you will have to survive where you are until such time as you can get to one. Remember that in a full TEOTWAWKI scenario there will be mass panic and chaos as people try to find food and survive. There will be a huge population die-off and there will likely be a delay of a year or two before food can be produced. You have to survive from the one to the other. Even after the die–off there will still be good and bad guys out there. Good guys probably living in those sustainable retreats or locations, bad guys marauding and living off what they can loot and pillage. There may be other complicating factors, such as civil war or foreign invasion.

So, if you survived the event and were not already in that ideal retreat, you then have to move. Did you hide and protect your bug out vehicle with a supply of stored gas? Are you going to have to walk, or use other modes of transport? The key thing is that your group will have to make it to somewhere where they can be accepted by a current sustainable community, or move onto land where they can create one. This will involve travel of some sort and also the ability to defend your group while moving from A to B.

If it is true TEOTWAWKI, then it could go on for years and you may have to travel to establish a farm somewhere. If you are going to be taken in by a community or small town that is sustaining itself, then you have to show your worth in some way. This can also become relevant to those who find themselves in the 'gold standard' prepper retreat location, because some of the factors may change to make that position no longer tenable.

So, at some point it may be relevant to all that they will have to move in vehicles in a post collapse environment. If you have to conduct vehicle movement then you will need to assume an extant threat. Such a threat will take the form, in simple terms, of armed groups and individuals who will seek to impinge on you and your family's freedom, property or life for their own ends. There could be road blocks, ambush, mobs, tricks and all sorts of threats.

You will also have to consider the extent that any law enforcement remains active, which could also include emergency or martial law. For example, if you are moving you will have to assess the situations as they appear and decide whether you are facing a legal checkpoint (i.e. military/law enforcement) versus perhaps an illegal roadblock with bad intent versus perhaps an 'illegal' one with simply defensive intent, such as one set up by a community militia to defend a town. Therefore, you will need to consider the adoption of defensive tactics and capabilities in order to mitigate against the threat.

Please put out of your mind any assumptions that you may have already about how you will move in this kind of environment. This is not about advocating the use of children as 'shooters', the open display of weapons out of car windows, or even the positioning of a 'shooter' in a sunroof. In short, this is not about going 'Mad Max'. You will need to consider the 'profile' that you adopt, which means how your vehicle packet appears as you are moving along the roads and at halts, and will also have implications for the professionalism that you display.

You can adopt either a 'high' or 'low' profile (or posture) and in this situation, as a family or group of civilians moving in a potentially hostile post collapse environment, it is likely best to adopt the lower end of the profile scale. This does not impact your defensive capability, but granted it could be said you make you a more inviting target if you look 'softer'. However, you do not want to incite action against you by hostiles and there may well still be elements of military or law enforcement working out there and you don't want to find yourself arrested or engaged by these elements because you yourselves are seen as a lawless threat. This is not a discussion about creating tactical teams or quick reaction forces, which will be useful in other circumstances and comes later in this book; it is more about mitigating risk to a family or friends group moving cross country.

Consider how you can maintain a defensive capability while also presenting a low profile. For example, consider your vehicles. Families often have minivans. These are not seen as cool or tactical at all, but if you put the seats down in the back you have a huge cargo space. Loading this with supplies would allow you to carry them while not making it look so obvious, less obvious than loading a pick-up or a trailer for example.

Wear your load/ammunition carrying equipment in a way that is comfortable for sitting in a vehicle but less obvious – perhaps putting a shirt over top of a load carrying vest, and keeping weapons down but accessible. If you have to get out and stand by your vehicle you can do so with your weapon in a ready position, but you can also leave it on the seat next to you and readily available, depending on the situation and the profile you wish to portray. Consider these things.

Remember that your vehicle gives you no protection. The only 'hardened' areas in a normal civilian vehicle are the engine block and the metal parts of the wheels. This is why if you are taking fire position next to a vehicle, you want to shelter by the engine or wheel wells; preferably you will then move away from the vehicle into a fire position in hard cover. You should consider how you may be able to change this by creating better ballistic protection in the vehicles.

As you are moving, the driver's job is to drive and he should preferably be capable as a 'shooter' but primarily the vehicle is his 'weapon' and the means to keep people safe. The other 'shooters' will be assigned observation sectors of responsibility as they move along the route. You should adopt a safe tactical speed that will give you warning of any dangers ahead and hopefully allow you to avoid them. Your primary focus should be on safety and the avoidance of danger.

Invest time in route planning. Don't be afraid to stop and move forward on foot to observe the route ahead, or turn around and go another way. Make sure you adopt the tactical bounds between vehicles and if you stop for any reason, such as to change a tire, fill up gas from your stored gas cans, or even for the night, you need to adopt a good tactical position and cover your sectors to protect the convoy. For longer term halts, such as overnight, conceal the vehicles off the road and post sentries.

As you move, you will need to have any music off and consider having the windows open in unarmored vehicles in rural areas in order to be able to hear and get a better feel for the environment, particularly if you stop for any reason. But if you are anywhere where there is the potential for people or mobs then you need to have the doors locked and the windows up to reduce the risk of entry and even people getting snatched from vehicles.

If you are driving and you come under enemy fire ('contact') then you are in the enemy 'killing area' also known as the 'X' and the key thing is to get off the X as rapidly as possible. You may take casualties but you still need to get out of there and consolidate at a secured rally point. This is where any added ballistic protection will be priceless. A problem you may have is if you have a vehicle(s) immobilized by enemy fire on the X.

These situations and the counter drills are covered in detail in this chapter. Briefly, you have to get the personnel off the X and this can either be with a rescue vehicle moving back into the killing area under cover fire and 'cross decking' the personnel, or alternatively the personnel in the immobilized vehicle(s) will have to fire and move off the X to rejoin the group under covering fire.

You will want to consider whether you are moving by day or by night. The situation will dictate but in general if you don't have night vision equipment for driving, which means driving with headlights, then you should move during the day. This will allow you to scan and observe and your movement will also be less obvious without your headlights as it would be at night. You will need to give consideration to the threats you may encounter and drill your team accordingly. You may have to respond to roadside ambush, and this may be with the road open or blocked and with your vehicles perhaps becoming immobilized or receiving casualties. You will also have to work out how you will respond to roadblocks, both legal and illegal and what you will do if you observe them early of if you drive into one without prior warning.

It is important that your practice these 'actions on' drills so that you will be able to respond in a crisis. You should even practice 'cross decking' and getting the kids out of the vehicles in an emergency, so that they know what to expect and are not surprised when you start giving them commands to 'get down' or get out of the vehicles. You can train this kind of muscle memory drill in the same way that kids do fire drills and 'stop drop and roll' at school.

If you do find yourself in a position where it is the protected vehicle that is immobilized and under fire, then there needs to be at least on adult acting as the protection person and directing the protected personnel to stay low and crawl, while the other spouse or team members provide covering fire. You should be able to identify what hard cover is (cover from fire, not just view) and also what is 'dead ground', which is ground that the enemy cannot see into i.e. folds in the ground and ditches etc. This will allow the protection person to identify areas where they may keep the kids while waiting for a rescue vehicle, or alternatively allow them to crawl out of the killing area in cover while others in the team fire and move.

The more vehicles and team members you have in your group, the more potential there is for covering fire from the flanks of the killing area, and the more people available to fire and move and also carry any casualties. The reality of a family or group of families or friends on the move is that there will be a mix of the tactically able, the young and the old and infirm.

Vehicle Movement Basics

i.e. some things to think about:

Threat mitigation: AVOID, AVOID, AVOID: How to? Stay put? In the long run, it may be riskier to stay put, so you may have to move to an alternative location. Think about advance planning, route selection: use back roads avoiding lines of drift and traffic. Timing: go at the right time, either early in the crisis when you first get alerted, or if you don't you may have missed the window when the roads were not clogged, so you may have to wait until the panic has subsided. Avoid panicked mobs on the main routes but certainly avoid too much of an area where there may be local militias or other types of threats where they may want to want to take your liberty or your property.

Move at a slow steady speed on selected back roads, maybe around 40 mph or slower; use slow speeds appropriate to the roads and the visibility. Make your speed such that you don't get surprised going round a bend. If necessary, stop short and conduct surveillance on the route ahead, even if that means getting out of the vehicles and moving up to an observation point. Utilize stand-off and observation. If necessary turn around and go another way. Primarily: AVOID.

Trailers can impact the ability to perform maneuvers, such as reversing under contact. AVOID situations where you have to do this, and consider not having a trailer if you don't have to; but you may need it for long term survival to carry gear and supplies. Consider kids car seats: these will keep them safe from a crash but sitting right up there strapped in during a contact? If you come under contact, anyone not operating a weapon, any children and elderly or sick non-combatants, should be down in the foot well taking cover. Consider having your kids in adult seat belts or free in the car but able to be placed into the foot well and also rapidly dragged out of the car as necessary. This therefore is another factor that implies not speeding along and therefore taking a steady approach to the movement.

A note on seat belts: in the early days in Iraq, it was considered the thing not to use seat belts. However, casualties were caused due to:

1) Road traffic accidents caused by roadside IEDs, which would otherwise be survivable except for the crash and

2) High speeds used as vehicles sped along trying to avoid ambush.

Later, it was considered safe to be strapped in and undo the seat belt if you needed to get out. Consider this with children and car seats: which is safer? So consider up-armoring the sides of the vehicle, even temporarily, where your children sit. Kids can't generally wear body armor, but if you have spare sets then prop it up in the doors next to where the kids are sitting. Or do the same with any other protective material, such as steel plates. Consider protection from enemy small arms fire coming from the roadside.

You can purchase 'ballistic blankets' which are close protection equipment to rapidly throw over someone if shooting starts. They are just soft armor without plates, therefore not protection against high velocity rounds, but they would have utility to place along the sides of a vehicle where the passengers sit. You could use something like ballistic blankets or steel plate materials to create a protected area inside a vehicle, even a steel open-topped box in the back of a mini-van. The challenge if doing that is to allow access to rapidly get the passengers out, which means having access doors or panels into the box.

If you were to create such a box, you would place all the seats down or remove them in the back, and then put the kids on the floor, possibly lashing down kids car seats to the floor of the vehicle. It is also important to note, on the subject of lashing stuff down, that all loose equipment inside a vehicle must be lashed down with ratchet straps to strong points. This is so, in case of a crash or rollover, the occupants do not get injured by such equipment flying around. All items such as jacks, ammo cans or other heavy stuff needs to be tied down.

The more team members, shooters and vehicles you have, the better. A tactic to use if you consider you are approaching a danger point, such as a potential ambush site, and you can't go another route to avoid it, is to use bounding over-watch with your vehicles. You have to have more than one vehicle to do this, preferably three. If a single family unit, consider using the second family car. Wife, kids and trailer on the rear vehicle, husband up front in the other - that is worst case.

Utilize a 'tactical bound' between vehicles - a distance that depends on the ground but means that one element will not be suppressed by the same effective fire as the other unit. The husband up front can stop short, scan the area and reverse out as necessary, in a recon function. The second car does not pull up behind, but maintains the tactical bound. If you were moving in one vehicle, maybe two, but you had protected personnel in all vehicles and no other way around the potential ambush site, your options are limited.

If you really had to go through then you could consider loading one of the vehicles with shooter personnel only and send it through, covered by other shooters. Alternatively you could send a dismounted team, even if it is only two people, to skirmish through with bounding over-watch and clear the areas of cover to the flank where you think the likely ambush will be. They can be covered by other people back at the road, with the protected vehicles and personnel pushed back into dead ground. If they make contact with enemy, they will simply break contact and fire and maneuver back to the main body and everyone will mount up and move out.

If you have more shooters and vehicles, then you can put more shooters in the lead vehicle and at the least a shooter riding 'shotgun' in the family vehicle in a close protection role. If your protection packet has three vehicles then you have a lead advance vehicle, a central 'client' protected family vehicle and a rear 'chase' or 'CAT' vehicle (counter attack team). This allows bounding over-watch, dismounted fire support positions, and for the CAT vehicle to move up to provide support for the lead or protected family vehicle to extract.

These tactics will be covered in more detail later. There could be debate about 'keeping all your eggs in one basket' with the non-combatants in the middle vehicle(s), but if you spread them out it is harder to protect them. Better to have front protection vehicles, central protected vehicle(s) and rear protection vehicles. Your packet could take numerous forms, but if we simplify to a three or four vehicle packet we probably have the lead and chase vehicles at the front and rear with the one or two protected vehicles in the center. The procedure for bounding over-watch:

- Identify the vulnerable point (VP) otherwise known as the potential ambush site. Pass the word to the convoy.
- Observe the location as best as possible to identify any enemy lying in wait.
- The lead vehicle 'goes firm' as fire support. This vehicle dismounts (except the driver) into appropriate fire positions.
- The protected vehicles remain a tactical bound behind, protection provided by integral shooters riding shotgun.
- The rear vehicle moves through the VP and moves to a suitable position beyond to cover forward and back into the VP.
- Now, both front and rear vehicles have the area covered with potential fire support from each side of the VP.
- The protected vehicles rapidly move through the VP.
- The lead vehicle pushes through, regains position at the front and the convoy continues.

The key thing in an ambush is to get 'off the X' as soon as possible. If you have not managed to AVOID, and you end up ambushed with no obstruction in the road, then try to speed up and drive through. Return fire from the vehicles if possible. If the way out to the front is blocked, and there is no feasible way forward, or around, or off to the side around the road block, then reverse out. If a route is blocked by light vehicles then you may be able to drive through it and ram vehicles out of the way: the technique is to slow down into low gear to approach the block, then gun the engine at the last minute and push, not smash, the vehicles out the way: strike at the corners to push the vehicles off to the side.

Shoot through your windscreen and through doors/windows as necessary to suppress the enemy. If the enemy is located at a front vehicle roadblock (like the stereotypical police type ones you see on TV) then you can drive at them firing through the windscreen, if you have to, or better still you can reverse away with the passenger shooter firing through the windscreen.

If a vehicle is immobilized on the X, then you have two options:

1) A rescue vehicle comes back, or forward from the rear, and cross-decks the passengers, bearing in mind neither vehicle is armored which lessens the protection you have from the immobilized vehicle as you conduct this maneuver; preferably you will have a third vehicle providing fire support during this.

2) The convoy having transited the ambush with the exception of the immobilized vehicle, the surviving support vehicles dismount outside of the X and take up a position of fire support while those in the immobilized vehicle dismount and fight back to them using fire and movement. If your babies are in the family car on the X, then clearly you are driving in to get them as per option 1.

If you are in a single family car immobilized on the X, then you have to get out and return fire while your spouse pulls the kids out and into the culvert/ditch/dead ground away from the enemy fire. Always get out of the car on the opposite side to where the fire is coming from, even though this means scooting across the seats. Then you will have to return fire and try and get off the X. Popping smoke would be useful to mask movement.

If possible, do not just return fire in the general direction (we covered that earlier) but use accurate fire to kill the enemy. Have the kids crawl out in whatever dead ground there is, with one of you providing close protection, guidance and supervision while the other makes fire and movement bounds and provides accurate covering fire. Crawl out to wherever the ground dictates. If there are other shooters or shooter teenagers involved on your side, then they can fire and move with you while the babies and mom crawl out. But, just because you armed a teenager or young adult, does not say or predict how he / she will perform under first time contact. Terrifying. Does it make you cringe just thinking about it?

If you just abandoned your vehicle and all your supplies on the road in an ambush, then you have survival priorities. If you could, you should have bugged out from the vehicle carrying 'grab bags' of essential ammo, water, food, medical emergency supplies. However, once the family is at a safer location and there is no sign of follow up, you may want to consider the situation and the strength of the enemy force. If they are looting your vehicle in the open, then you could consider a counter attack, preferably using stand-off weapons range and marksmanship. Put them down without mercy, they tried to kill your family. Take your stuff back. Get another vehicle, cross load, and get out of there.

Consider escalation of profile. Depending on the situation, you will either be wearing full battle rattle, (body armor, vest, assault rifle and handgun), or you will likely be wearing the same rig but in a low profile configuration. Consider how active you expect law enforcement to be as the situation deteriorates. It may not all be black and white, it may be shades of gray, with authorities stopping people who are armed etc. 'The Man' (i.e. the State/Government of any country) historically requires and needs to maintain the monopoly of violence and the use of force, even if that leaves citizens unable to protect themselves against the criminal element.

It is therefore possible, or likely, that law enforcement will not be taking courses of action that are best for the safety of you and your family, but will be based on other considerations, such as not allowing citizens to be 'armed and dangerous'. If you are in a vehicle, you can lower your profile by putting a large shirt over your body armor and rig. However, consider the law. Does a CCW cut it? What about a local Sheriff's Deputy who is trying to enforce the law against strangers coming onto his turf? How well trained and informed is he really? Maybe he has a police roadblock or pulls you over on the back road. If he wants to take your weapons or take you into the station, then this may be a lethal threat to the safety of your family, if the situation has really gone to complete disorder and the deputy is operating in denial on an old set of rules. How to deal with that? Do you let him? Ponder it.

Specific threats and TTPs:

Jammed Roadways: It would be best to avoid this in its entirety. Take alternate routes, either planned in advance or based upon a quick map assessment. Make sure you have the right paper maps available in your vehicles, showing detail down to small back roads. It may be that you are transiting gridlocked roadways sometime post event and the obstacle is simply parked vehicles, with the occupants long gone. In these situations you can try and use the road and find ways around. If it is a back road that is blocked by parked traffic, then consider ambush, (more below under unmanned roadblocks) but also consider your ability to push or winch vehicles out of the way to make a way through. Vehicles can also be 'bounced' out of the way by a team using the firefighter technique.

Law enforcement/military traffic control points (TCPs): If we are in a slow-slide gray area situation then you will need to adjust your profile and conceal weapons accordingly. Be legal and treat the personnel manning the TCP with courtesy and respect. Have your identity documents and vehicle registrations in order. Have a good reason for being on the road: where are you going and why? Make an assessment as you approach the TCP to whether you think it is legitimate. Try and avoid such check-points, but once you get close to them any avoidance type action will be perceived as suspicious and will likely trigger a pursuit or kinetic response.

Illegal traffic control points (ITCPs): Assess and avoid. Try to maintain stand-off. These can effectively be the same as roadblocks, see next item, and will likely be designed to relieve you of your property and / or liberty. If you end up pulling up to one of these, perhaps by mistake, then be prepared for action. It could be that it is manned by personnel impersonating police or military, and you don't realize until you pull up, or even police and military that are no longer in on official capacity. Try and stop short and avoid by reversing out, or if it is too late just keep going (see roadblock, below) or if stopped try and talk your way through.

Don't turn off your vehicle, even if instructed. Have your handgun ready to shoot through the door at the questioner that approaches your window if you can't talk or bribe your way through. There will likely be others standing by covering with weapons and any ITCP worth its salt will be covered by fire from a concealed position. If you do have to shoot, go to extreme violence instantly. Initially covertly, then openly, shoot out through the body of the vehicles and accelerate out of there, firing as you go.

Note: as a general rule, you won't be driving about with weapons protruding out of the windows of your vehicles. That is simply not cool. You will look like an Iraqi police car. Don't do it.

Manned Roadblocks: Avoid. If you are caught by one, it is effectively in ITCP, but you don't know the intention. It could be a roadblock set up by a civil defense group or militia defending a town or area. They will be suspicious and wary but they may or may not be hostile. The key issue is that depending on the strength of the physical roadblock, you may or may not be blocked from forward movement. Be aware of the use of vehicles to pull out and block you in from the rear, closing the trap. This is why keeping a tactical bound between vehicles is a good idea, so your whole convoy is not trapped. If you cannot move forward, you may have to reverse out: and clearly if you can avoid driving through a roadblock manned by goons with guns, then don't. Think outside the box: if the ITCP personnel are not that imaginative, they may have blocked the road but there may be ways to drive around the block and continue forward, if you need to.

You may also be able to use your vehicle as a weapon and drive at the enemy team members as you do this. If the block is made up of light enough vehicles, and your vehicle is fairly powerful, then you can push the block out of the way by slowing down into low gear, aiming for the corners of the vehicles, and pushing your way through. Whether you end up going forwards or rearwards out of block, then whichever vehicles are outside the X will be providing covering fire to those still inside and trying to get out.

If you don't spot the roadblock early enough to totally avoid it and you end up getting too close, try and avoid actually pulling up to the roadblock. It is better to stop a little short, with maybe just the first vehicle at risk. You can then reverse out. If they open fire then the passenger can shoot back through the windshield as the vehicle is reversing. Reversing can also be used as a tactic if you inadvertently pull up to the block. It may be your option if they seem hostile and there is no way forward. So, reversing will give you some protection from your engine block and will avoid either splitting your convoy or having the whole convoy have to follow you through the block, possibly under fire. Remember that as you take avoiding action, probably stopping short and reversing out, your CAT vehicle can pull up and provide fire support to suppress the roadblock as you move.

Unmanned Roadblocks: Avoid. You don't of know if the roadblock/obstruction is actually manned or booby-trapped, perhaps with a well concealed ambush. Consider that an ambush in a post event scenario will be set for a reason. A manned roadblock is set to either extort with robbery or tolls or to deny access to a defended area. An unmanned roadblock will possibly just be abandoned, or it will be there to slow down or stop you to allow an ambush from a concealed position off the road. It is more likely that some form of obstruction will be used in the road to slow you down prior to the enemy initiating the ambush: they probably will not have (but consider that they may have) the capability to initiate an ambush with an IED and thus stop your vehicles with that.

They therefore have to sacrifice the covert possibilities of an IED or mine for an obstruction, otherwise how to stop you simply driving through the ambush site? If you have to transit past an obstruction, use bounding over-watch, observe the area before moving, and try and find alternative ways around, even as simple as crossing the median to the other roadway (if a dual highway) and travelling against the probably non-existent traffic for a little while. Think outside the box.

Ambush - Static: If an ambush is set right, you won't know you are in it until you are fired upon. You also should not be able to get out alive. However, we rely on friction, the mistakes of others and the limitations of their tactical abilities and resources to find ways through the gaps to survive in a combat situation. Get out of the ambush and return the enemy fire where you can positively identify (PID) the enemy. More will be covered on specific drills below.

Ambush - mobile: It may be that an ambush is not purely static and will incorporate mobile elements, whether that is just moving vehicles to block you into the killing area. It may also be that has no static ambush element and is just in the form of vehicle(s) chasing you and trying to run you down. Remember that you can fire out of your vehicles, either through the windshield or the rear window. Try not to let the attack turn into a breakneck chase where you are using speed to get away and risk crashing and losing it all. Move away at a steady pace and use firepower to attempt to break contact; fire into the cab of the chasing vehicle in order to kill or deter the enemy.

The rear CAT vehicle will not allow the pursuing vehicle past and will block them from threatening the protected vehicles in the center of your convoy. If you are unable to stop them by fire, try to use some useful ground such as a bend in the road to break contact, pull into a likely location, and dismount into fire positions where you can really 'light up' the chasing vehicle, perhaps as it comes around a bend. This is where you could use your chase or CAT vehicle to stop and set a snap ambush while the protected vehicles speed away out of the contact area to a safe rally point.

If you are moving as a three vehicle convoy and you are pursued by attacking enemy vehicle(s), then don't let them make you speed up to crash / disaster speed. Keep a vehicle, such as your rear chase vehicle, between the enemy and your central protected vehicle(s): this vehicle will be raining accurate fire into the cab(s) of the pursuers. That may stop them. If it does not, then send your front vehicle only speeding ahead to a suitable snap ambush site, and have them dismount into fire positions. When the chase comes round the corner, they will let your vehicles pass and hammer the pursuers with accurate fire, hopefully allowing you to break contact. The convoy can stop further down the road to RV with the snap ambush vehicle(s).

Urban Areas: if possible, avoid any sort of urban area. This would include small towns as you transit though the countryside. There will no doubt be increased population, mobs, gangs or defense forces, and an increased risk of ambush.

Mob: Any situation where there are crowds can be extremely dangerous to your convoy. It does not take much to crowd in a vehicle and when that happens, your options are very limited. You could go kinetic but if you are truly being mobbed the people may not actually be able to get away from you so although you may kill a large number, they may have no option but to tear you apart to save themselves as the ones on the outside try to push in. Again, avoid. If you find yourself in some sort of flash mob that poses a risk, then try and keep the vehicles going. All doors locked and windows up. There is a fine line between inciting mob violence and getting out of there. If the mob is focused on you, is trying to get into or onto the vehicles, then you have no choice but to try and keep going and when necessary open fire to get people off or away from your vehicles.

Trick or Con: this could take many forms and may be the precursor to some sort of ambush or heist. Think of the old classic fake car accident, or maybe the attractive hitchhiker or distraught mom by the side of the road. Maybe even a stroller with or without baby pushed under your wheels as you are moving through. Don't think it would happen? Think about 'crack mom'. Essentially, the bad guys will think up any sort of trick or con where they can get you to stop, get you off guard, and take advantage of you. Charity is one thing but be aware. Hungry looking kids may be sent to tug on your heart strings, any number of things. If you are going to stop, do so under your own terms. Be aware, observe and assess the situation, try to read people, and ensure you have security.

Counter-Ambush Drills: Consider the following for vehicle mounted counter ambush drills. The following are proven techniques for various contact situations and outcomes. They can be modified as appropriate to the threat and vehicle number/type employed. They can be viewed as templates to be adapted as necessary. The following factors need to be considered and planned for as part of vehicle drills. SOPs adapted to your situation will dictate how you utilize these drills:

Casualties: Casualty treatment and movement will severely hamper the smoothest of break contact drills. Have a plan for casualties.

Communications: Where possible, install some sort of radio communication between vehicles. This can be simple VHF radios. You can install a vehicle kit that everyone will hear on load speaker, and/or individual radios carried on personal equipment with earpieces and mikes. The personal radios will go with you when dismounted and also if you have to abandon the vehicles, so there are definite advantages to this approach.

'Cross-Decking': The rapid movement of personnel, casualties and equipment from an immobilized vehicle to a rescue / extraction vehicle. This drill needs to be practiced and 'grab bags' prepared to facilitate the process. The nature of cross-decking means that the extraction vehicle will end up overloaded as it leaves the killing area. However, that can be dealt with and practiced for, and further distribution of personnel can happen at a rally point out of enemy contact.

Reaction to Contact Drills

The following are some standard vehicle mounted reaction drills to contact:

Simple Contact, **Route Open**: "CONTACT, DRIVE, DRIVE, DRIVE!" In this simple contact situation, no vehicles are immobilized and the convoy is able to continue to make progress and drive through the killing area (The X). Vehicles should speed up to exit the area rapidly. Fire can be returned if Positive Identification (PID) can be made of the enemy at a firing point or firing at the convoy. It is possible that there may be casualties. If possible, care under fire will be performed by CLS without stopping any vehicles. Once the convoy is clear of the area, a plan can be made to further treat and evacuate the casualty(s). Steps:

1) "CONTACT, DRIVE, DRIVE, DRIVE"

2) Return fire if possible, PID enemy.

3) Initial Contact Report: voice radio.

4) Reports from vehicles: "Vehicle 1 OK, Vehicle 2 OK…." or "Vehicle 1 mobile, 1 casualty…" etc.

5) CLS treat casualties on the move: tourniquet 'high & tight'.

6) Rally if necessary in secured location.

7) Continue mission or make a casualty extraction plan.

Note: this drill could include an obstacle to the front, but the convoy continues forward because they can either knock it out of the way or drive around it. The road is therefore not totally blocked to egress forwards. It is always easier to continue forwards in vehicles rather than try to turn around.

Contact, Route Blocked: "CONTACT, REVERSE, REVERSE, REVERSE!" In this situation, the contact may come from the front, or from any direction, but the egress route to the front is blocked either physically, by weight of enemy contact, or both. In this situation, the way out is the way the convoy came in. Fire will be returned as appropriate and according to enemy PID. All vehicles will reverse until out of contact, or when the rear vehicle finds a spot to turn around in, whichever is better under the tactical situation and the ground.

The best way to turn around is to do a 'K turn' – this can be done simply on the road if it is wide enough, or into a suitable turn point. Turning around can be difficult, depending on the size of the roads and any banks or cliffs on each side. The K-Turn is simple: turn the wheel to reverse the vehicle to the verge of the road, and then drive out in the opposite direction. If you are super 'high-speed', and have been trained, you could do a 'J' or 'handbrake turn', but considering that most people don't know how to do this, it is best to stick with a K turn. Steps:

1) "CONTACT, REVERSE, REVERSE, REVERSE!"

2) Return fire if possible, PID enemy.

3) Initial Contact Report: voice radio.

4) "K-TURN, K-TURN, K-TURN"

5) Reports from vehicles: "Vehicle 1 OK, Vehicle 2 OK....etc" or "Vehicle 1 mobile, 1 casualty…" etc.

6) CLS treat casualties on the move: tourniquet 'high & tight'.

7) Rally if necessary in secured location.

8) Continue mission or make casualty extraction plan.

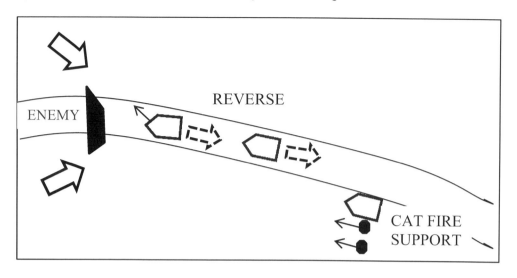

Figure 7 - Route Blocked – REVERSE

Note: The depiction in Figure 7 of the Counter Attack (CAT) or rear chase vehicle dismounting and providing fire support for the extraction is an option not described in the outline above. It is an option which you may decide to employ depending on the drills you develop.

Vehicle Immobilized: In this situation a vehicle in the convoy has sustained damage in a contact and becomes immobilized in the killing area. For the purposes of this drill the assumption is the worst case: complex ambush. It would be ideal in a post-event situation to have run-flat tires so that if your tires get shot out, you can keep going. With run flat tires, it is possible for a vehicle to sustain significant damage while remaining mobile: in this case, if the vehicle can limp out of the killing area, it should keep going so that ideally the convoy can rally at a safer location 'off the X' rather than stopping within the potential complex ambush.

A sense of urgency and fast action is the key to this drill. Ideally, when a vehicle is immobilized, the vehicle to the rear of it becomes a rescue vehicle. This is faster. If the rear vehicle is immobilized, then the vehicle in front will have to reverse back to it. Because you will likely not be in armored vehicles, and therefore your rescue vehicle is not effectively shielded from enemy fire and is very vulnerable, then there are two variants to this drill. One involves a rescue vehicle and the other involves those in the immobilized vehicle fighting out under covering fire. If one of your protected vehicles is immobilized, then the crew will largely be non-combatants and thus you will be limited to using the rescue vehicle approach to go in and get them out. Steps using a rescue vehicle:

1) "CONTACT, DRIVE, DRIVE, DRIVE!"

2) Return fire if possible, PID enemy.

3) Initial Contact Report: voice radio.

4) Reports from vehicles. Example:

>"Vehicle 2 immobilized"

>"Roger, vehicle 3 assist"

>"Vehicle 3 assisting"

5) Evacuation vehicle pulls up next to the immobilized vehicle. If contact is initiated mainly to one side, then pull up on the opposite side to gain maximum protection from the immobilized vehicle.

6) Other vehicles take up cover positions and return fire to PID enemy, as necessary. Throw smoke as appropriate.

7) Evacuation vehicle leaves a space between the two vehicles wide enough for both vehicles to be able to open their doors.

8) Evacuation vehicle crew takes up cover positions. Driver remains in the vehicle. One person assists the crew of the immobilized vehicle (can call for more assistance if there are serious casualties).

9) Personnel, weapons and equipment rapidly 'cross decked' into the evacuation vehicle. Personnel accounted for.

10) All vehicles "DRIVE, DRIVE, DRIVE!" An option is to blow vehicle horns as a signal that cross decking is complete, to recall all cover personnel and get everyone mounted up and mobile.

11) Evacuation vehicle sends update.

12) CLS treat casualties on the move: tourniquet 'high & tight'.

13) Rally if necessary in a secured location. Redistribute casualties and equipment.

14) Team Leader decides on course of action; makes casualty extraction plan.

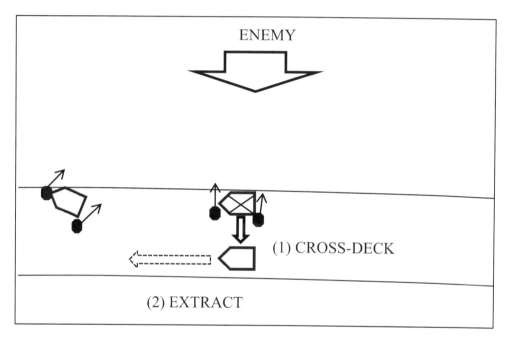

Figure 8 - Vehicle Immobilized - Cross Deck

Steps utilizing fire and movement:

1) "CONTACT, DRIVE, DRIVE, DRIVE!"

2) Return fire if possible, PID enemy.

3) Initial Contact Report: voice radio.

4) Reports from vehicles. Example:

"Vehicle 2 immobilized"

"Roger, all vehicles go firm, provide covering fire"

5) Immobilized vehicle crew get out of the vehicle on the side opposite of the ambush. They take up initial fire positions at the vehicle wheel wells while assisting other team members. Throw smoke as appropriate. Casualties, weapons and equipment 'grab bags' are dragged out of the vehicle. Move into better cover on the road verge. The only treatment for casualties at this point is tourniquet high and tight as appropriate.

6) Other vehicles take up cover positions and return fire to PID enemy, as necessary. Throw smoke as appropriate. Protected vehicles will be moved out of the way to a safe rally point while the fire fight continues.

7) Immobilized vehicle crew begins to fight out along the road verge, forward or back depending on where the convoy moved to. Utilize fire and movement techniques and peel out. If you have casualties, you will either have to drag them each time you make a bound, or if there are more of you a team can be designated to carry the casualties and others can provide cover.

8) Upon fighting off the X, the immobilized vehicle crew will mount up in the other vehicles, supporting fire positions will begin to be collapsed, and the convoy will begin to move out by bounding over-watch/fire and movement.

9) All vehicles "DRIVE, DRIVE, DRIVE!"

10) Evacuation vehicle sends update.

11) CLS treat casualties on the move: tourniquet 'high & tight'.

12) Rally if necessary in secured location. Redistribute casualties and equipment.

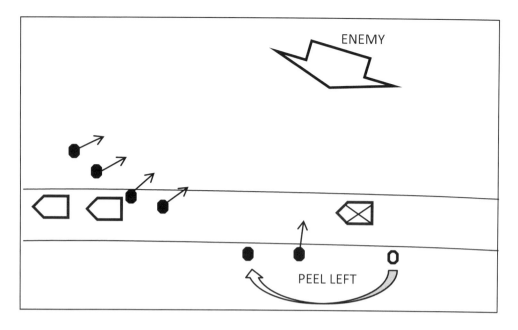

Figure 9 - Vehicle Immobilized - Fire & Movement

13) Team Leader decides on course of action; makes casualty extraction plan.

For an immobilized vehicle, there can be any number of reasons why it is stuck on the X. Maybe the engine was shot out, or the tires, maybe an IED knocked it out. It is likely that if an unarmored vehicle is immobilized, there is a high chance of casualties. One of the potential reasons that a vehicle is immobilized is that the driver becomes wounded or killed. In this case, the vehicle is not truly immobilized and can be driven out. You will need to think about how to do that with the vehicles you have.

If the driver is wounded, you can drop the seat back and drag him into the back of the vehicle and take his place. It may be that with an automatic transmission you can simply put your foot on the accelerator pedal and drive from the passenger seat or similar. It will be harder to get off the X in a manual transmission, and you will have to move the driver to take his place. If you take too long doing all this on the X facing heavy fire, then you are better getting out of the vehicle and taking cover, because the longer you mess about, the more likely you will be shot because the vehicle will become a magnet for enemy fire.

All Vehicles Immobilized: In this situation the convoy sustains significant damage and all vehicles are immobilized, or alternately the situation is such that even though not all vehicles are immobilized, the team has to leave the vehicles and extract on foot. As for 'vehicle immobilized' above, the worst case will be trained for. It may be that the convoy limps out of contact and becomes immobilized outside of the killing area. However, the assumption here will be for a complex ambush with the vehicles stuck on the X. It is important to remember the principles of fire and movement, over-watch and 360 degree security that are described above. Steps:

1) "CONTACT, DRIVE, DRIVE, DRIVE!"

2) Return fire if possible, PID enemy.

3) Initial Contact Report: voice radio.

4) Reports from vehicles. Vehicles are immobilized.

5) Take up cover positions as best as possible and return fire to PID enemy, as necessary.

6) Team Leader makes the decision to extract on foot. Sends direction to move i.e. "RALLY LEFT 200 METERS" or "RALLY REAR 300 METERS"

7) Vehicle crews dismount and take up fire positions around or close to the vehicles. Return fire as necessary. Throw smoke as necessary.

8) Casualties, equipment and weapons taken from vehicles: 'grab bags'. Care under fire for casualties only - tourniquet 'high and tight' as required.

9) Crews begin fire and movement away from vehicles to the designated rally point. Shoot, move and communicate. Team leader and crew leaders

keep the teams in touch and ensure no team or individual becomes isolated. Casualty extraction will be a challenge and command and control will have to be established between teams to designate personnel to carry casualties while others provide fire support. Physical fitness and the ability to aggress the enemy with rapid accurate fire are valuable commodities at this point.

10) At a suitable covered location, preferably once contact is broken: "RALLY, RALLY, RALLY!"

11) Teams establish 360 degree security and conduct rapid tactical field care on casualties as necessary.

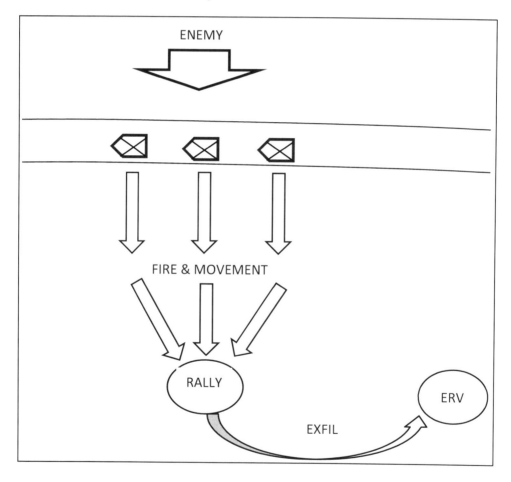

Figure 10 - All Vehicles Immobilized

12) The Team Leader decides on an egress route and moves the unit away from the ambush site to an ERV (Emergency Rendezvous), prior to establishing security again and making a rapid plan for further movement or action. At this point the team should move to a defensible location and establish security planning for further movement.

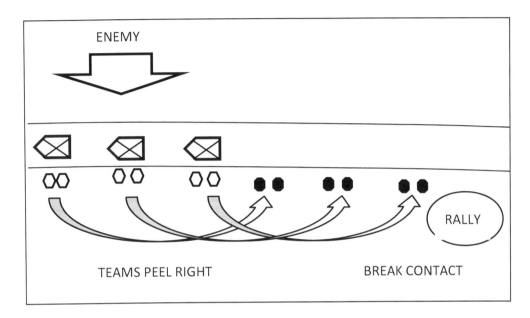

Figure 11 - All Vehicles Immobilized - Peel Out

Actions on Halts

The actions on halts will be largely determined by the nature of the task and the team SOPs developed. There are some basic principles that should be adhered to:

360 degree security: All round defense should be achieved. This will include allocated sectors for weapons to ensure continuous coverage and mutual support around the perimeter.

Vehicle positioning: Tied in closely with weapon sectors, vehicles must be positioned to provide cover, allow any mounted weapons to cover the perimeter, and allow rapid egress as necessary. Vehicles should be positioned, space dependent, to allow them to physically protect the interior of the position. This could mean circling the vehicles, or making a box formation. Thus, when the team is conducting tasks or giving orders within the halt position, the vehicles themselves provide cover from attack.

Vehicles can also be used (see cross decking, above) to provide temporary cover in a contact situation. Consideration should be given to using vehicles to move out and physically cover & recover casualties: a vehicle, even to some extent an unarmored one, will provide some cover from fire if a team member has been hit by a sniper and cannot be recovered without sustaining further casualties.

Use of Ground: A halt could be a quick stop, a tire change, or an overnight LUP. Best use of ground should be made and consideration be given to achieving a dominant position, cover & concealment, coverage of avenues of approach and fields of fire.

CHAPTER EIGHT

DISMOUNTED TACTICS

"If you're gonna be a bear, be a grizzly."

Introduction

Dismounted drills are important in the following situations within the scope of this manual:

1) When conducting break contact drills, such as in the 'all vehicles immobilized' scenario described above.

2) When conducting dismounted movement to and from the vehicles and a location to be visited, such as a site for barter, forage or whatever other kind of meeting may be envisaged.

3) When conducting infantry tactics as part of a tactical team.

Dismounted drills cover normal movement and also contact situations. It is likely that for a dismounted site visit drivers (and possibly gunners if you have it set up that way) will remain in the vehicles. This has the advantage of allowing mobile extraction (and fire support by gunners) in the event of a contact, but the disadvantage of reducing boots on the ground moving onto the site. In a situation such as a dismounted site visit, this is not altogether dissimilar from a close protection task; it is possible that the team will have with it key personnel for the site visit, such as some of the teams protected or non-combatant personnel, who are along to contribute their own specialty or skill to the completion of the task.

We are concerned with the integral capability that you can muster within your team. As in a close protection task, it is likely that the team will be responsible for escorting personnel onto the site, or simply protecting yourselves as a tactical team. In the case of protected personnel, they should be assigned an individual who will be responsible for these personnel, to be known as the Principle Protection Officer (PPO) and will not be the Team Leader; the Team Leader will be in a position to be able to command the formation in a contact situation.

The drills remain the same whether or not protected personnel and a PPO are present or utilized; simply, the PPO keeps the protected personnel in the center of the formation and in the event of a contact independently moves them within and behind the protection provided by the team, in order to move them back to the vehicles and get them away from the scene. For the example here, we will initially assume a team of four moving from the vehicles onto the site, with or without a PPO present in addition to those four.

Formations: With a four man team it would be possible to use any of the number of infantry formations, such as the squad wedge. It is more useful in these circumstances to use formations such as the diamond or box, simply because these provide all-round protection and are readily adapted to contact from any direction.

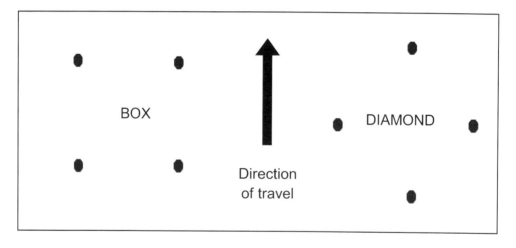

Figure 12 - Formations - Box & Diamond

Action on Contact: Using the diamond formation as an example, the drill is that once the contact is initiated the team will take immediate action by reacting to contact and returning fire to PID enemy. They will get 'on line' facing the direction of enemy threat and fight back to the vehicles using fire and movement. Usually, if the contact is from the front, the drill is for the diamond to split into two buddy pairs, and each pair will provide cover for the other pair as they bound back using fire and movement.

The PPO, if one is used because protected personnel are present, will remain central and to the rear of the formation, covering the move of the protected personnel back. If the contact comes from the right or left, the team will again react to contact and get on line. They will then peel back towards the vehicles.

If the situation is more complex than simply fighting back to the vehicles, such as contact on the way out of the site and the way is blocked, then the team will take up a covered position and have the vehicles come to them or to an alternate egress point. Of course, fire support will be provided at all times by the gunners in/on the vehicles, if present, and if the ground allows it the vehicles will move up to pick up the team and reduce the distance over which they have to fight.

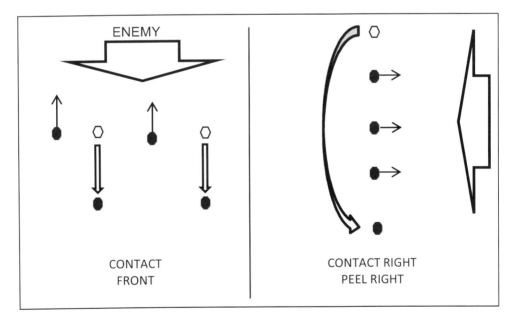

Figure 13 - Contact Drills

In a situation where your vehicle is immobilized and you have to fight out of the killing area, you will do so in the vehicle crew team based on who was in the vehicle. This is probably not more than four and may be only two. The same principles apply and you will fight out with fire and movement bounds. If there is a casualty then someone needs to be carrying or dragging that casualty out; if you have more people available then you can designate a casualty extraction person or team and leave others to cover the move with fire and movement. If it is two of you dragging out a third, then you will have to drag that casualty with each bound that you make, covering them physically as you give fire support for your other buddy to move.

The Squad

As previously stated this manual is not intended to be a re-hash of current U.S. Army doctrine and available manuals. The standard U.S. Army squad consists of nine soldiers: one squad leader, two teams of four each with a team leader. For your purposes, it makes sense to remain flexible depending on the numbers that you have and the way you are organized.

For the purposes of a site visit as explained above, a four man protection 'bubble' is used with additional PPOs, plus the drivers and gunners remaining in the vehicles. If you are moving in vehicles, then you should plan your 'actions on contact' based around vehicle crews, for example you may have three vehicles each containing two or three people, or a mix of this. These crews when dismounted will act as individual teams to cover each other as they move, and in the tactical bigger picture each of the crews will cover the other crews as they maneuver.

A dismounted squad could contain six people in two teams of three. That is a useful number if you have a patrol of two vehicles each manned by three people. For the purposes of the dismounted drills demonstrated here we will assume a squad of eight. The eight man squad will be divided into two teams of four. The squad leader will be integral to one team that will be named 'Charlie' and the squad second in command will be integral to the other team, to be known here as 'Delta'. Call them what you want: 'chicken' and 'biscuits' may confuse the enemy, it really does not matter!

Depending on what you are doing and what weapons you have available, you may also want to consider the potential of an 'attachment' to this squad of a 'gun group'. A 'gun' is the generic name given to a 7.62 x 51 support machine gun, what used to be the M60 and is now the '240 Bravo'. If you have weapons such as the 'Squad Automatic Weapon' or 'SAW' this should be kept at squad level. This 5.56 machine-gun is an excellent easily carried weapon at squad level, with one in each team and used to boost the firepower generated by each team as it maneuvers and supports the other. A NATO 7.62 x 51mm weapon, such as the 240B, is excellent to provide additional fire support and with the right fitness levels can be happily carried dismounted at squad level.

If you have access to this capability, having additional two man 'gun groups' that can be 'attached' to squads is a very useful force multiplier. This would make a temporary ten man squad, two four man 'rifle' teams and one two man 'gun group'. The gunner carries the weapon and he should carry it in such a way that there is a limited amount of ammo belt on the weapon and ready to go for an initial engagement. The 'gun' should be carried with the sling not over the shoulders but hooked just over one shoulder so that it can be brought into action immediately. The other gun group member carries the extra ammo and is the 'number two' on the gun.

A 240 can actually be fired from the 'hip' in the standing crouched position for short close range engagements, but for correct use as a fire support weapon it should be carefully deployed to a flank and sited so that the gun group can support by fire the maneuver of the two rifle teams. There is an incredibly reassuring feeling to hearing the beat of a 240 as it provides support fire and tears up the enemy position.

The eight man squad will look something like this:

      Charlie Team: Squad Leader

	Rifleman
	Rifleman (possible designated marksman)
	Rifleman (possible SAW gunner)

Delta Team: Squad 2 I/C
              Rifleman
              Rifleman (possible designated marksman)
              Rifleman (possible SAW gunner)

(Gun Group: If Available and allocated)
              Gunner
              No. 2

For dismounted tactical movement there are various formations that will be used. Single file, file and line were already mentioned. Generally, the 'order of march' will be Charlie team followed by Delta team. The squad can either move as one unit together with no effective separation between the two teams, other than the natural spacing between each person that will be dictated by the ground and thickness of cover.

If the squad leader deems it useful, he can create a tactical bound between the two teams. This is known as travelling over-watch as per U.S. Army tactics. The idea is to keep a small separation so that the rear team is free to maneuver if the front team comes under enemy contact or vice-versa given that contact can come from any direction. However, the squad leader should be careful because a good rule to live by is to not split the squad too far or on opposite sides of an obstacle. A good squad leader will keep an account of his team and keep them together in contact.

Satellite Patrolling

An exception to this rule about not splitting up further than a tactical bound is if you decide it is appropriate to move a little further away from conventional tactics towards more counter-insurgency or counter-terrorist tactics. This will depend on the threat that you are facing and the tactics that the enemy employs. If you expect to come under contact from groups operating as consolidated units in a more conventional way, then keep the squad together (this does not preclude splitting teams to maneuver and flank the enemy).

If you are facing a more irregular type threat, perhaps a 'shoot and scoot' type scenario, then there is value in organizing your squad into separate teams that work together but apart. An example would be the 'satellite' model with perhaps three teams of four, which can be rapidly switched to two teams of six to confuse the enemy or adapt to a tactical situation.

With the satellite model there is a primary team containing the overall leader. The other two teams act as satellites and move around the primary team in a designated manner. As part of the orders given prior to the mission, roles and positions can be designated to these satellite teams for each task the patrol will carry out. For general movement the primary team will be moving along an axis or route. The satellite teams will be moving either 'two up' forwards and to the flanks or 'two back' rearwards and to the flanks of the primary team. Thus it is a triangle shape between the teams as they move.

The idea is that using a limited amount of stealth and good use of the ground it will be difficult for the enemy to locate all the teams and also if one of the teams is engaged then the other teams will be in position to move up and to the flanks and outmaneuver the enemy. This is an effective deterrent against small enemy groups that will employ shoot and scoot type tactics and expect to live. It is not as effective as a deterrent against those that will throw away their lives, because they will engage you anyway. Given that we are planning for a post event scenario in America, it is more likely that the enemy will be of the type that will want to inflict damage and then run, rather than suicide types.

This satellite technique is useful to employ of you are engaged in any sort of 'ground domination patrol' (GDA) activity around your secure base. If your base is not of the covert type but perhaps a bigger retreat, small town or defended compound, then this is useful if there are bad guys out there trying to raid you for supplies. Run regular GDA patrols of the satellite type to dominate and deter in the surrounding area. The satellite model also works in urban areas where teams can be moving on parallel streets and will be able to interdict fleeing enemy who have engaged one of the teams and fled out of the back of a building.

To be really effective, the satellite model needs to be done with an offensive mindset. If a team comes under fire it will return fire and communicate the location/direction of the enemy. The satellite teams will go 'hard and fast' into depth in the direction of the enemy in order to either cut off escape or bring them under flanking fire. The contacted team will also move hard and fast onto the enemy firing point once effective fire has ceased. This is a good way to capture or kill harassing type attackers. It means running towards the sound of the guns, so it is not for the faint hearted.

This technique can also be used for patrols with vehicles, or in some combination with vehicles in support. Thus you will have a vehicle mounted 'mobile' element and a 'foot' element in support of each other; this all ties in with the principles of threat mitigation, avoiding patterns and confusing the enemy. It also relies on good planning and orders, effective map reading and navigation skills, and communication. However, if communications do fail, all is not lost: plan for rendezvous points along the route where the teams will come together in concealment and therefore if communications are lost, teams can link up, check in and then continue on mission.

Trust is also involved: you need to know that when you are on task at a location, your satellite teams are out there providing over-watch as you do what you need to do.

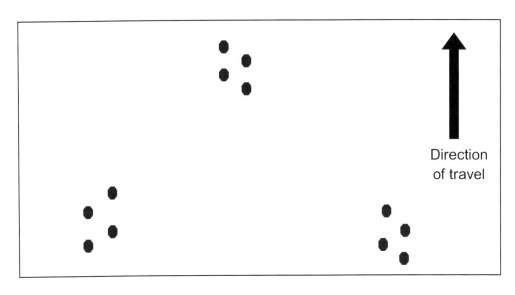

Figure 14 - Satellite Patrolling – 'One Up'

A satellite patrol may look something like this:

Primary Team:	Squad Leader i.e. callsign "Alpha One Zero"
	Rifleman
	Rifleman
	Rifleman
Satellite Team:	Team Leader i.e. callsign "Alpha One One"
	Rifleman
	Rifleman
	Rifleman
Satellite Team:	Team Leader i.e. callsign "Alpha One Two"
	Rifleman
	Rifleman
	Rifleman

In a patrol, every person is a sensor and every person is a 'link man'. It is very important that signals are passed back and forwards along the line. For hand signals there are two distinguishing types. If the signal is given for a change in formation, such as between single file and file, then it is important to only pass back the hand signal when you get to the place where it was given. Otherwise, if you pass it back down the line, people will change formation right then, which will be inappropriate to the ground.

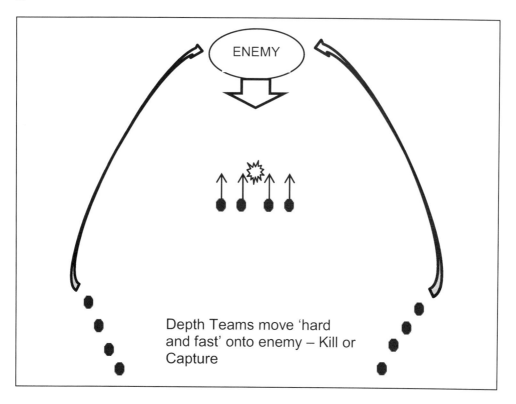

Figure 15 - Satellite Patrol - Reaction to Contact

Communication & Movement

If it is another signal, such as stop or enemy seen, then it needs to go back immediately. When the situation goes noisy and you are in contact, there is no need for quiet anymore unless you are engaged in moving around to a flank and want to retain an element of tactical surprise. When it goes noisy, every man is a link man and extraneous chatter and shouting needs to be minimized. When an order is shouted it should be shouted down the line so everyone gets it.

Also, leaders should be vocal because it will help to break any freeze and also if you order the squad to take action, such as engage the enemy, then they are more likely to do it if you have ordered them, rather than being left to figure it out on their own for the first time: the danger here is the potential for freezing and also for a non-firing response.

Train well, condition the team to respond aggressively, and WTSHTF get vocal and reinforce all the drills with shouted orders to take action. Depending on what comes at you, it may be shocking and violent and you need to hit back aggressively and avoid the potential for people to cower.

Communication is very important and you should plan for the following types:

- Radio
- Voice
- Hand signal
- Visual signal i.e. flags or flares, depending on the situation and requirement.
- Audible Signal i.e. whistle or horns, depending on the situation and requirement.

When moving you can be in single file, file, arrowhead or half-attack. Extended line or 'skirmish line' is usually used when advancing into an attack, or perhaps for searching or sweeping an area. Squad wedge is an arrowhead formation used within a team as per U.S. Army tactics. Often, the lead team in travelling over-watch or perhaps both teams will adopt the squad wedge. It is perhaps just as or more useful to move in file, which is effectively a box formation within each team, and allows greater all round security. That's just an opinion, do with it what you want. Arrowhead at squad level is simply an arrowhead formation with Charlie team on one side and Delta on the other. Each team slopes back from the point of the arrow, one to the left and one to the right. It can be used short of a full extended line when moving towards expected contact.

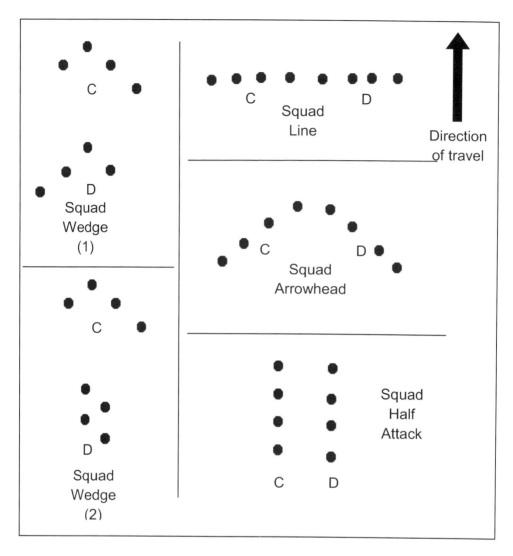

Figure 16 - Squad Formations

Half-attack is a very useful formation that can be used when moving towards contact in closer country or if you are echeloned back from the point squad and want to move tactically in reserve. Half attack looks just like file, except Charlie is on one side (left or right) and Delta is on the other (right or left). Remember that in file, each man steps left or right but Charlie is still at the front and Delta is at the rear. Half attack can easily be pushed out (i.e. imagine extending the wings) to an arrowhead or extended line formation.

Squad Battle Drills & The Quick Attack

We are considering a post-event survival scenario, not deploying to combat. However, battle drills will be covered here because they perform a useful training function and illustrate the process. You should train and be competent in them in case you need to use them as a response to the scenario you may find yourself in, and perhaps need to create tactical teams. The next section is primarily offensive; later, break contact drills will be covered as actions on enemy contact under patrolling. Those dismounted break contact drills more closely follow the techniques described under the vehicle drills already covered, and are primarily 'run-away' techniques to get you out of contact. However, if operating in a tactical environment, you should be familiar with squad battle drills.

Squad battle drills are useful as part of your preparation for any operation but are primarily aimed at an 'advance to contact' situation where you are moving cross country and expect to come into contact with the enemy. You may or may not ever have to do this, but the techniques within these drills are applicable across all tactical situations. The steps of the squad battle drills are as follows:

- Preparation for Battle
- Reaction to effective enemy fire
- Locate the enemy
- Win the fire fight
- The Attack
- The Reorganization

Preparation for Battle: The mnemonic was already covered: SAWPERSO.

- Security: make sure you are either in your secure location or that wherever you are has been secured by your integral security. This may be a patrol base that you have set up and have been occupying, or it may be a stop in the woods where you place security out. Normally, for a tactical halt, you will have 50%

security up with the team preparing in buddy teams, while one provides security.

- Ammunition: ensure it is distributed and loaded into magazines. Make sure each team member has enough and there should be a reserve carried. Consider ammunition requirements for whatever weapon systems you have.

- Weapons: ensure that they are clean, zeroed and serviceable. At a minimum conduct functions checks and if possible test fire the weapons if the tactical situation allows.

- Personal Camouflage: consider clothing and equipment and if they are appropriate for concealment for the mission. Are you using ghillie suits (sniper / hunting suits), natural camouflage and/or camo face cream? If you are using any of it, make sure it is correctly applied.

- Equipment: make sure each team member has the equipment appropriate to the task, including the right personal equipment, clothing, rations and water.

- Radios: check operation, batteries, spares, frequencies and callsigns.

- Special equipment: whatever you have decided to take along for the task. Maybe breaking and entering gear for a forage mission into a distribution center? Make sure the designated individuals have the gear they are supposed to have.

- Orders: This will take the form of a briefing by the team leader to his team. Depending on the size of the operation the orders group may get bigger and more complex. Some suggestions for orders headings are:

- Situation:
  - Enemy: what do you know about them:
    - Numbers
    - Weapons
    - Intentions
    - Capabilities
  - Ground: specific to the task:
    - Map coordinates and area of operations
    - Terrain type
    - Vegetation type
    - Roads and features.
  - Weather: relevant to the task:
    - Rain
    - Heat
    - Cold
    - Sunset/sunrise/moon state.
  - Friendlies: any friendly force operations expected in or around the area of operations. Supporting troops or activities?
- Mission: i.e. Alpha squad will conduct a GDA patrol in sector 5 <u>in order to</u> deter further enemy indirect fire attacks against the home base.
- Execution:
  - Intent: what is the commander's intent?
  - Concept of operations: how do we intend to achieve this? This may include phases of the operation or similar and scheme of maneuver.
  - Tasks: specific tasks to sub-units.
  - Coordinating instructions: times, locations, rendezvous points etc.
- Summary of Execution: everyone puts their notebooks down and looks in to the map or model of the ground and the commander reiterates how the task will be done.

- Service Support: admin instructions. Rations, water etc.
- Command and Signal:
  - Frequencies
  - Callsigns
  - Location of team leader and chain of command succession
  - Hand Signals
- Questions:
  - From the team
  - To the team to check on understanding
- Rehearsals:
  - Noisy (day)
  - Silent (night)
- Pre-combat inspections (PCIs).

Following the preparation stage the patrol will head out on mission in whatever way was designated: walking out of the base, being dropped off by vehicle, or perhaps taking their own vehicles and establishing a secure vehicle rally point ('Zulu muster'). They will then take off on foot and patrol via the route out, the objective and the actions on the objective, and the route back. Formations will be changed and adopted according to the terrain they are crossing and the designated route. The route will be via a series of nominated 'RVs' which are rendezvous points.

When moving cross country in an advance to contact mode, the squad leader will move the team along an axis. This axis will provide a reference point. Before setting out on a leg across relatively open country, it is useful for the squad leader to get the team together in cover and point out the route ahead, the axis, and any relevant reference points, if the opportunity arises. If not, the axis is simply the direction the patrol is heading in. This becomes relevant because as the squad looks at the axis, the ground in front can be broken up into left (90 degrees left of the axis), half left (45 degrees left of the axis), axis, half right and right. This helps with target indication.

Reaction to Effective Enemy Fire: when the squad comes under effective enemy fire, the squad leader will give the executive order to take cover. This can be "TAKE COVER!", "CONTACT FRONT!" or "ENEMY RIGHT!" – whatever works for you and has come to mind in training. The squad will react by taking cover by one of the two methods outlined: dash, down, crawl, observe, sights, fire or RTR. If at this point any squad members actually see the enemy, they should immediately begin returning fire and communicate this to the rest of the squad.

Bear in mind that if you come under fire like this, there may be casualties and also the enemy has chosen to engage you on ground of his choosing and therefore you are currently on the X. This means that the squad leader may have to make initial corrections to the position of the squad, depending on the available cover. This may take the form of maneuvering the squad, individual teams or individuals off the X and into cover to the front, rear or flanks. This is not an attack at this point; it is simply an adjustment into better cover.

Also, at this point the squad may choose to retire and fight out, which would be breaking contact with the enemy. If you have taken casualties, then at this point they are not a priority: engaging the enemy is the priority and you must not tend to casualties if the tactical situation does not allow it. The most you can do right now is to have them return fire, crawl to cover, lie still or apply self-aid. Self-aid at this point is a tourniquet high and tight on a limb as required. If they are next to you and you can, whip a tourniquet onto them high and tight, then get on with the battle.

Note: Near & Far Contact: it is generally considered useful to divide contact (or ambush) ranges into near and far. A near ambush is one where the enemy is within grenade range. A far ambush is where they are further away. Reaction drills will vary and it may be that for a near ambush the best drill will be to immediately fight through the enemy with the team nearest to the contact. This will be discussed further in actions on contact drills, under patrolling.

Locating the Enemy: Before you can go any further, you have to locate the enemy. This will be done by observation and potentially hearing. You may be able to see muzzle flash or the dust kicked up by the enemy weapons firing. You may actually be able to see the enemy. You may still be under contact or it may be that the enemy shot and scooted. Try to locate the enemy by:

- Observation: if that fails then;
- Fire: fire into likely cover to try and get a response. If that fails and the fire has stopped;
- Movement:
    - Initially, short rushes by individual riflemen to see if it draws fire.
    - If no response, begin bounding over-watch, hard targeting out of positions.
    - If no response, continue the mission.

Assuming a situation where the enemy fire continues and we are able to locate the enemy, once a rifleman locates the enemy he must give a target indication and begin to engage. The target indication will be passed by the squad as link men to the whole squad. As they locate the enemy, riflemen will engage. A target indication can be given in a number of ways, usually with a range, direction or indication and description.

Note: you will need to practice estimating distance, so that you can give accurate target indication ranges.

Target Indication Methods:

- Simple: "Enemy front, 100 meters, tree line!"

- Range, Direction, Indication:
    - 200!
    - Half right!
    - Enemy in ditch!

- Clock Ray Method: This method utilizes a clock face overlaid on a reference point (not your location). Example:
    - 200!
    - Half Right!
    - Right corner of building!
    - Three o'clock, 2 fingers*, enemy in gap in wall!
        - Three o'clock is from a clock face laid on the right corner of the building,

*Note: The finger or knuckle method: hold up your outstretched hand and lay your fingers or knuckles on the object and estimate how many fingers or knuckles the enemy is away from the object. It works very well.

- Strike: Use the strike of your rounds:
    - 200!
    - Half Right!
    - Watch my Strike! – fire multiple rounds in the area of the enemy to kick up dust and indicate the position. This works better if you have loaded tracer as the top few rounds in your magazine.

Winning the Fire Fight: This is about gaining fire superiority over the enemy to allow you to maneuver. This is where it becomes very important to use accurate fire to kill, suppress or neutralize the enemy positions to allow you to maneuver, either to break contact or to assault the enemy. To win the fire fight, the squad leader must utilize the weapons systems available to him to suppress the enemy. There may be more than one enemy position and location so he must direct his elements to fire where he wants them to fire. If you have designated marksmen he will be putting precision fire out to kill the enemy. Machine gunners will be suppressing the enemy position with accurate volume of fire. In order to win the fire fight the squad leader must issue fire control orders:

Fire Control Order: **GRIT**:

- **G**roup: which group or weapon he wants to fire.

- **R**ange: range of target.
- **I**ndication: target indication
- **T**ype of Fire: rapid or deliberate

Example:

- Delta!
- 200!
- Half right, enemy in gap in wall!
- Rapid…..FIRE!

Note: rapid fire is a rate of 30 rounds per minute, or one round every two seconds. Deliberate fire is ten rounds per minute, or one round every 6 seconds. Slow hey? If it's accurate, it's all you need. If it's not accurate, then you are just wasting rounds anyway.

Types of Fire Control Order: **FBI D**etective:

- **F**ull: a complete order, as above.
- **B**rief: short version, usually at close range: ENEMY FRONT, RAPID FIRE!
- **I**ndividual: selecting individuals in the squad to fire at select targets.
- **D**elayed: a full order, but using the words "AWAIT MY ORDER….(pause)…..FIRE! This is used where you see enemy moving and want to wait till they get to a certain place before you open fire.

How a Fire Control Order should be given: **CLAP:**

- **C**lear
- **L**oud
- **A**s an order, with
- **P**auses

Locating the enemy and winning the fire fight requires that your team has personal courage and will be willing to put their heads up while under fire to observe and return fire. If they don't, then you will be 'pinned down'. Also remember that if you are there for any period of time, you need to adjust position to frustrate the efforts of the enemy to see where your head keeps popping up so he can't get a bead on you.

Methods of military training in some elite units are designed to select for aggression and the ability to keep the head up while taking punishment. This often takes the form of some form of loose boxing or brawling type training where you have to deal out punishment while not being able to defend your head.

The British Parachute Regiment employs 'milling' which is one minute of two adversary's straight punching each other without being allowed to defend themselves. They are not being selected for boxing prowess, but rather for their ability to keep their head up and accept punishment while dealing it out.

Other types of similar scenarios deal in creating situations of stress and fear and requiring that the candidate react to orders under those conditions. This is training and conditioning control of fear and reduction of the freeze response, so that in combat these individuals will have been selected and conditioned to react aggressively and respond to orders in the face of fear.

Once the fire control orders have been given the squad will work on suppressing the enemy. The squad leader will hand over control of the fire to the 2 I/C (usually the Delta Team leader) who will take it over and orchestrate it as necessary. The squad leader then needs to take a moment to do a combat estimate. This is an assessment of the ground, enemy and situation. He may decide to withdraw or to assault the enemy position. When doing his estimate he will be looking at the location and strength of the enemy, the shape of the ground and cover from view and fire. He will try and identify a fire support location and a mechanical process for adjusting the position of his squad by fire and movement to establish a fire support element in position and a route to the objective for the assaulting element.

This estimate takes practice and experience and requires an eye for the ground and a logical understanding of fire and movement and weapons placement. The squad leader ideally wants a fire support location and an assault position that are at 90 degrees to each other. He wants some cover in the fire support location and he wants a covered and concealed route around to the assault position.

Note that for a near ambush type situation it is possible that if a decision is made to assault, rather than withdraw, then a frontal attack may be possible, or feasibly the only alternative if there is no room to maneuver. Such a 'two up and bags of smoke' attack is not ideal. For such a near ambush response, the team or teams closest to the enemy will simply launch into the assault, with whatever fire support allowed by the relative angles of the other team. Depending on your formation when attacked, and the relative location of the enemy, will decide for an immediate assault if you can launch one team, or both teams side by side, and whether there is any angle there for effective fire support. A near ambush is grenade range, so it is no going to be any further away than about 30 yards. For anything beyond this, it is better to conduct a flank attack, as outlined below.

The Squad Quick Attack: The attack phase is broken down into the:

- Approach
- The Assault
- The Fight Through the Objective

The squad leader will in simple terms break the ground down into left, center and right and identify routes to the objective. He will then make a plan based on the best option available. The actual process of the attack is a drill so he does not need to give verbose orders. He issues QBOs (quick battle orders) which are a series of instructions that are passed down the squad by the link men.

To keep the example simple, we will assume that the location where the squad is located while winning the fire fight is suitable as a fire support location, so he will leave Delta there as fire support. He will take Charlie on the right side route to assault the enemy position. The following is an example of the squad leaders QBOs:

> *Delta prepare to give covering fire!*
> *Charlie prepare to go RIGHT FLANKING!*
> *Delta, FIRE!*
> *Charlie, MOVE!*

Delta team leader will order his team to rapid fire to cover the move of Charlie. Smoke will be popped as necessary.

Charlie peels out to the right behind the squad leader and he leads them at a steady pace through the covered route up to the objective.

The squad leader reaches his previously identified Forming Up Point (FUP), which is in cover at right angles to Delta Teams fire support position. He lays or kneels down facing the enemy and points his weapon in the direction of the enemy position. He will look to his left and right and ensure that his team has got on line (skirmish line) on either side of him.

He will signal to Delta to give rapid fire and will stand up and move off with his team in a skirmish line across the Line of Departure (LD), which is the forward edge of the FUP, towards the enemy position.

As soon as Charlie team breaks cover in sight of the enemy position (hopefully his route was covered and he achieved tactical surprise) Charlie will take cover and initiate rapid fire onto the enemy.

> *Enemy Front, RAPID FIRE!*
> *FIGHT THROUGH! FIGHT THROUGH!*

Charlie team will break down into fire and movement and assault towards the enemy position. They can either do this in left pair and right pair moving in synch or the left and right pairs moving on their own. It just depends on the drills you train. The team will stay in lane and try and remain on line.

When they reach the forward edge of the enemy position (FEEP), Delta team will begin to switch their cover fire to the left (or to the right if it was a left flanking attack).

Charlie will assault and fight through the enemy position.

When Charlie reaches the limit of exploitation (LOE) on the far side of the objective:

STOP, STOP, STOP!
CHARLIE GO FIRM!

Charlie team will go into all round defense and establish security on the objective while the squad leader calls Delta team in. Once Delta arrives the squad will go into all-round defense in a pre-established drill i.e. Charlie will take one side of the circle, Delta the other.

The enemy may be dead, wounded, surrendered or fleeing at this point. While on the objective the squad must be observing for any depth positions and any further threat, including from the position they just fought through.

Note that the sort of ranges that we are talking about for a squad attack will be for anything out to about 300 yards. It all depends on the ground, but when you move to the flank you are likely to have an FUP situated no more than about 100 yards from the enemy position, and you would hope to be closer or be able to move through cover or dead ground to closer to the enemy position so that you do not have to fire and maneuver over that whole 100 yard distance. This is to give you an idea of the sort of ranges this will take place over.

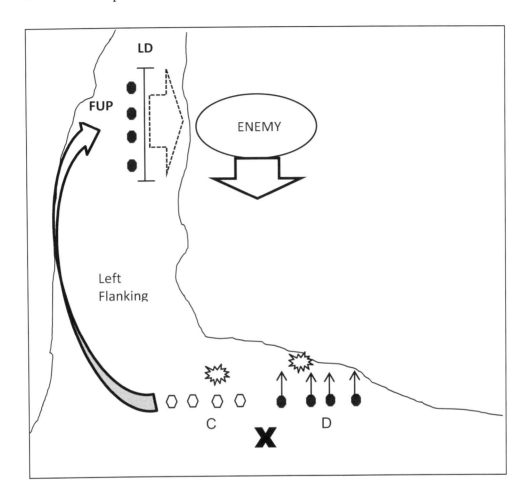

Figure 17 - Squad Quick Attack

Also note that US Army squad attack drills have a very mechanical method of the assault and rejoining of the fire support team: the first team will fight through from the flank, and go firm on the far side of the enemy position, the fire support team will then fight through in a second clearance straight ahead and go firm on the far side, leaving both teams at right angles to each other. In my opinion, this is too mechanistic and idealistic and fails to take account of difficulties of ground, visibility and how exactly the assaulting team ended up: it leaves open the possibility of the fire support team going 'blue on blue' with the assault team.

Alternatively, the fire support team can either rejoin the assault team on the objective by following the same route they took to the flank, which is theoretically cleared of obstacles and booby traps, or they can just head straight in. Either way, rather than having them do a second assault/clearance across the same objective, it is perhaps more useful for them to be met and guided in to a security position, so the squad covers 360 degrees around. The objective can then be thoroughly cleared and secured.

The Reorganization: At this point the squad is re-formed on the objective and they have a lot to think about. The squad leader will go around the perimeter and ensure that he places the squad members down to establish 360 degree security. The 2 I/C is primarily concerned with getting ACE reports: Ammunition, Casualties, Equipment and doing any organizing that he needs to do, such as have casualties treated and re-distribute ammunition. The squad leader and 2 I/C need to be vigilant for multiple things at this point, not an all-inclusive list:
- Enemy counter attack.
- Surviving enemy on the objective.
- Squad members who are wounded but don't realize it.

Once the squad leader and 2 I/C have done the rounds, they will have to organize:
- Treatment of casualties.
- Ammo redistribution.
- Prisoner handling.
- Searching and clearing enemy dead.
- Searching and clearing the objective.

Once the reorganization is complete, the squad can police themselves up and either continue the mission or return to base.

Casualties & Prisoners

Just because it's TEOTWAWKI doesn't mean that we forget our humanity. You can't murder prisoners and enemy casualties will require treatment. Officially casualties are treated as equals in order of severity of wounds for triage purposes. Post-event you may not have the resources for this but you should act humanely and do what you can even though your people will be a priority. You may have just violently assaulted the enemy in their position, but it's just business, so don't get over-excited about it.

If you are forced to actually fight through an enemy position, then this can result in some serious operational and moral dilemmas. You can't leave live enemy behind you, but you can't murder prisoners. It is also an ineffective tactic by any enemy to wait till you are that close to try and surrender, because at that point you are fighting through and the battle is on. It is also hard to take the surrender of a group of enemy if other enemy positions continue to fire on you. If you are maneuvering onto an enemy position and the enemy does not flee or surrender before you actually fight through their position, then generally they are in for the whole deal; however, consider the situation and if they have an opportunity to flee. Did you trap them?

When searching enemy dead, be aware of enemy shamming death. Search procedures will involve two people, one to cover and the other to search. As you approach and one covers, the searcher should give the body a hefty boot to the groin area: if they are shamming, you'll know about it then. Then the searcher gets on top of the enemy body and rolls it away from the cover guy. If it's clear, he says "Clear!" and the searcher can roll the body back down and conduct a search. If there is a grenade or booby trap, the coverer calls out and the searcher drops the body back on top of it, they then both dive away, and take cover in the prone position, feet towards the booby trap. Hopefully the enemy body absorbs most of the blast.

Grenades

Post-event, you may or may not have access to fragmentation or phosphorous grenades. You may be able to fabricate improvised grenade type devices such as small pipe bombs with fuses. Molotov cocktails would be of limited use for mobile operations: you would have difficulty carrying them in an assault. If you do have grenades, then you should think about how to utilize them. A grenade incorrectly used will be as dangerous to the user as to the enemy.

Grenades are best used in an enclosed space. If you are assaulting a bunker or a building then you will want to place the grenade into the bunker or room that you are assaulting. This is done by 'posting' the grenade: physically put your fist with the grenade in through the aperture and drop it. You don't want to try and toss or throw grenades at an aperture because they will likely miss and bounce back. If the enemy is in the open then it is possible to get to a position within throwing range and hit them with a volley of grenades before assaulting through the position. It is also possible to 'grenade your way up' a feature, such as a hedge or ditch-line.

Also, you may want to think about utilizing a couple of grenades, slightly spaced, so that if the enemy leaves the bunker or room and tries to re-occupy it after the grenade blast, they will be caught by the second blast. Grenades are not as destructive as you may think. You only have to get on the ground to avoid the shrapnel. You will get more concussion effect in an enclosed space but if there is any sort of cover in there then there will be unharmed survivors. Phosphorous is worse, and is nasty stuff, and will burn the enemy out. But if you use blast or fragmentation (or stun 'flash-bang' type) grenades, then you need to follow it up rapidly with an assault into the room or bunker to take advantage of the shock and disorientation the grenade will create.

Bunker Drills

If assaulting an enemy in a bunker or dug in position, there are variations to the drills previously mentioned under squad battle drills. The key thing is that a bunker will provide protection to the defenders but will restrict their fields of fire due to the firing port opening. This means that to suppress a bunker, you have to be in a position to fire through the firing port, which also places you in the killing area of the bunker. The good news is that it only takes a deliberate stream of accurate rounds fired through the bunker opening to kill or neutralize the machine gun crew inside. Volumes of inaccurate fire will have no effect whatsoever on the performance of the enemy gun team, but accurate fire through the slit will keep them suppressed.

To assault a bunker, conduct the squad battle drills as outlined above and move to a flank. When you are to a flank, the bunker cannot get you, but you will have to worry about any depth or mutually supporting positions. The mechanism of the assault phase is amended to take account of this. If you find yourself attacking a network of mutually supporting bunkers with your squad, then you will need to rethink what you are about and go and get some support. For the purposes of this instruction, the type of bunker envisioned is a dug-out trench type with overhead cover and firing ports, not the kind of concrete monstrosity that you will have seen in Second World War movies.

Once you move the assaulting team to the flank, you will split the four man team into two teams of two. The squad leader and another will be the assault team; the other two will be the 'point of fire'. You will need to make a decision as to whether your point of fire is best deployed to cover 'inside' towards the bunker you are assaulting or 'outside' to cover any depth or mutually supporting positions.

For the inside option, angles of fire may be an issue and you may be best supported by your fire support team, which should be situated at close to a 90 degree angle to your assault and best able to get fire in through the bunker opening. As you move up towards your FUP you will make a decision on where to place your point of fire team and they will go down either to provide more intimate support firing at the bunker, or to look outwards from the assault into depth to cover you from that direction; situation and ground dependent.

You will place the point of fire and continue on towards the flank of the bunker. The assault team will then crawl up to the side of the bunker. The squad leader can lead from the front or he can act as backup to a competent rifleman. Either way, one assaults while the other is behind them to act as a backup in case the assaulter is wounded or has a weapon stoppage. Ideally, you will have grenades and the assaulter will post a couple of grenades into the bunker and once they detonate he will follow up by crawling in there and finishing off any enemy inside, followed by the other rifleman as support. This second rifleman can also cover to the rear of the bunker to catch any fleeing enemy. Bayonets are ideal for this but you may not have them.

As the assault team crawls up to the bunker it is an important trust point between the assault team and the fire support team. The fire support team should put accurate fire through the bunker opening even as the assaulter is laid there by the side preparing his grenade to post. Only at the last moment should fire switch away from the bunker to cover any depth positions or fleeing enemy. Once the position is taken it may not be possible to use the bunker to occupy and cover to the rear because it may not be set-up like that, so you may just have to use the ground around as cover as the fire support team joins.

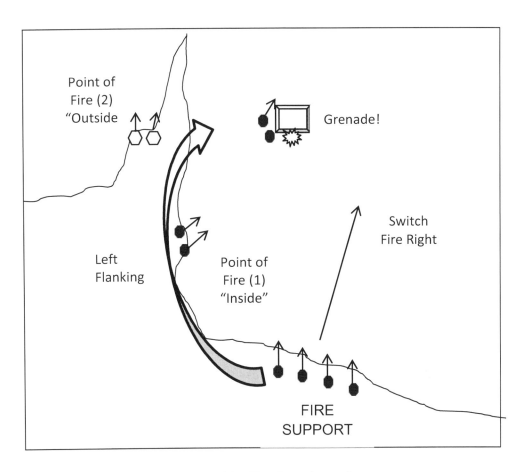

Figure 18 - Bunker Assault

Secondary Positions

For the purposes of a squad assault you should only really consider attacking two separate enemy positions with perhaps two or three enemy in each, so long as you feel that you have a chance of your accurate fire being able to win the fire fight and suppress the enemy to allow you to assault.

The simple drill for a second position is for the assault team to take the first position and then bring fire support onto the second position, thus allowing the fire support team to maneuver and become the assault team for the secondary position. Depending on the ground they will either move through the first position if the second is in depth, and launch from there, or they will launch from their fire support position and take a separate route to an FUP relevant to the second position.

If both positions are mutually supporting, which means they can both cover each other with fire, then both will have to be suppressed to allow the assault to go in on the first position. This is where fire control orders and the use of a point of fire buddy team come in, to suppress these positions while the first attack goes in, and continue to suppress the second position throughout as the fire support team transitions to the secondary assault team. It may be possible for the assault team to take on both positions, with fire support remaining in place, but that is a lot to handle for a spent team.

Potentially, the assault team could provide fire support from the first enemy position to allow the fire support team to maneuver to a secondary fire support position, and then the original assault team could assault the second position. There are multiple iterations depending on the situation, enemy and ground. The important thing is not to bite off more than you can chew and to ensure that there is never movement without effective suppressive fire. The key to all of this is use of ground and use of accurate suppressive fire.

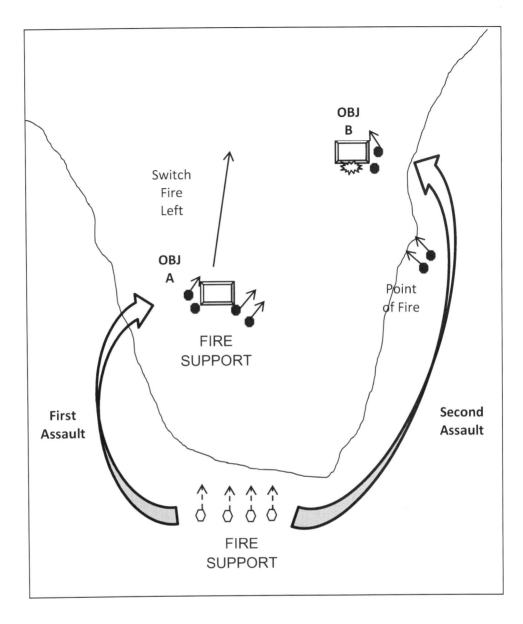

Figure 19 - Secondary Objective

CHAPTER NINE

DEFENSE

"He who defends everywhere, defends nowhere."

Introduction

Defense of your family/team and location is one of the key skills for a post-event situation. You are far more likely to be conducting defensive rather than offensive activities, although you should know how to do one in order to best do the other. The purpose of this chapter is not to recommend a best strategy to adopt in your prepping plans, in terms of moving to the 'American Redoubt' or staying in Suburbia, or living in an RV, but rather to give you the knowledge and skills to best defend wherever you are, and also to help you make choices about which locations to set up in. It is true that for many, they will have no choice to at least <u>initially</u> remain in situ in a less than ideal location, such as suburbia. It may make no sense for those that do not already own or live at a redoubt, to try and head out into the mayhem following an event. It may be best to remain in place, wait it out for a little bit, then make an extraction plan once the initial chaos is over

The Principles of Defense

The following are the principles of defense:

- Offensive Action, in order to seize or regain the initiative.
- All Round Defense, in order to anticipate a threat from any direction.
- Depth, in order to prevent penetration or its effects
- Mutual Support, in order to increase the strength and flexibility of a defense
- Concealment and Deception, in order to deny the adversary the advantages of understanding

- Maintenance of a Reserve
- Administration

And to add, because we are not a military force:

- Numbers of trained personnel
- Weapons and equipment
- A watch system for early warning

We will also discuss the types of defense, which are static and mobile, which will tie in to a discussion of point and area defense and how we can best incorporate these principles.

Remember, the best form of defense is to AVOID THE FIGHT. But, that may not be possible and you have to always plan and prepare for that fight.

It is true that most family homes and locations where we live do not hold up well to a defensive plan. It is one thing to react inside your house to intrusion in the night by burglars. It is another to be inside your house and be targeted by a raiding party intent on killing you and looting your house.

Most homes do not lend themselves to defense. The structure is vulnerable to high velocity rounds which will pass through multiple frame, wood and plasterboard walls, and also simple mechanical breaches are possible with tools and even vehicles used as rams. If you try and defend your house from the windows, then you will not be protected by the walls framing those windows and the room can be filled full of high velocity rounds by an attacking group. If you stay back from the windows, then you limit your fields of fire and unless there are enough of you defending then the enemy will be able to take advantage of blind spots to close with and then breach the house. It is limited what you can achieve even by running about from room to room.

This would make it very hard for a single family to defend itself from a determined attack from inside of a family home. You better hope you have a basement or other safe room ballistic protected for your protected personnel to be inside while you have this fight, otherwise they will not be protected from the violence and from the high velocity rounds ripping through the walls.

One of the key things for a prepper defense of a location is to have a decent number of trained personnel with weapons and equipment to defend. If we look at a single family situation, then you may have a husband armed and acting as the defending force, with a wife also armed but doing close protection of the kids in a specified safe location such as the basement. That one man on his own is very vulnerable and once he is wounded or outflanked then there is only the wife left between the attackers and your children.

If you are defending your suburban home, then it would be better if others on the street were armed preppers, and then you have the potential for a mutual defense with killing areas between properties. But we like to keep our prepping secret, so our neighbors don't come looting us when they are starving, and we don't want people to think we are crazy, so maybe you don't know any preppers on your street. But there may be some like-minded armed citizens who you can get with pre or post-event and set up a neighborhood defense group.

You may even be able to set up positions and roadblocks to defend a neighborhood such as a dead end road. If you are forced to defend in limited numbers then consider having at least one of you outside the property in a position to over-watch and fire onto raiders trying to breach the building; how you do this will depend on the ground.

You will also have to take measures to harden the building to slow down attempts to breach. You need to consider whether or not you want your property to look derelict; this could be good or bad in the circumstances. It would be worthwhile to consider boarding up at least the ground floor windows and think about putting up door bars or even board up some of the doors. This will also help with light discipline; external boards can make the place look derelict and will also help if you have to abandon the property and hope to come back to it one day, but looking derelict will also encourage squatters. There a lots of pros and cons each way. You could put up the boards internally, or something similar, in order to maintain a low profile, slow any breaches and also help with light discipline. Perhaps boards on the lower floors and light proof curtains/cloth upstairs?

The important point is not so much what approach you take for the appearance of your property, which is tied in with your survival tactics; rather, for the purposes of defense you need to harden both a low or high profile property if you intend to defend it against a raid. When boarding up doors, ensure that you have at least two independent exits that can be used both for routine tasks but also for egress if you have to bug out. You may decide to make your front door entirely impassable, keeping the lower profile back door for normal use, but then you will need an alternate exit in case of fire or hostiles at your back door. This could even be a ladder (solid or rope) that can be used as an escape from an upper floor if necessary.

But even boarding up your windows and doors does not make them ballistically hardened. Again, we encounter questions of pre-event storage and low and high profile measures. You could have sandbags ready to go, but then you will need to consider a big pile of sand to fill them from. Sandbags need to be at least two deep in order to protect against high velocity rounds. If you try stacking these on a modern upper floor, or even a ground level floor with a basement beneath, then the weight of a constructed fighting position may cause a collapse! You could stack sandbags externally around designated window fighting positions on the ground floor, but you will need a lot of them.

Other alternatives would include filling a chest of drawers with soil to create firing positions, or maybe even material such as steel plate that will weigh less but will provide ballistic protection. A basement has excellent protection, but you usually can't fight from it; perhaps you can from the small basement windows but your fields of fire will be very restricted and if the enemy get to the walls, they will be able to approach your 'bunker' and post a grenade, Molotov cocktail or other nasty down into the basement with you.

Let's look in detail at the **Principles of Defense**:

Offensive Action, in order to seize or regain the initiative: This is effectively the saying 'the best form of defense is attack'. This principle says that you should have an offensive mindset. This would mean that you will proactively take measures to actively defend your property, and to counterattack the enemy where possible to seize the initiative. Offensive action could be something as simple as putting some of your group outside of the property in static or mobile fighting positions, which could be permanent watch observation posts (OPs) or perhaps temporary 'stand to' positions that will be deployed to as a response to observed enemy approach and may also depend on the direction of that approach.

All Round Defense, in order to anticipate a threat from any direction: You cannot simply defend from one direction. You defense should cover all approaches. If you imagine defending a central point in a military sense, then the trench or bunker system surrounding that point would go around that central point in a 360 degree circle. If your defense only points in one direction, for instance the driveway or street approaching your house, then you are not defending against flanking attacks or covert approaches to the other sides of your property. This means that you must have fighting positions that orient 360 degrees around your property.

Now, if you are limited in numbers you may not be able to occupy those positions at all times, but you need to have 360 degree observation so that if those positions come into play, the observer is able to communicate this and defenders can be deployed to the right area. Again, if you are limited in numbers a position outside the property may be able to provide this level of over-watch and early warning. But an external OP itself needs to be either well defended all round, or covert.

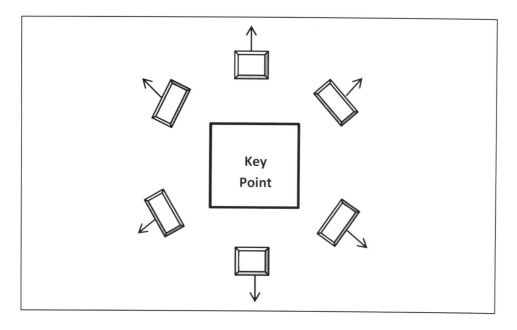

Figure 20 - All Round Defense

Depth, in order to prevent penetration or its effects: The idea of depth is to ensure that if the enemy breaks through the outer line of defenses, then there are more defenses in depth to stop them. Your defenses should be able to absorb an attack, like a sponge, rather than be a brittle line like an egg shell. If we look to the military example above in all round defense, with the ring of trenches or bunkers around the central defended point, then to include depth there would not just be one outer ring of positions, but a staggered line of inner positions so that if the outer ones are overwhelmed, the enemy is not free and clear but still faces further positions to get through.

For our more limited purposes, we can think of fall back positions in depth so that if we are being overrun, we can fall back and have an opportunity of further killing areas to defend against the overrunning attackers. Depth also means stand-off distances and fields of fire. Going back to the idea of having people posted outside of the building, if you have ground dominating area (GDA) patrols out, observation posts, check points and external fighting positions, then you are creating stand off and depth to the building(s) themselves. If the outer skin of your defense is the walls of your house, then you will only have the fields of fire available to you from your windows and once the enemy breaches the walls, you can only create depth by fighting back through your house, which is also a tactic with options but not as good as keeping them away from the house.

A note on depth: if your house is breached, there is only so far back that you can fight until you are cornered. That location may be the place where you stashed your family. In this type of situation, where you are being overwhelmed by raiders, there is little utility in 'safe rooms'. This is not a situation where you can phone law enforcement and wait until they arrive. No-one is coming, and the raiders are at leisure to take as long as they want to breach your safe room. They may want you or your family, and they will expect that the most valuable booty is in the safe room with you.

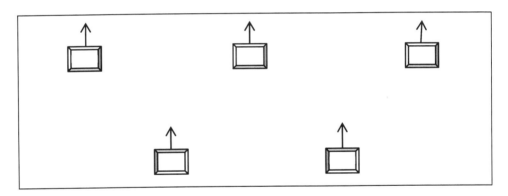

Figure 21 – Depth

If they become frustrated and can't get in, they will likely burn it down around you. Either way, it's end game for you and your family. Therefore, make sure you have egress routes and if you decide to make a stand and your defense is becoming overwhelmed, get out. Depth in terms of stand-off is also very useful because if you can keep the enemy away from the buildings, they are less likely to be able to use fire to burn you out.

Mutual Support, in order to increase the strength and flexibility of a defense: mutual support requires that fighting positions are able to support each other by fire. This means that a position is not responsible alone for fighting of an enemy assault, but that other positions can fire onto enemy attacking that position and vice versa. The implied task from this is that you need the right numbers of defenders to occupy mutually supporting fighting positions tied in with the requirement for defense in depth.

Remember the movie 'Platoon', where they are in the Fire Base prior to the final climactic enemy assault at the end of the movie? The squad leaders complain that the foxholes are too far apart ("You could run a whole NVA Regiment through them." or words to that effect) and when the platoon leader tells his Company Commander he is falling back, the reply is to ask him where he is falling back to. This is a lack of mutual support and depth on this position as portrayed in the movie. 'Arcs (or sectors) of Fire' are used to create mutual support. There are two types of mutually supporting arcs of fire:

- Overlapping: This is where the arcs of fire completely cross over and positions can fire in front of other positions. This is the best case.
- Interlocking: This is where just the edges of the arcs touch, which means that there are no gaps in the sectors but that there are areas where only the weapons system at one position will cover the area to its front.

Ideally, support weapons systems, such as machine-guns, will have overlapping arcs of fire while individual riflemen will likely be allocated interlocking arcs.

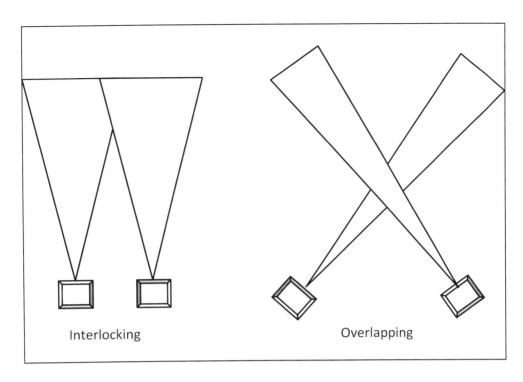

Figure 22 - Mutual Support

Concealment and Deception, in order to deny the adversary the advantages of understanding: Whether or not you have a low profile suburban house where you are hunkering down in the basement, or a multi-family compound retreat, you will be well served by concealment and deception. For the low profile retreat, you are trying to avoid becoming a target on a looter's radar, so all your preparations will be covert. For a strong defended location, you may not be trying to hide the location in entirety, and you may also have sufficient strength so that part of your defensive tactic is to portray that strength, but even so you should conceal your positions and deny a reconnoitering enemy the ability to map out your defensive plans.

You will want to consider your cover and concealment. If you are concerned by snipers creeping up on your property, you may also want to consider vision screens. Cover, will protect you from enemy fire, but you may want to tie that into a concealment plan so, for instance, your guard in the hard bunker is simply not shot while on duty in the bunker or walking/running to and from, either to change shifts or to deploy into a stand-to position as a reaction to contact. Use of natural vegetation can provide concealment, but you can also put up vision screens created by items such as cloth or camouflage netting, placed in strategic positions so that your people walking around your property are not in plain sight from an observer or sniper.

Vision screening is used on deployment military bases to cover areas where hard cover is lacking, perhaps to obscure the view into the base where the wall is low, maybe where there is a dip in the ground or similar. It makes it harder for an enemy sniper or mortar team to get 'eyes on' into the base. For example, if you had a fence around a property or compound, if you put vision screening on that fence, perhaps even raising it up in places to cover the view from high ground, you aid in concealment and protection from snipers.

Maintenance of a Reserve: it is essential to have a Reserve, even if it is just a couple of people located in a designated spot in the center of your house. In pure doctrinal terms, a reserve cannot be allocated any other tasks. Practically, it may well be your Quick Reaction Force (QRF). However, once you have deployed the QRF, you need to stand up another reserve. In purely defensive terms, when there is a danger of being overrun, the reserve will be all you have left and you must keep it ready to be used when necessary.

You should deploy your reserve to plug gaps in the defense. However, be wary of committing your reserve in defense unless it is absolutely necessary, because you may not be able to pull it back out again. Ideally, you could deploy your reserve in a 'firefighting' type role, plug the gap, and then send the personnel back into reserve. Be aware of feints and demonstrations by the enemy that may be designed to distract you and perhaps cause you to deploy all your forces to once side of your perimeter, before the main attack comes in from the other side.

Administration: This is a key factor. While you are maintaining your defense you need to look after the welfare of the people, equipment and the site itself. Administration is what preppers usually concentrate on. This is your 'beans, bullets and band-aids'. One thing about administration is that this is an area where those that are non-combatants can really pull their weight and make a difference.

You must maintain a watch system which will be tied in to some form of QRF, depending on the resources and numbers available to you. Your watch system can be augmented by other early warning sensors such as dogs and mechanical or electronic systems. However, day to day you will need to keep the machine running. Tasks will have to be completed, such as food will be prepared, clothes washed, latrines emptied, water collected.

Depending on the extent of your preparations and the resources within your property, this will have a knock-on effect to your ability to remain covert and the requirement to send out foraging patrols. Directly tied to your storage preparations will be the time you are able to hunker down in concealment before you have to go out and replenish supplies. People will also start to get cabin fever, particularly kids, and you will need to consider how to entertain them. It may be that they can be allowed into an outside area under guard for periods of time; you will have to consider the situation and the factors of noise and visibility.

We should be realistic about our modern day habits and it would be really useful to have some way to recharge batteries or provide a limited amount of power so that both kids and adults can have the opportunity to watch limited amounts of movies, possibly on portable devices, as well as reading, playing and playing board games. If you bugged out to a hidden location and are camping, you will be able to either use an in car DVD system or recharge portable devices, whether audio or DVD, from your vehicles 12 volt system.

If you are hunkered down in a cabin, apartment or basement, then it would be ideal to be able to get some exercise. You don't want to overdo it, because calories will be critical, and you don't want to cause too much sweat or smell inside the limited environment. But something that allows quiet exercise such as a stationary bike or water-type rower will allow you to keep the blood circulating. Even doing yoga, calisthenics or stretching will help, along with push-ups and pull-ups. If you are really savvy you could tie this in with some form of electricity generation. A stationary bike would be ideal for this. It would also be ideal to have some sort of camping laundry detergent, of the type that will wash in cold water, so that you can do some laundry in a bucket.

If you have a wood burning stove (be wary of the smell of smoke) then you will be able to boil water for purification, heat food and water, and also heat water to add to a solar shower so you can wash. If water is very limited, then you should at least have baby wipes to clean up with: 'hit the hot spots'! Foot hygiene should also be carefully looked at, utilizing foot powder and changes of socks; when back at the base in administration mode something like a TEVA type sandal will allow your feet to breathe and dry out but also allow you to react to an emergency.

Females also need to consider feminine hygiene product availability, cleaning of such items if they are recyclable, or disposal. Keep some basic medications to hand separate from your trauma kit for primary care: for example any medications people are taking (when you run out, that's a reason for a forage patrol); anti-histamines for allergies as well as Epipens for anyone with anaphylactic shock allergies to bites and stings, athletes foot cream/powder, pink-eye medication, antibiotic cream and oral pills, band-aids, anti-inflammatories (Motrin), and Tylenol, both adult and kids.

When you are hunkered down in your hide location to wait out the initial crisis, think of yourself as the crew of a ship out in the ocean; you need to have a watch rotation, someone on 'mother watch' taking care of the cooking, a work detail for anything that needs to get done (trash, laundry, water purification or fetching etc.) while other crew will have down-time for sleeping and relaxing. The more self-sufficient you can be, with stores and supplies, the more you can limit outside forays or contact until you are literally operating like a ship alone in the ocean. Be on watch for boarding pirates!

Back in the cold war, Long Range Reconnaissance Patrols (LRRPs) were trained to dig a bunker ahead of the approaching Soviet shock armies and wait it out inside this hidden underground hole for fourteen days prior to emerging and conducting operations behind enemy lines. If they can do this in a hole, you can do it in your basement with all the luxuries afforded to you. Depending on the size of your location and the numbers you have (make sure you don't pack it too tight or with not enough resources for the numbers of people you have there), you may have to consider being able to have separate locations within your hide for sleeping, entertainment, eating, washing, cooking etc.

You will want to be able to separate people so they can get a little bit of a break if they get at each other's throats as a result of the stress of the event and the tight living conditions. This is also why the ability to exercise or work at chores is good. Go out and split wood if you need to take out frustrations!

You may have a house with a basement and you will perhaps establish a watch position in an upper window. You may have boarded up and/or blacked out the ground floor windows and you may therefore use the kitchen and some ground floor locations as your work and administrative areas, with the back door acting as access to the outside and for chores such as latrine and trash dumping etc.

If you have a basement this can be where some of the noisier activities take place, such as kids playing and watching movies. It is also your sleeping area and the 'stand to' emergency rendezvous for your non-combatants if you are attacked. If you have a generator then think about location, noise and how to soundproof it, as well as times to run it. You won't be able to sound proof it effectively on a still quiet night.

Regarding your 'non-combatants' or protected personnel; what you do with them depends on who they are. The younger kids will need to be protected in the safest location you have. Others will be useful to do tasks such as re-load magazines, distribute water and even act as firefighting crews. Note that you need to have fire-extinguishers and buckets of water and /or sand available at hand during a defense to put out any fires. You may have, for example, a Vietnam era relative who may not be able to run about but may do very well in a fire position with a rifle as a designated marksman, or alternatively to protect the kids.

The more tasks you give people during a crisis, the more the activity will take their minds off the stress of the situation and the team will be strengthened. Ammunition replenishment, water distribution, casualty collection point, first aid, watching the rear and looking after the younger kids are all examples of tasks that can be allocated to make people a useful part of the team when personnel resources are tight.

Static (Key Point) Defense

Static or Point defense refers to a situation where you are defending a key point and your defenses are situated around that key point in static fighting positions. An example would be defending your vital ground, which may well be your property or retreat location. Remember that if you decided to go for concealment, you may therefore not have occupied actual vital ground or key terrain in your vicinity, such as being down in a dip with a hill or elevated ground overlooking you. In that situation, the hill becomes key terrain (even the vital ground) and you will need to make a plan for a static defense of it, perhaps by establishing an OP/fighting positions(s) on top of it.

Elevation does provide a marked advantage to a defender, it will make the enemy attack uphill towards you and you will have the advantages of 'plunging fire' down onto them (refer to the definitions of forward and reverse slopes) but you should be careful how you occupy it. If you are in open trenches or behind linear cover then you should consider how your heads are sky-lined from the perspective of the attacker. Consider moving forward off the crest so that you have the ground behind you as a backdrop. Alternatively, if you are in bunkers with overhead cover and a backdrop, you will have to worry about sky-lining your head less.

If you are in a house window, you need to be back from the window, never protruding your weapons outside. You should cover the window with some form of tattered curtain or burlap stripping so that you can see and fire out but it darkens and obscures the visibility into the room. Remember that you need hard cover and a bedroom wall will not provide this, so build some sort of protected fire position inside the room back from the window.

Mobile (Area) Defense

Mobile or Area defense refers to a situation where you are defending an area. To defend this area you cannot simply have a huge amount of static positions because you will not have the resources, hence 'he who defends everywhere defends nowhere'. The idea of an area defense is to establish a limited amount of static defensive positions around your vital ground and then utilize mobile resources.

This requires sensors, such as OPs, which can detect a threat and activate a decision response. Such OPs will be sited to cover the approaches to your position and will overlook NAIs (named areas of interest). These NAIs will be decision points for approaching enemy forces and also decision points for your mobile defense forces.

Once the OPs report back that the enemy is approaching via a certain decision point the mobile force will be activated to a TAI (target area of interest) and will establish a blocking position. This blocking position would usually take the form of some sort of ambush, locations which will have been scouted and prepared in advance so that they can be rapidly occupied and await the approach of the enemy.

Key to this form of defense is coverage of possible enemy approaches by well sited and concealed OPs equipped with surveillance and communication equipment, as well as the necessary stand-off distances to allow deployment of your mobile forces to cover the activated TAI.

You consider doing this sort of defense in a situation where, let us conjecture, you have moved to a bug out location as a survivor group to a large forested area. You have established a hidden and defended base camp where you have safely stowed your protected personnel and stores. You establish an area of influence around this concealed base with GDA patrols combined with static OPs covering the likely enemy approaches in to your area, which would be any roads or trails and the related road/trail junctions and decision points. You may have an ideally vehicle, maybe ATV or horse, or worst case foot mounted defense force either situated at the base camp or more likely at a strategic rally point (patrol base) which is best to act as a jumping off point for deployment to the TAIs. When an enemy approach is detected, the force deploys to a pre-designated and prepared ambush/blocking position to engage the enemy.

Static/Mobile Combinations

In this case you will combine your defensive tactics to create a 'hammer and anvil' approach. The anvil will be your static point defense location. The hammer will be a mobile element that may be your QRF. This mobile element will deploy to offensively engage the enemy preferably in the flank or rear while they are engaged with the static defensive location.

The idea is to maintain an offensive spirit, regain the initiative and exploit tactical surprise to unbalance the enemy and cause them to flee or break off the attack. If you are interested in causing casualties, historically a fleeing enemy is most vulnerable and if you engage in a pursuit you will be able to cause considerable damage.

Defensive Operations in Built Up Areas (OBUA)

Some of the techniques for defensive fire positions in buildings have already been covered. Remember that modern housing is relatively flimsily built and will not stand up to a lot of damage, or act as hard cover for high velocity rounds. If you are defending a retreat in an urban environment then you will need to consider establishing a stand-off area, which is an area of influence that you will control with GDA patrols and outlying defensive positions. You will decide on where your strongpoints are going to be and defend them accordingly.

In an urban environment any street and open spaces will become fields of fire and killing areas for weapon systems. If you are defending your strongpoint then you will site your firing positions and weapons to cover the approaches and open spaces around that strongpoint. To establish an outlying area of influence you will push out OPs to surrounding streets to give you early warning of the approach of the enemy. You can create a mobile area defense effect by doing this, with positions set up for urban ambushes.

When defending an area around a strongpoint, don't consider moving in the streets. You should consider alternative areas to move along and create covered routes. Such covered routes could include backyards, sewers and through houses. Such routes are known as 'ratlines' and will allow you to engage the enemy at an outlying position and fall back without being caught in the open. You can establish roadblocks and obstacles, both outside on the streets and also in areas inside that you will fall back through, in order to slow the enemy and provide greater opportunities to catch them in your killing areas.

If you are moving back through houses and backyards you can create ratlines by making holes in walls so you can move through the houses. You can create covert fire positions at various locations, ideally so that two groups can move back through a series of ratlines while covering the move of the other group and slowing the enemy down.

If you use automatic weapons and snipers to make the streets deathtraps, then you will force the enemy to move into the cover of the buildings. If they have armored vehicles then your obstacles will need to be sown with IEDS and ideally you will have anti-armor weapons to use to conduct urban anti-armor ambushes. If they have armored vehicles then you can only slow them down with obstacles and it will be hard to prevent them from making 'thunder runs' down the main avenues of approach to your strongpoints, and then demolishing them. If you have to fight Main Battle Tanks and APCs, then you have to have the right weapons, otherwise you will be outmatched and your defended locations turned to rubble around you.

For attacking forces, the doctrinal plan usually follows along the lines of 'investing' or surrounding the urban center, making thrusts or thunder runs down avenues of approach to take key strongpoints, followed by a detailed clearance. An alternative approach, perhaps when they don't have the armored ability to do thunder runs, is to fight systematically through the houses to clear areas and move into position to assault enemy strongpoints.

For any kind of vehicle mounted gang or post-event raiding party they will likely attempt mobile thrusts into urban areas with the aim of overwhelming any poorly prepared defenders; with correctly sited fields of fire and obstacles you will rapidly bring such a move to a halt and force them into the cover of the buildings. The buildings themselves will also be obstacles: you will know where your ratlines are and they will not be obvious to follow.

If the enemy tries to move conventionally through the buildings to approach the strongpoint or follow you, they will be met by fire from sequentially falling back firing points, obstacles and booby traps. Booby traps and obstacles can be high tech such as trip wires and IEDs, or they can be low tech: think nailing doors shut, filling rooms with furniture or barbed wire, smashing out floors or stairwells, putting down nailed boards or nailing boards to the stairs and oiling them. Think 'Home Alone' without the comedy factor!

When it comes to your strongpoint, this is your main defended location where all forces will fall back to once the enemy has been slowed and thinned out on the approach. This is the Alamo, but again hopefully you will not have to fight to the death here and you will leave some escape routes, even if it is into the sewers. The strongpoint will be equipped for a siege and will have built up ballistically hardened fire positions. You can even put positions in an attic and remove some tiles or roofing material to make an OP and sniper hide.

Make sure you remove as much flammable material as possible and have firefighting equipment to hand, as well as pre-prepared ammunition/magazine dumps at strategic locations. Make sure that all the ground floor windows and doors are inaccessible. You should create alternate ratline routes even within this building by knocking out holes in walls and using ladders through holes in the floor instead of the stairwell. Ladders can be pulled up out of the way of enemy on ground floors.

Create grenade chutes out of gutter piping material so that you can drop grenades, explosives (IEDs) or Molotov cocktails down onto enemy below as they try and fight their way up to you (make sure you don't burn yourself out). Make sure that fire positions are hardened from fire coming from the floors below!

Fire positions should be protected all round so that even if the enemy gets into the room with you, you can still fight from the bunker. You can also create grenade 'coffins' which are coffin shaped sandbagged bunkers in the corner of the room to allow you to take cover if a grenade is tossed in. When it goes off, the enemy will rush the room and you have the option of tossing your own grenade out or popping up and engaging with small arms or both (you can sit up like Dracula from his coffin if you have a sense of humor).

You should make the usual routes in the house impassable by creating obstacles such as filling rooms with furniture or wire, taking out the stairs or completely blocking them up or nailing oiled boards to them. Make sure that the enemy cannot get in by the ground floor but also (see OBUA offensive operations later) if they attempt to get in at a higher floor and fight down, make it so they cannot easily access upper floor windows. Place obstacles over the windows such as netting, wire mesh or nail boards across that will prevent entry but allow you to fire out.

Give some thought to the types of weapons that you will utilize inside the building. You will need your long rifles and machine-guns to fire out of the building and engage enemy outside in your fields of fire, but inside a building long barrel length becomes unwieldy. You may not be able to have additional sub-machinegun type weapons available but you can at least have your backup handgun readily available.

Also consider getting really 'medieval' and having weapons like hatchets available for when it gets really up close and personal and they get into the room with you, particularly if your magazine is emptied and you have no time to reload.

You may also want to consider leaving an entry point less well guarded so that the enemy will use it and create a killing room inside that they cannot easily get out of, perhaps even booby trapped. Make sure that any booby traps that you use inside the building with you are not able to take you or the building out when they are initiated!

If you create a defense like this, it will take an extremely motivated enemy to follow through with an assault and take it off you. They may try and stand off and use either fire as a weapon or larger caliber weapons like tank guns or artillery in a direct fire role, or even anti-armor weapons; but if you are against that type of enemy, which would only really happen if you decided to mount an insurgency campaign against a foreign army that has invaded post-event, then at that point you are outmatched and will have to withdraw to fight again another day.

You can make your strongpoint harder to set on fire, even dousing it in water beforehand if you have enough available, but eventually a building will set on fire unless it is made of concrete, at which point you have to get out. Such a defensive location is also not suitable as a colocation for your retreat and cannot house protected personnel i.e. in the basement. However, you should know these techniques because it is a sliding scale of tactics that are available to you and depending on the threat and what you are trying to achieve, there will be elements that you may be able to utilize.

Entry Control Points

If you have a defended location on any sort of property with standoff, such as a farm, compound, small built up area or town, then you will want to establish Entry Control Points (ECPs). This is a slightly more thought out version of the 'roadblocks' or 'barricades' that you may envisage blocking routes in to towns post-event.

An ECP is designed to allow the control of traffic into and out of the location. It is not simply a block, although it needs to be able to be closed when it is necessary to seal up the location, perhaps when facing an attack or incoming horde of refugees. You can establish an ECP at your remote farm property, or at the entrances to the town you are defending. Note that if you have an ECP, then you will want an alternate egress route, not only to allow your patrols to vary their routine, but also to provide an avenue for a counter attack if the main entrance is under attack, and also to allow a break out and withdrawal as necessary. Think the 'sally port' on an old castle.

An ECP needs to be able to slow down and stop approaching vehicles, provide standoff, and also cater to pedestrians. Also consider the need to be able to conduct 'public order' operations at your ECP should you have a situation with an unarmed but starving and desperate mob, something that may not necessarily immediately escalate to the use of lethal force. You may want to consider Tasers, riot guns and CS gas if you can get it. If you are defending a town, one would hope that the local police department would be equipped and willing to help out, and if they were gone, perhaps you could get hold of their equipment.

The components of an ECP will be:

- Standoff
- Warning signs
- A 'chicane' (S-Bend) to slow down approaching vehicles.
- Ability to stop vehicles and/or close the ECP
- A sentry to check the vehicles for ID, recognition etc.

- A close cover person/searcher
- A cover fighting position or bunker
- A search bay
- Reserve or QRF
- Somewhere to turn around for those denied entry.
- Access to flanks denied

The warning signs will let approaching vehicles know to slow down and that lethal force will be used if they do not. There will be a physical 'S' type chicane built into the road that they will have to negotiate. They will slow down and approach the sentry, who will be in the road or at a guard shack. There may be a vehicle across the road, a raising barrier, or perhaps caltrops pulled across the road, to deny entry if the vehicle keeps going. If there is trouble the sentry is backed up by the searcher, and if there is bigger trouble the fighting position will be covering the ECP and if necessary the QRF can be called.

It is important that the areas around to the sides of the ECP do not allow vehicle access. For example, if you had a ranch property, then you could situate the ECP perhaps 75-100 yards back from the entrance to the property. This would create standoff and also perhaps some concealment for the ECP from the road.

You would build up the ECP but to the sides you need to create obstacles such as berms, felled trees, or wire strung between trees or pickets to prevent vehicles and personnel simply avoiding the ECP. If you don't have the resources you need to put the ECP up close to your gate with no standoff, and this will help for the vehicles but without an effective perimeter obstacle, such as a good fence, you will be relying on observation of your perimeter alone to stop ingress from dismounted persons.

An ECP needs to be run like any other rotating position, such as an OP, in order to allow rest. Below is a simple schematic showing a possible ECP setup:

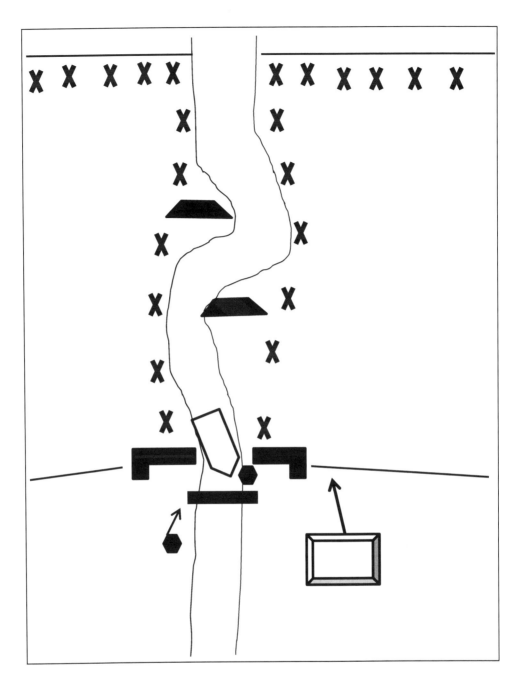

Figure 23 - ECP Schematic

Traffic Control Points (TCPs)

Traffic Control Points (TCPs) are most likely to be conducted by you as part of Ground Domination Activity Patrols, or Satellite Patrolling, around your secure base as a form of clearance and extension of your sphere of influence into the surrounding area. There are multiple ways of conducting these but for our purposes here we will concentrate on a couple of methods that can be used for temporary TCPs when patrolling.

It's important to note that if you go out and establish a TCP then in fact it is an Illegal TCP (ITCP) unless it has some form of legitimacy established by the situation and the fact that you are establishing some form of law and order. To gain any form of legitimacy you have to be representing some form of defense force that has taken responsibility for an area and you must keep it lawful. You can't profit or loot from a TCP!

So, really you are establishing temporary TCPs on routes and maintaining them to check passing traffic. If they are good guys, then they go on their way, if they are bad guys then you can take appropriate action. The need for TCPs does assume that there is still sufficient traffic on the roads and routes: another use for TCPs is to establish a checkpoint inside or on the outskirts of a town or area, similar to an ECP but perhaps simply just a two way checkpoint where IDs and business can be checked, which may have the effect of reducing crime and looting.

When establishing a TCP, you need to consider security, the ability to stop vehicles, and cut offs. A TCP is a little like an ambush, in that vehicles will come into your area and if they do any 'bad stuff' then you have cut off groups to prevent escape. You also need to site your TCP well: it is no good if incoming traffic can see it a long way off and evade you. You likely want to have some kind of concealment and perhaps site it around a bend in the road, preferably so that the approaching vehicle is past your cut off groups before they see the TCP and can evade it.

You can use vehicles to physically block the road for a TCP but if you are trying to maintain a flow of traffic this may not be ideal. You can use your vehicles to establish a temporary chicane in the road and a good method for stopping any escaping traffic is to use caltrops. Caltrops are some form of chain or maybe rope with spikes on, which can be pulled across the road so that it punctures the tires of an escaping vehicle. Cut off groups can have caltrops at each side of the TCP, on the opposite side of the road from them with a piece of paracord across the road; they can then pull the caltrops across on command.

In a TCP you need a road guy for each side of the road, with cover persons. There needs to be a security group and then there will be the cut offs pushed out sufficiently far to provide security. There are two easy methods to do this, which you can amend to fit your needs:

Mounted: Leave the vehicles in the center of the TCP to form a chicane to slow traffic. Have the TCP conducted in the center where the vehicles are, stopping traffic both ways. Have two separate cut-off groups each side of the TCP.

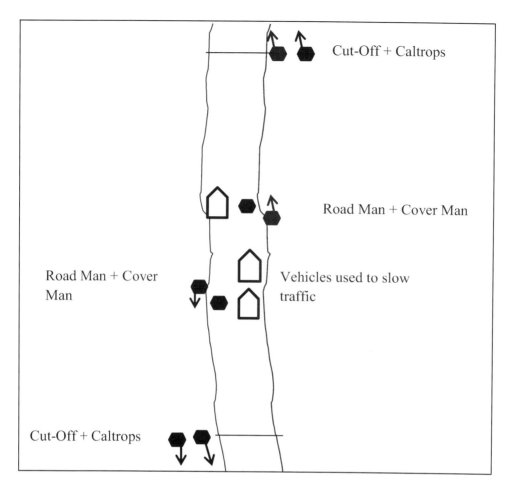

Figure 24 - Vehicle Mounted TCP

Dismounted: if you are conducting a satellite type patrol than a simple way of doing it is to leave one team in over-watch, preferably on high ground dominating the area of the TCP. The other two teams for their own separate TCPO teams: effectively there is no 'middle' to the TCP, one team checks traffic coming from its side; the other team checks it from the other side. Each team works as a cut off for the other team from vehicles speeding through. This is a weaker method in terms of stopping approaching vehicles if they spot the TCP and try and evade, but you can push the cut offs a little further out than the stopping group.

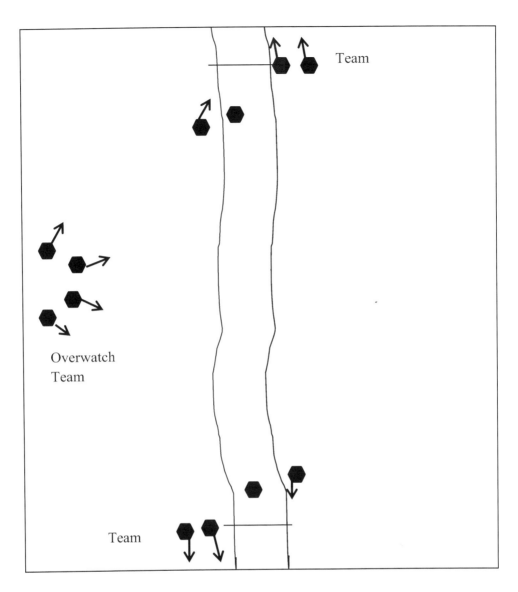

Figure 25 – Dismounted Satellite Patrol TCP

Key Point Defense Orders

The following is an example of key point defense orders that will be useful to you in organizing a defense force around a retreat location:

PRELIMINARIES   Admin: any relevant points
Security of the Orders Group
Task Organization: Appointments, positions, equipment etc.
Ground Orientation: use map/model

1. **SITUATION**

ENEMY FORCES	FRIENDLY FORCES	ATTACHMENTS/ DETACHMENTS
Likely Threat Numbers locations Weapons Equipment Morale Gangs Influence of drugs/alcohol Refugees Subversive Civilian Orgs Air Threat NBC Future Intentions	Mission and Concept of Operations (incl. Intent and Main Effort) of Commander Civilian Police Paramilitaries Military Militia/Defense Groups Neighborhood watch Locations and future actions of neighboring forces which may affect the operation.	Only if not covered under Task Org

2. **MISSION:** Task(s) plus unifying purpose. Always repeat twice when giving orders.

262

3. **EXECUTION**

   a. **Concept of the Operation**: Commanders Intent. Scheme of Maneuver: how the group will achieve its mission. Main Effort e.g. prevent enemy force breaching defensive perimeter etc. Key timings.

   b. **Missions/Tasks:** Given to individual team members or group leaders and their groups in turn. The Reserve will be given planning options, not tasks (i.e. "Be prepared to ....A, B, C.")

   1) Squad/Groups/Individuals
   2) QRF/Reserve
   3) Gun Group(s)
   4) Sniper(s)
   5) Reactive OPs/Over-watch positions
   6) Recce Team
   7) Dog Handlers
   8) Armored Vehicles
   9) Non-Combatants
   10) Medical Personnel/CASEVAC Teams
   11) Fire-Fighters

   c. **Coordinating Instructions**

Timings	Civilian Police/Military	Control Measures
Defensive works complete in Key Point (KP) Ground Domination Activity Patrols	Tasks Locations Roadblocks TCPs	Boundaries Sectors of Fire Legal Powers Use of Force Access list to KP Lethal Force Notices

Rules of Engagement	Deception/Security	Field Defenses

Profile
Weapons Carriage
Opening Fire
	Patrols
	STAP (Surveillance Target Acquisition Plan)
	Specialist Equipment
	Stand To Positions
	Sentries/Watch System
	Weapon Security
	Movement inside KP
	Counter Surveillance Measures
	Camouflage/Concealment
		Mines/IEDs
		Trenches
		Bunkers/fighting positions
		Reactive OP/Over-watch
		Wiring:
		  Concertina Wire
		  Low Wire Entanglement
		Priority of Work
		Defensive Stores

Action On	**NBC**	**Public Info/Media**
IED Intruders Mob Dismounted Attack Armored Vehicles Indirect Fire Sniper Air Attack NBC Warning POW Civilians/Refugees	States Detection Plans Alarms Reporting Protective Measures Contamination Control	

    d. **SUMMARY OF EXECUTION**

4. **SERVICE SUPPORT**

SOP Variations Dress Equipment Weapons	Logistic Support Replenishment Ammo Rations POL Water IPE Batteries	Medical Locations CASEVAC Stretchers Med Packs IFAK CAT Tourniquet Pain Meds	Transport Location of Echelon Fire Equipment

5. **COMMAND AND SIGNAL**

HQs Chain of Command Locations Alternate Command	Communications Comms Plan Changes Telephone Numbers Orders if Comms Fail	Liaison CivPol/Military Other KPs Other Defense Groups
Codes Codewords Nicknames Nick Nos Phase Lines	**Password** **Synchronize** **Questions**	

CHAPTER TEN

PATROLS

"No plan survives contact with the enemy."

Von Moltke

Types of Patrol

It is generally considered that there are two main types of patrol. One type is the fighting patrol and the other is the reconnaissance patrol. More usefully, think of patrols as overt / aggressive, or covert / passive (potentially aggressive). A fighting patrol will usually be a larger formation, militarily something like a platoon sized operation, and a recce patrol will be smaller, maybe squad sized or perhaps smaller. Patrols will be equipped and sized depending on the action that is expected and the aim of the operation. Also, the aim of the patrol will usually define what the 'actions on' will be: either oriented to be aggressive offensive or aggressive extract 'run-away' drills.

Some types of patrol:

Fighting Patrols:

- Raid / Deliberate Attack
- Ambush
- Hostage rescue
- Capture
- Ground Domination Activity
- Clearance Patrol

Reconnaissance Patrols:

- Close target reconnaissance (CTR)
- Observation Post (OP)

- Standing Patrol

Forage can be under both, depending if you are doing a covert or overt operation.

Patrol Planning

It is important that all patrols are well planned. An outline procedure for planning and executing a patrol could look something like:

- Decide on the mission
- Issue a warning order to allow your team to begin concurrent battle preparation
- Conduct map and ground studies
- Reconnaissance (could be a recce patrol for a fighting patrol)
- Orders Group
- Rehearsals
- Conduct the Operation
- After Action Review (AAR)

Patrol Execution

A patrol will consist of the route out to the objective, the objective rally point (ORP), the 'action on' the objective which will consist of the aim/task of the patrol, the return to the ORP and the route back. It is important that the team receives a detailed set of orders delivered by the team leader. When receiving the orders the team will sit around a sand table type model, usually created in the dirt on the ground with sticks, various vegetation, objects and labels to create a representation of the ground that the patrol will cover.

There will preferably be a model of the area in general and a model of the objective in detail, set next to each other. The model will include a north pointer, a scale, and will preferably be oriented to the ground with the team sitting facing the model in a way where they can best be oriented to the operation.

The route out: This will depend on how far the patrol has to cover and whether there will be any kind of preliminary vehicle move to a drop off point (DOP). The patrol will then move through a series of pre-planned Rendezvous (RVs) towards the ORP, depending on the route planned by the team leader. It may be that the patrol will halt in these RVs, but it is not necessary, some may be passed through and simply indicated by a hand signal. If the patrol does halt, they will usually go into a herringbone formation.

Formations will be dictated in orders and when they are changed the necessary hand signals will be passed back along the line. A patrol move is a silent tactical affair. Whenever the team stops, all personnel will get into a fire position. No talking, shouting, laughing, smoking or generally goofing off. If the patrol is moving at night then care needs to be given to light discipline.

For map checks the leader and any additional navigators will need to have small flashlights with the lens covered with tape with a small pinhole in, either a red or green filter. When checking the map, they will need to get low to the ground and pull over a poncho or similar shield so that no light escapes. The red or green lens is to preserve night vision: be aware that under a red or green light, items of the same color on the map will be hard to see, such as contour lines (red) or woods (green).

ORP: this is the final RV of the route out and some sort of additional activity will take place here depending on the patrol. It may be that a team will remain at the ORP as a rear security element and perhaps the patrol will initially stop in herringbone but then will be re-deployed into a different formation. Because this is the rally point short of the objective, activity will happen such as a recce group going forward to the objective perhaps followed by an occupation plan, depending on the task. The ORP is also a location to cache heavy rucksacks, moving to the objective with daypacks only. More will be covered under specific patrol types below.

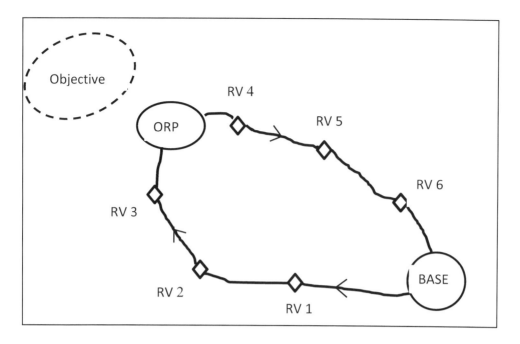

Figure 26 - Patrol Route Out & Back

Actions on the objective:

Raid / Deliberate Attack: This is likely to be a larger formation patrol than a simple squad patrol, perhaps more like a platoon sized task depending on what numbers and resources you have. A rear security element will be left at the ORP and the patrol will have been planned as a deliberate attack. There will be a fire support element, and assault elements. There may even be an indirect fire support element if you have the weapons systems and resources.

Prior to a deliberate attack you need to have already conducted a recon patrol. This may have been done by the patrol commander as a prior operation in the form of a reconnaissance patrol, or perhaps by a separate specialized recce patrol element. Either way, it is better if those that conducted the recce were able to return to base to brief and add the feedback to the orders preparation, rather than simply meeting them on the ground. If it happens the latter way because of time, the commander will have to trust the recce team to lead his elements into the identified fire support and FUP positions prior to the assault.

Also a less than ideal situation, but you could conduct a final recce from the ORP position, perhaps to confirm fire support and FUP locations, which will make it more of a hasty attack with quick final briefings for the team; however ideally you will have conducted a separate recce in advance and had the opportunity to make a plan and fully brief and rehearse that plan with the team prior to moving out on the patrol. This will make your rehearsals more informed to the actual ground and plan of the assault.

Once you have reached the ORP for a raid or deliberate attack you will then conduct any final confirmatory reconnaissance and then the elements will move to their respective positions. A raid is only different from a deliberate attack in that a raid is a quick operation with possibly larger enemy forces able to respond and therefore you will need to get in, accomplish the task, and get out. A raid is similar to an ambush in this sense, in that it is a covert attack followed by a rapid extraction away from potential follow up.

A deliberate attack in contrast may have less urgency about extraction and it may be that you intend to stay at the location, perhaps for a detailed search, forage, or perhaps occupation for a period of time. For the attack you will need to identify a suitable fire support position, for both direct fire assets and also for indirect fire assets if you have them (i.e. mortars). You will also identify an FUP (forming up point) which will incorporate an LD (line of departure) at its forward edge and will be where you launch the assault elements from. If you have to break up the attack into stages with phased objectives or phase lines then you will have assault elements allocated to those stages and they will move through the FUP 'in echelon'.

To set up an FUP at day or night you can use the 'NATO T' method which is standardized; however, what it essentially comes down to is a 'T' shape utilizing markers or lights at night (cyalume sticks or right-angle flashlights) to mark out the shape. Decide on what lights you want to use and rehearse it. The troops will be led in up the base of the T and will then peel in along the top of the T facing the LD, in preparation for the assault. The NATO T is slightly old-school in that it is best utilized for two formations, such as two squads or two platoons, one peeling to the left and one to the right of the top of the T. This was a slightly older school tactical usage which could still have relevance: you advance across the LD 'two up', allowing both elements to maneuver side by side onto the enemy position.

In more contemporary use, one element (squad or platoon) would cross the LD and the other would wait in reserve and then assault 'in echelon' (which basically means in series rather than in parallel) once the first element had secured its objectives. This all the while as the fire support element suppresses the enemy.

When selecting your various locations for the attack you should do your best to select a fire support and assault FUP position at right angles (90 degrees) to each other, as per the squad quick attack drills already covered. The deliberate attack will be covered further under offensive operations below.

Ambush: Again, ambush will be covered in more detail under offensive operations. An ambush is a surprise attack, launched from a concealed position, in order to overwhelm and destroy an enemy force. The difference between an ambush and a deliberate attack or raid is, in simple terms, that an ambush takes place from a static concealed position and depends for initiation on when the enemy shows up.

A deliberate attack is a moving operation that is initiated by the attacker's choice of timing. Once at the ORP the ambush will be reconnoitered and then there will be an occupation and work phase as the ambush is set up. The ORP will be occupied as a rear security base. The ambush will either be sprung on enemy contact or if not it will be collapsed and either way the elements will move back to the ORP.

Hostage rescue: this would take the form of a deliberate attack or raid but the emphasis would be on the safety and recovery of the hostages rather than simply on the destruction of the enemy. Supporting fire and the assault will therefore need to be more targeted and not indiscriminate, but the same thing will effectively happen where a fire base is set up and assault/recovery teams will move onto the objective, extract the hostages, and recover them back to the ORP.

It may be that you have conducted a recon of the location and identified where the hostages are being held, plus enemy positions and guard locations and routines. You would then be able to plan an assault with the limited objective of reaching the hostages, establishing blocking fire positions to suppress the enemy, allowing you to free the hostages and withdraw off the site. The limited objective in this case would be the rescue of the hostages, rather than the clearance of the entire enemy position.

Capture: this could be a situation where you have decided that you need to capture enemy forces for information, or perhaps an enemy leader for negotiation purposes. It is a snatch operation and can look like an ambush or raid but the idea will be to capture some of the enemy rather than kill them. If you are planning on capturing enemy, make a plan to get unhappy people back with you, who may not want to cooperate. The alternative is a covert type capture which would take the form of a covert patrol where you feel that the situation is such that the person can be taken without the firing of weapons and alerting the enemy.

Ground Domination Activity (GDA): these patrols have been discussed in terms of creating stand-off and depth to a location. They are not full strength fighting patrols but neither are they fully covert. If they spot enemy in the vicinity they will engage and offensively target them. Consider the option of satellite type patrolling as described above.

Clearance Patrols: these are similar to a GDA patrol but a lot smaller in scope. A clearance patrol will go out around a location, such as a patrol base or a defensive position, usually after a stand-to in order to check for enemy in the immediate vicinity.

Reconnaissance Patrols: these types of patrol are by their nature smaller and more covert than fighting patrols. The main objective is to gather information and they will seek to avoid contact with the enemy or compromise of their position.

Close target reconnaissance (CTR): this type of patrol is conducted when you need to obtain detailed information on the enemy or location. You may conduct one of these prior to a deliberate attack, raid or hostage rescue. The patrol will be smaller, maybe four to six persons, and will move to the ORP and establish security there. From the ORP small team(s) of perhaps two will go out and recce the objective.

Although it is termed a close target recce, you must be careful of compromise and if you can gather the required information from further away utilizing surveillance devices, then do so. A technique that can be used for CTR is the 'petal method' where the team or teams will circle the objective, moving in closer to gather information, circling out and continuing the process until a 360 has been completed and all information gathered.

You need to be camouflaged, move stealthily and with patience, and be aware of enemy sentries and counter-surveillance. Also, be aware of barking dogs, sensor devices, booby traps and early warning systems in general. Be aware of random acts such as the enemy sending out a patrol or even someone relieving themselves out in the woods.

If there is a danger from tripwires, then a technique that can be used is to move forward slowly holding a light stick or wire between thumb and forefinger. When it touches a wire you will feel it in the movement of the stick.

While the teams are out on the objective, the remaining patrol will hold security at the ORP. Make sure you have rehearsed actions on compromise and return to the ORP, including identification signals and passwords. A returning team approaching the ORP at night can, for instance, hold out their arms 'akimbo' with weapon held in one hand, to assist in identification.

Observation Post (OP): an OP will covertly watch a designated area and gather information from a distance. An OP patrol will be designated an NAI that they must cover and they will have to establish a position from which to covertly watch that area. This will be done initially from map study and then reconnaissance from the ORP. Once the site has been established, there will be an occupation and work phase during which, while maintaining security (always!), the OP will be built and camouflaged.

A simple OP can be created with natural cover, poncho (tarp) and cam netting; however it may be necessary to dig an OP in for both concealment and protection, but this will need to be done covertly. Once the occupation and work phase are completed, the routine will be established. Depending on location all personnel may be located in the OP or there may be a separate admin area a short distance to the rear in better cover, perhaps to allow administration.

There will need to be enough people at the OP to allow a routine, which will include someone observing, someone on rear protection, plus rest and admin. You should not have to observe for more than an hour, after which concentration will degrade rapidly, so a useful routine is to go from rest or admin to observation, then move to rear protection and then back to rest.

If you have a rear admin area, you will need more people and the OP and rear area will effectively become separate areas with rotations happening within each area and then both swapping over perhaps after 12 or 24 hours, depending on the duration of the OP. There are many ways to skin the cat! For instance, you could have a squad of eight on OP patrol with four in the OP and four in the admin area getting more rest. The four in the OP will have two on observation (the tired one perhaps writing the log), one on rest and the other on rear protection (if required and not covered by the rear admin area).

The four in the rear area will have perhaps three on rest and one on protection. Both groups will swap perhaps after 24 hours. Depending on the cover available at your OP location, will determine the comfort level and ability to conduct admin. For any OP, you should carry out anything that you carry in. This includes bodily waste, and you may have to get used to defecating in close proximity to your buddies, into a bag. If you have an admin area, you may be able to dig a latrine.

Once the OP is complete you will take it down leaving no sign and extract back to base. Be aware that if you cut natural foliage for camouflage, it will degrade and you will have to replace it, perhaps every night.

Standing Patrol: This is a sort of hybrid between an OP and a fighting patrol. It is a static patrol that deploys to a location and remains there for a specified time, intended to provide early warning, security or perhaps to guard a geographical feature, such as dead ground that cannot be covered from a defensive position.

The Route Back: specifics of this will depend on the type of patrol that you have just conducted. General principles are that a route back is similar in execution to the route out, with the patrol moving through a series of RVs from the ORP back to the home base. Ensure that the route back is not the same as the route out to prevent enemy observing you on the way to the objective and laying an ambush to catch you on your return.

Post Patrol Actions

On returning to base it is not a case of dumping your gear and racking out for a few hours. A debrief and AAR will be conducted. The debrief will be for commanders and any personnel performing an intelligence or collation function to gather information from the patrol members. Every person is a sensor and may have valuable information. The AAR is for the patrol to assess the conduct of the operation and improve as necessary. Administration will then be a priority ("First my weapon then myself.") with cleaning of weapons and gear taking place to ensure that gear is ready to go for the next task, then feeding before release to personal admin and rest time.

After Action Review: the AAR process can be pretty detailed but at its basic it is a mechanism to determine what went right, what went wrong, and to incorporate any lessons learned into future operations. It should not be a personal criticism session and criticism should be constructive. A simple way to do it is to look at first 'sustains' followed by 'improves' and then a positive summary. Sustains are things that went well and should be continued, improves are things that were not so good and need to be worked on. Leaders can then incorporate this into future missions. For instance, it may be that the AAR highlights the need for greater concentration on a certain aspect during rehearsals, which can be incorporated for the next mission.

Patrol Equipment

Let's take a moment to consider the type of equipment that will need to be carried on patrol. This will move the discussion on a little from the equipment and profile considerations that we already covered earlier in the manual. There are many factors here, such as whether you will be operating from vehicles, always dismounted, or a mixture.

If you are out tactically patrolling them the assumption is that there is no longer any necessity to appear non-military or covert; the only covertness required is the tactical covertness and desire to remain unseen by the enemy. Therefore, at this point you are effectively a soldier. You will need to consider that there is a requirement for camouflage and concealment but not necessarily uniformity. Therefore, you may be wearing camouflage, but for its concealment properties not necessarily to appear uniform.

You may also decide that uniformity is desirable, but they are not necessarily one and the same thing. Your patrol team may be camouflaged but wearing a mixture of styles and even just drab clothing – this may also be a more realistic view as time goes on, maybe as more people come into your group, and also as clothing wears out and availability diminishes.

We already discussed that if you are sitting in vehicles, you will need to minimize the equipment on the rear of your belt. For vehicles, either a light belt with the pouches to the side on your hips works, or a chest/vest rig works very well. Temperature and climate are an issue here and it may be that for long term operations you don't want to be wearing body armor or you want to minimize the equipment on your torso. For extended patrolling and operating in the heat a full belt rig combined with a daypack and pack is the best way to go.

Body armor is either not worn or carried in your pack and worn when the threat increases (i.e. intent to carry out an offensive operation) or worn at all times at which point you may as well wear your pouches on top of the body armor, or a combination of belt and armor pouches. You may also want to consider a plate carrier for extended operations; these do not incorporate the soft body armor vest that covers your torso and makes you really sweat, it just incorporates plates, which will make you sweat less but will provide less protection. Remember that it is only the plates that provide the protection from high velocity rifle rounds anyway, usually the soft armor provides protection against fragmentation and handgun rounds (types depend on the specification of the vest).

If you are acting as dismounted infantry then you will be well served with a complete belt rig and yoke/suspenders. You have the option of wearing or not wearing your body armor, but the belt rig will remain in place. This is an old school thing, because currently the military wears body armor at all times in hostile environments and the pouches go onto the armor, so there is no need for belt rigs unless you wear both to distribute the load across your body more.

A belt rig, or battle belt, will be squared away and tight with no pouches hanging off or generally looking like a cluster. You will probably have rifle ammo pouches on your left hip (if right handed), with handgun ammo pouches on the front; Handgun holster on the right with IFAK behind that. Behind those pouches will be a canteen pouch and on the back will be a butt pack or alternatively a separate couple of pouches with 24hours worth of emergency food and any spare equipment.

You will also carry a daypack and a rucksack. The daypack should be able to be strapped under the lid of the rucksack when you are carrying the ruck. You will consider carrying on your belt rig/person something along the following lines:

- Rifle magazines x 8
- Handgun Magazines x 4
- Radio if carried
- IFAK
- Canteens x 2 and/or Camelbak replacing 1 Canteen
- Water purification tablets
- 24 hours of rations – emergency type
- Solid fuel burner/cooker
- Knife or machete
- Rifle cleaning kit
- Spare socks
- Foot powder
- Tactical orders and quick reference guide
- Model making cards
- Notebook
- Bug repellant
- Cam stick
- Comms cord 50 yards (550 cord)
- Spoon, 'racing type', secured
- Compass
- Map in case

To set up a standard ALICE belt rig system with suspenders (yoke), a suggestion is as follows, looking at the belt laid out flat and from left to right from the rear of the belt:

- Handgun magazine pouch x 3 (3 pouch combo).
- ALICE 5.56 AR ammo pouches x 2. 6 mags. Situated on left hip.
- Canteen pouch, canteen with metal mug. Puritabs.
- Admin pouch. Rations. Solid fuel stove. Commo cord. Basic weapon cleaning supplies.
- Fit in another AR mag pouch somewhere if you can
- IFAK
- Belt/sheath knife/bayonet
- Handgun holster
- Leatherman if you want in its pouch.

Note that with the exception of small pouches such as pistol magazines, equipment should not be further forwards than your hips. The pouches should be well secured and situated on the belt. Using some kind of belt pad or hip pad is ideal because it makes the gear more comfortable, reducing chafe from pouches, and also increases the size of the belt so you can get more pouches on it. Having the pouches off your front will allow you to get into the prone position and crawl.

Also, the only time in your life that you will be allowed to 'sag' anything (most definitely including your pants) is with this belt: don't have it up by your belly button but have it situated over the outside of your hips, a little cowboy style. This is a better place for weight distribution and rather than cinching the belt in to your belly situating it over your hips will allow you to fit more equipment on it, and have better access to the ammo pouches. Distributing the weight on your hips is more efficient and will be supported by the suspenders.

Along with the equipment you carry on your belt or vest rig, anything that you carry on your person should be secured with 550 paracord so that you don't lose it. That includes your racing spoon, very importantly.

Camelbaks/hydration bladders are great; carry them if you have one. Carry a canteen or two and puritabs also when out on patrol; you may find it easier to fill from available water sources and sterilize with the purification tablets than you would with a bladder. You can always use the canteens to fill the bladder.

If you carry a metal mug and solid fuel stove (or gas camping stove in your daypack) then this is ideal for making hot beverages, which can be a morale winner if you are partial to a cup of coffee, tea or hot chocolate. Carry the required beverage in single serving packages with sachets of powdered milk and sugar to taste. If you carry MRE entrees with the heater, then that is another alternative.

If you are eating any other kind of food, such as 'boil in the bag' or dehydrated rations, then you can use the metal mug and solid fuel stove to boil up the water. With boil in the bag rations, it is really convenient because you can heat them up in the mug and then use the water to make a hot drink. If you have to go 'hard routine' then do so, but 'any fool can be uncomfortable' and if you can plan your activities to include a tactical stop during daylight you will be able to get at least one hot meal and drink in per day.

In your daypack you will carry additional items that you can't fit on your belt. Suggestions:

- Spare clothing
- Warm clothing
- Waterproof clothing
- Spare batteries
- Water
- Food
- Additional ammunition
- Mission specific gear
- Binoculars or surveillance equipment
- Entrenching tool

In the ruck you will have:

- Additional spare clothing
- Dry footwear
- Sleeping system
- Tarp
- Rations
- Additional medical supplies and aid items, plus medications
- Wash kit/wipes plus tactical small towel
- Any other administrative equipment you need.

A note on chafing and clothing: consider the type of pants that you are wearing, along with your underwear, and how well they fit. It is common to get chafing between the thighs which can rapidly become debilitating. You can use Vaseline between your thighs. Another method is to wear 'spandex' or 'lycra' shorts, of the tight fitting thigh length style. These get criticized for heat retention but in fact they are ideal for reducing chafing, particularly in hot humid environments where you are doing a lot of walking and where chafing can result in infection. So, the place where you may think they are too hot to wear is precisely where they may be most useful – i.e. places like the jungle or any hot environment.

In terms of clothing, your environment may be hot and there is no real reason why you can't wear a pair of decent combat boots and a pair of cargo shorts. In places where bush wars were common, such as Rhodesia and South Africa, wearing of shorts was very common (even though it was the 70s and some of those shorts are worryingly short and tight from a modern perspective....). However, if you wear shorts and short sleeve shirts and t-shirts, consider the threat from biting insects and you may wish to review the clothing choice around dusk where long pants and rolled down shirts will keep the bugs off better.

'Actions On'

'Actions On' covers a host of Standard Operating Procedures (SOPs) that you will adapt and adopt to suit your circumstances. These actions on

SOPs need to be drilled so that they become standard and you can then brief them in orders 'as per SOPs'. Actions on cover a host of conceivable situations and no doubt they will have to be adapted to the situation post-event. The following is a series of standard ones with possible reaction drills:

Halts: the patrol will stop in the designated formation, usually herringbone, and conduct security until either the patrol moves on or alternative instructions comes down the line, such as to drink or eat, at which point this will be done in buddy pairs with one providing security while the other conducts the designated admin. Even when doing admin, that soldier should be looking out of the perimeter, rather than facing in or paying no attention.

Obstacles: this can be a situation where the obstacle is an actual obstacle, such as a river, or it may simply be a vulnerable point (linear danger area, LDA) such as a road that needs to be crossed. Whichever it is, there are basic principles that need to be adhered to but the way the drill is conducted is up to you and you should experiment with the best way of doing it.

If you have to cross an LDA, select a good point where there is maximum cover from enemy observation and potential fire. The principle is that as the formation moves, the lead scout identifies the LDA and calls a halt, passing back the relevant hand signal. Once the hand signal is passed back, the patrol will snap into the drill you have practiced. First, the 'near bank' is secured by riflemen covering across the LDA and to the flanks. Then a group will cross and secure the 'far bank'. Once that is done, the main body will cross and the whole formation will continue.

A technique is to use people from the rear of the formation to initially cross the LDA so that as the formation moves across, they can simply join back in at the end. Another option is to create a 'tunnel' effect (center peel) by moving in file formation. The patrol peels in to the obstacle, crosses it and peels in on the far side, with the following patrol members continuing to walk through the tunnel that the file formation creates, until they in turn peel in and face out, providing security. Once all have crossed, the first people remaining on the near back get up and walk through the tunnel, and the whole formation peels back out of itself and continues walking. This is better with smaller groups. With larger groups, you may want to use a team to secure the near bank, another for the far bank, cross the main body and have the teams fall back in to the formation.

Lost or separated: you will need to make provision for this eventuality as part of your patrol orders. A useful SOP to adopt is to nominate each RV that you pass through as the emergency RV (ERV). Thus, if you are contacted and the patrol is separated, then the squad will make its way back to that ERV. A drill like this will work if you specify that they will wait perhaps an hour at the last ERV and then perhaps another hour at the previous ERV.

Also, if the patrol becomes separated in the darkness due to link men losing contact with each other, then reforming at the ERV will work. In case of a full on disaster where you have been ambushed and had to fight out, your ERVs may not be accessible. For these circumstances it is good to have a nominated safe haven or 'War RV' which may be your retreat or base. The patrol and any separated personnel will separately escape and evade back to this location.

Enemy Pre-Seen: this is a circumstance where you spot the enemy in an unexpected location prior to your own presence being compromised. You will need to have a hand signal for enemy; a thumbs down followed by a five finger point in the enemy direction works, and the patrol should seek concealment. At this point you will have the initiative, but your follow up action will depend on your mission. You could observe and then move away, you could attack, or you could set up a hasty (snap) ambush or OP.

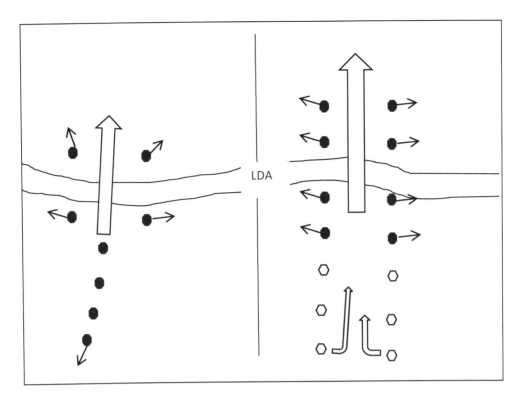

Figure 27 - Crossing an LDA / Obstacle

Actions on Contact

Your reaction will depend on the type of patrol you are on and the overall situation. You may be a fighting patrol on the way to an ambush, but you may still include actions on contact that plan for withdrawal from contact, or you may decide to act offensively. Generally, smaller recce patrols will always attempt to break contact and withdraw from the enemy.

Offensive Drills

These types of actions on enemy contact will depend on what you decide about your objective, the size of your patrol, and also how the skill of your team compares to that of the enemy in historical contacts.

Squad Size offensive reactions: for a far ambush, which is one outside of grenade range, so we will say over thirty yards away, an offensive reaction to enemy contact would be the same as the squad quick attack drills already covered. One of the teams, usually the team that was contacted if you are moving a tactical bound apart, will win the firefight while the other team conducts a flanking attack.

If it is a near ambush, which is within grenade range or less than thirty yards away, then the drill is for an immediate assault by all elements of the squad that can engage. For a contact in the frontal or rear axis, this may mean only the lead or following team is able to engage, but the other team will attempt to push out to a flank to provide supporting fire or flank protection to the assaulting team.

This is certainly not as ideal as a far ambush, with only one team assaulting at close range without benefit of fire support, but it may be the only option if surprised by the enemy. If at all possible, it is preferable to be able to react as per a far ambush: maneuver your teams to the best covered positions possible and then leave one as a fire base while the other flanks. If the near ambush comes from a flank, then it may be that both teams can turn to face the threat and then fight through side by side.

If you generally over-match the enemy then this may be a useful tactic; think Rhodesian Fireforce skirmish lines which were overwhelmingly able to gain the upper hand and skirmish through enemy contacts, usually due to better fire accuracy and personal drills.

For formations larger than a squad that are moving in linear formations, such as a fighting patrol on the route out to the ORP, then a useful offensive drill is for the group in contact, for example the lead squad, to go firm and return fire while the following elements, such as the remaining squads of the formation, will go into an immediate flanking attack and attempt to roll up the enemy from the flank.

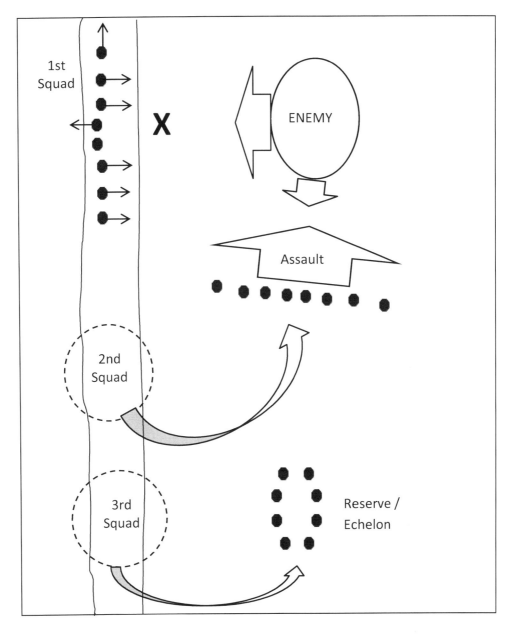

Figure 28 - Platoon Reaction - Ambush – Offensive

Note: Not shown in Figure 24 is the location of the Platoon Leader (PL) and the Platoon Sergeant (PS). The PL will mobilize the 2nd squad into the flanking assault and the PS will remain with the 3rd squad in reserve, ready to pass them to the PL as required for the assault through the enemy position.

For a close ambush, for instance coming right from the side of the trail you are on, an old school drill is to simply turn towards the enemy and run through their line firing your weapon from the hip into the ground ahead of you. This does require brass balls but is not as crazy as it seems. If the enemy has not done their job and put you down in the initiation of the ambush, then you charging towards them may unbalance them and also get you out of their fire quicker.

Of course, to digress, you may not be one of the lucky ones who make it out, felled as you charge. As you crash through the veil into Valhalla, weapon in hand, you will be greeted by the roar of the feast hall, the heat of the hearth fires on your face and the crash of thunder and lightning as the Norse Gods battle above!

Break Contact Drills

For smaller recce patrols, or even squad or larger sized patrols that plan to break contact and extract if contacted by the enemy, then these drills are more suited. Break contact and extraction drills are similar to those described under vehicle movement and consist of fire and movement away from the enemy. There are various techniques that can be used. In terms of your SOPs you will need to decide what you are going to do and in which direction you are going to move.

You can either plan to simply move directly away from the enemy or back the way you came. A contact with the enemy can take numerous forms, from a meeting engagement with another patrol, bumping a sentry at an enemy location, or walking into an ambush. However, you should decide on what your actions are going to be so that you can react as a drill.

Fighting out the way you came in is generally a good idea because you have just traveled it and you should be able to get out, but remember that if it is an ambush the enemy may have placed cut-off groups out, and you may have just walked past them as you entered the ambush killing area. But fighting directly away from the ambush may just keep you under fire for longer. Fighting into the ambush was covered above. It is usually helpful to base your drills on the direction of enemy contact, so it will be "CONTACT FRONT!" or LEFT, RIGHT or REAR. Let us imagine a squad sized formation on patrol, either moving together or in travelling over-watch with a tactical bound between teams.

CONTACT FRONT! An example of the drills that you can do for a contact front would be for the front team to return fire, with the two rearmost riflemen of that front team stepping out to the sides to allow them to fire: effectively 'getting on line'. These two pairs would fight back utilizing fire and movement. The rear team would take up security positions and then begin to move back, utilizing bounding over-watch, to secure a rally point.

Alternatively, the center peel or tunnel method can be used. With this method all the patrol members step to the left or right accordingly to create a file, or tunnel formation. This will only allow the front two riflemen to engage but it is useful for withdrawing along linear features or where fire is coming in from the front but also to the front and flanks on both sides.

The front people will return fire and then in sequence they will turn and run through the center of the tunnel, peeling back in at the other end. This allows the next front people to fire and the process will continue with the tunnel turning itself inside out all the way to a suitable rally point. It is effectively a peeling technique with two lines.

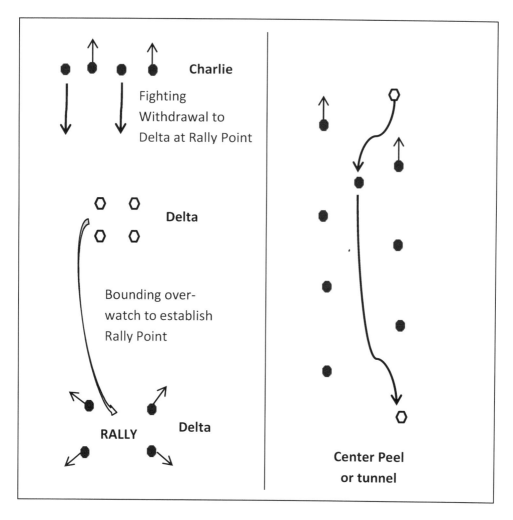

Figure 29 - Contact Front

CONTACT RIGHT (or LEFT)! In this situation the squad will turn to the threat and get on line to return fire towards the threat. A note here: recent experiences in Iraq and Afghanistan have shown that they enemy is not shy about ambushing from all points and therefore it is imperative to maintain 360 degree security. Therefore, designate riflemen to face the opposite way when practicing these drills so that the rear is protected.

The squad will then peel out back down the trail the way they came. For contact right the man on the left would move first, running behind the other patrol members and peeling back in to the right side of the line, with the whole process continuing as the squad peels out back along the trail until a suitable rally point is reached.

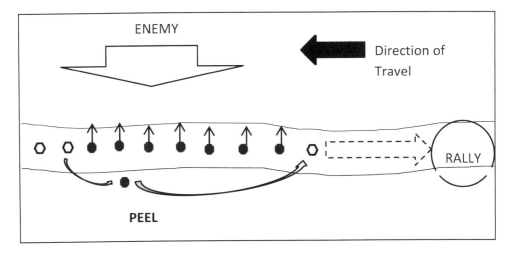

Figure 30 - Contact Right

CONTACT REAR! This drill is carried out as per contact front, but with the exceptions that the team will have to turn around and face rear to engage the enemy and then will have to break contact by continuing on the direction they were moving.

RALLY, RALLY, RALLY! Once the squad leader feels that he has successfully broken contact and has reached some suitable ground, he will give the command to rally. The squad will get into the rally point and get on line facing the enemy direction, with some of the squad covering rear. The squad leader will conduct a rapid assessment of the squad, the situation and make a rapid plan.

If the enemy is following up, or you are still under fire, then a healthy dose of rapid fire at the enemy will prepare for further movement and the squad will continue to fight away as per the quick battle orders (QBOs) from the squad leader. Once contact is actually broken and the squad leader feels that he has made sufficient ground on the enemy, he will halt the patrol and secure a defensive position before tending to the welfare of the patrol and making a plan for further movement or extraction.

Patrol Bases

If you are conducting operations as an independent patrol away from your home base then you will need to set up patrol bases for rest, admin and to conduct the operations if you are out for anything more than one night. You will preferably move into a patrol base in daylight, so you should identify an area on the map and move towards it in good time.

In some circumstances it is a good idea to cook and eat at one location before moving on and establishing a base and sleeping at another location. This will not be possible if you plan to occupy a patrol base for several days, but may be used if you are moving in jungle-style or heavily wooded terrain and are looking to eat an evening meal then move to an overnight spot before moving on again in the morning.

It should be noted here that for any of these tactical operations described here there cannot be any wood fires, particularly at night. Also, if you have solid fuel or fuel stoves in order to heat rations, then they should be dug in and only used in daylight. In severe circumstances in close proximity to the enemy you can do 'hard routine' with no cooking but in any other circumstances it is advisable to look after yourself well and eat hot food and consume hot beverages to maintain both body and spirit.

Most patrol base drills are designed for platoon size formations containing three squads and as such as based around triangular shapes. You may well not have three squads and either way it does not really matter what formation you create. A three squad platoon can occupy a triangular harbor but they can just as well occupy a linear one with the three squads next to each other.

It may also be that you use these drills adapted from a woodland setting to occupy a building for a short period of time, and you can adapt them accordingly. It may also include vehicles in a similar concept. The triangular concept is a way of simply creating 360 degree security with three elements, with platoon headquarters in the center for command and control.

Look at the formations that you have and decide how best for you to achieve this effect. The phases for the occupation of a patrol base are as follows:

- Hasty Ambush
- Recon
- Occupation
- Stand to
- Clearance patrols
- Sentries
- Work Phase
- Routine

Snap Ambush: As the patrol is moving along, perhaps along a small trail, the leader gives the signal for hasty ambush (hand covering the face for ambush) and points to the side of the trail. The squad breaks track 90 degrees to the trail, heads off the trail a short distance, and then peels back another 90 degrees back parallel to the route they just walked up, peeling in on line into a hasty ambush (don't forget rear protection).

The idea of the hasty ambush is to wait for a period of time to ensure that you are not being followed or tracked. The idea of breaking track and peeling back is so that by the time any tracker realizes that you left the trail, he is already in the killing area of the snap ambush, in front of you. If this was a platoon move, they would have peeled into a triangular ambush, with a squad on each side of the triangle.

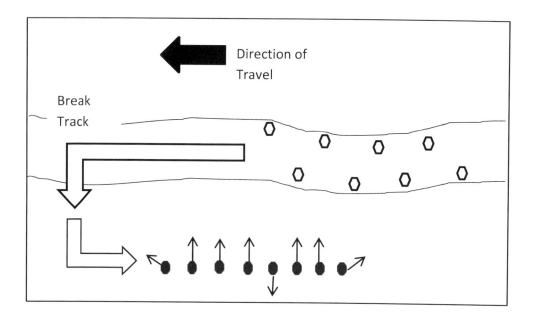

Figure 31 - Break Track & Occupy a Snap Ambush

Recon: Once a suitable period has elapsed, the leader will depart on a recon of the potential patrol base. At platoon level he will take with him security to place down at each apex of the triangle and a buddy pair to send back and lead in the patrol. At squad level you will not be able to spare so much manpower so he will likely take a small security element and perhaps return to the snap ambush himself.

A patrol base is not designed to provide a dominating defensive position or fields of fire, but rather it is designed for concealment. So, ideally the leader is looking for an area in deep cover, perhaps with an accessible water supply, on a reasonable slope and without any obvious trails or tracks through it. The idea is to get hidden in the woods.

Occupation: The patrol peels out of the snap ambush and moves to the patrol base location. For a platoon level triangle, there are specific drills as to how the three squads move into the position and you will have to play with the occupation procedure to make it work for your group. For smaller formations you will decide how the patrol base will be laid out, either in a line or perhaps in a small circular perimeter. Usually the patrol is led in through the base, or 6 o'clock position. For a triangle, the apexes and thus sentry positions would be at the 6, 10 and 2 o'clock positions (upside down triangle). For a small group, it may only be possible to have one or two sentry positions and if only one it should be at 6 o'clock which is the direction facing the greatest enemy threat. The leader places each buddy pair down in their position and they will take off their packs and use them as fire positions as they watch out and cover their arcs of fire.

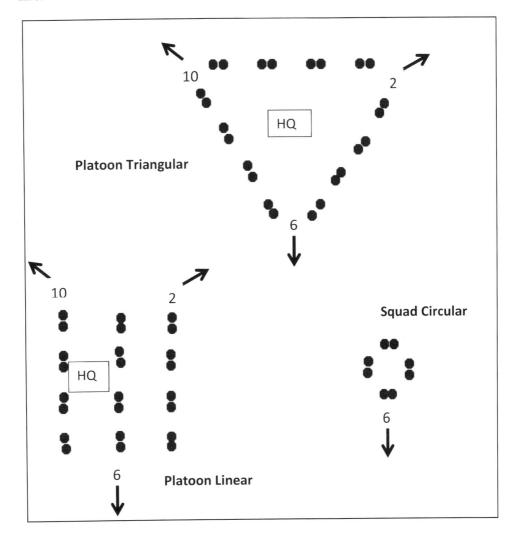

Figure 32 - Patrol Bases

Stand To: the patrol will remain silently at stand to for a suitable period of time, probably 30 minutes, listening for any enemy activity or follow up.

Clearance Patrols: at the close of the stand to period, clearance patrols will be sent out. These should only consist of two or three men and the idea is to clear the immediate area around the patrol base. A simple technique, given that you are likely in the woods, is for the first man to move out to limit of sight from the base, the next to limit of sight of him, and the third to limit of sight of the second man; they will then circuit the base and return inside. The patrol remains 'stood to' throughout.

Sentries: on completion of the clearance patrols sentries will be posted. These will initially be posted at the limit of sound from the patrol base due to the requirement for the coming work phase. There will be two different sentry positions in a patrol base, which will be day and night. Night time sentries are brought in to the base and at daytime the positions are pushed out.

Work Phase: once the sentries are posted then the patrol will stand down and begin the work phase. There are various things that may or may not happen:

- Track plan: Use paracord or string (green) as comms cord to mark out a track plan inside the perimeter around the position, linking the sentry position, buddy positions and the command location. This will allow the track plan to be followed at night and prevent people wandering off into the woods. Clear brush and sticks from this track.

- Positions: in conventional warfare shell scrapes should be dug and the buddy pairs will live in these. They are 12 inches deep and large enough for two people to stretch out and sleep with all their equipment, which should be covered by a tarp or poncho at night against the rain. Tactically you may not do this but individual positions are still laid out with arcs of fire allocated. Your tarps will only go up at night, after evening stand to, and will come down again in the morning, prior to dawn stand to. If you are not digging in then do something to camouflage and build up your location and fire position, maybe using logs, branches and leaves etc. Also, clear your sleeping area of ground cover to reduce noise and keep away the bugs on the forest floor.

- Latrines: a deep drop latrine will be dug. This should be just outside of the position and yes unfortunately under the eyes of the sentry position. You can get behind a little cover for privacy, and if you have a mixed gender post-event infantry team then you will have to make other allowances, but the latrine must be covered by the sentry because people using it are vulnerable and you do not want them snatched.

- Defenses: if you have any defenses such as claymore mines or improvised equivalents, and also trip-flares etc., these will be placed out during the work phase to protect the base.

Routine: Once the work phase is complete the patrol base will go into routine. A sentry roster will be written and once that is done there will be time for weapons cleaning, admin and sleep. There should be stand to for at least 30 minutes spanning dawn and dusk which marks the change from day to night routine. There should be a clearance patrol after dawn stand to. This is now the time when the patrol will rest and administer itself in the patrol base and also conduct any operations that it has planned, such as recce missions. There should always be a security element left at the base when a mission goes out, so long as the patrol intends to return to the base.

Bug-Out Plan & Battle Discipline: A patrol base is a covert affair, a temporary base to conduct operations from. It should not be seen as similar to a contemporary 'Forward Operating Base' (FOB) or even the Firebases of Vietnam era. That would be a different animal, the establishment of a defensive position. The patrol base will need an ERV and will usually plan to stand-to for any enemy threat or incursion. If the patrol base is 'bumped' by the enemy then there will be a plan for a withdrawal under fire to the ERV and then break contact.

If true battle discipline is applied, then shell scrapes will be dug as fire positions and all gear that is not in use will be packed away ready to go at all times. This means that when you are woken in the night for your turn on sentry, you will not doze back off but waken, get out of your sleeping bag and pack all your gear away in your pack silently in the darkness, without use of light. You will re-deploy your sleeping gear once you get off duty. When dawn stand to comes, everyone will pack away their gear, take down their tarps (also known as ponchos or 'bashas') in the pre-dawn and be ready in their fire positions for the dawn.

It is useful to rig up your basha with bungee cords attached which can rapidly be used to put up and take down the tarp using nearby trees; make sure that when you set up the basha, it does not sag in the center or it will collect rain water and collapse on you. Strategically located bungees will help with this, including one or two to hold up the apex. If you are bumped, then the patrol base will be stood to and all gear will be rapidly packed away in buddy pairs, stuffing sleeping bags away etc. If the order is then given to withdraw, packs will go on and the patrol will fire and maneuver out to the ERV.

The triangular patrol base has also been successfully used as a long term ambush position because it conforms to the principles of defense, and has also been used to defend against overwhelming numbers of enemy attacking. With the triangular configuration it is usual to have any support machine-gun weapons systems at the three apexes of the triangle, where they are able to cover down the front of each side of the triangle with enfilade fire.

Sentries: Sentries need to be alert and motivated and should not be on watch for more than two hours, which can be less depending on environmental conditions. During the day sentry positions are usually pushed out and can be occupied by a single sentry, but ideally a buddy pair. At nighttime there will be two sentries and the position will be brought back in to the perimeter.

All patrols will usually leave and return via the 6 o'clock position and sentries must be familiar with passwords and recognition signals. Sentries must be alert, not asleep or distracted, and must watch and scan their sector.

There should be a challenge system in place for situations where the sentry is not sure who is approaching. There will also be rules of engagement so that if the sentry recognizes an enemy approach, he will engage without hesitation. If an unknown patrol approaches the sentry, he will challenge them to halt at a suitable distance. If he has some sort of communications system he will also alert the patrol leadership who will stand-to the patrol base. He will then advise the approaching group to "Advance one and be recognized." At which point he will either be able to recognize them or give his part of the password and wait for a response. Once he has identified the group as friendlies he will ensure that he gets the number count from the leader and counts them back in to the patrol base, in case of any 'tag-ons'.

The watch rotation should be staggered so that there is always a fresh sentry in his first hour, and another who is in his second hour. The off-going sentry can wake the next on the roster 15 minutes prior to his duty, in order to give him time to pack his gear, put on warm clothing as necessary, and make his way to the sentry position.

Sentry rotations should be written down, depending on the level of trust in your team and the numbers involved, because there is always a temptation among less well-disciplined soldiers to skip rotations and if the specific names and times are not written down there is no way to really check this when you are woken at, for example, 3am.

Infiltration

In the sense of tactics, an infiltration is to move your group in smaller elements via separate routes to an RV where they will join up to proceed with the mission. This is not the same sense of the term that is used for, for example, for an undercover cop infiltrating a criminal group, although this tactic may also have its merits post event.

For example, a platoon may wish to conduct a platoon sized fighting patrol but wishes to move to the ORP covertly. They may decide that a platoon is too large a formation to conceal on the route out to the objective so they may split down into squads and move via separate routes to the ORP, link up and conduct the mission.

Possible disadvantages to this are the use of multiple routes, which may or may not be feasible, and hence the consideration of discovery via using multiple routes in smaller groups, versus using perhaps one excellent concealed route in a larger formation.

Perhaps an option to use that lies somewhere between moving as a platoon snake and completely dispersed is the satellite style patrolling with the three squads separated but close enough to provide mutual support should one be contacted, moving as a sort of widely dispersed platoon advance to contact. The circumstances will dictate the best option to use to achieve your mission.

Patrol Orders

The following is an example format that can be used for giving patrol orders:

PRELIMINARIES   Admin: any relevant points
Security of the Orders Group
Task Organization: Appointments, positions, equipment etc.
Ground Orientation: use map/model

1. SITUATION

Enemy Forces	Friendly Forces	Attachments/Detachments
Strength Positions Weapons Equipment Morale Obstacles Surveillance Devices Defensive Fires Patrols Routine NBC Future Intentions	Commanders Mission & Concept of Operations (Incl. intent and main effort) Defensive position layout Field defenses Trip Flares Defensive Fires Other Patrols Outline fire support plan	Only if not covered under Task Organization above **Civil Refugees** Friendly/Unfriendly Locations Movement Intent

2. MISSION: Task(s) plus unifying purpose. Always repeat twice when giving orders.

3. EXECUTION

   a. **Concept of Operations.** Patrol Commanders intent. Scheme of Maneuver (How patrol will achieve its mission). Outline Phases.

   b. **Sub-Unit Missions/Tasks.** (If Applicable)

   c. **Phases:**

Preparatory Move	Route Out
Method of Movement	Order of March (OOM)
Load Plan	Navigation
Time of:	Formations
Rehearsal	RVs
Leaving Base	Obstacle Drills
Out	Action On:
Route to Drop Off Point (DOP)	Enemy
Location of DOP	Prisoner of War
Arcs of Fire (Sectors)	Casualty
Order of March (OOM)	Lost
Action at DOP	Separated
Action on Enemy	Confirmation of ORP

ACTION ON ORP	
Incl. initial recce of ORP	
Recce Group	**Remainder**
Composition	Composition
Tasks	Tasks
Position for Cover Group	Arcs
Route In	Signal to open fire
OOM	Action On:
Formations	Enemy pre-seen
Arcs	Ambush
Signal to Open Fire	Groups not return
Actions On:	Recce group contacted
Enemy present	
ORP Move	
Ambush	
Remainder located by the enemy	
Return to remainder	

Action on Objective	Withdraw to ORP	Route Back

See separate action on objective paragraphs following*	Signal to Withdraw
	OOM
	Action in ORP
	Head Check
	Exchange of Info
	Signal to move out
	Action On:
	  Enemy
	  Prisoner of War
	  Non return of group
	  ORP Move
	  In ORP
	  Being surprised
	  Mission not achieved
		Navigation
		Formations
		RVs
		Obstacles
		Action On:
		  En pre-seen
		  Ambush
		  Casualties
		  Separated
		  Lost
		  At Base
		  At Pick Up Point (PUP)
		  Friendly Force Location

d. **Coordinating Instructions**

Timings	Actions On	Fire Plan	Rehearsals	Deception
Meals Rest Rehearsals Weapon Test Inspections Times out/in Debrief	Halts Lights Flares Obstacles POW Civilians NBC Lost Comms Contact	Defensive Fires Illumination Light Mortar	Location Equipment Dress	Preparatory Move On Objective On Withdrawal
			Public Info/Media	

e. **Summary of Execution:** This is a "Put your notebooks and pens down and look in to me please gentlemen." moment. To ensure that the plan is understood following the depth of information that has just been relayed, this the time for the Patrol Commander to go over it and tell the story of the patrol as a summary, going over what will happen and painting a picture that will be further reinforced during rehearsals.

4. **SERVICE SUPPORT**

SOP Variations	Equipment	Medical
Dress Weapons Ammo Equipment	Special Equipment	Medic Locations CASEVAC Stretchers Med Packs IFAKS CAT Tourniquets Pain Meds

5. **COMMAND & SIGNAL**

Command	Radio	Debrief
Location of Patrol Commander Location of HQ Chain of Command	Frequencies Call-signs Check Comms	Location Conducting Officer

Codes	Password
Codewords Nicknames Nick Numbers Phase Lines	**Synchronize Watches** **Questions**

*ACTION ON OBJECTIVE PARAGRAPHS

RECCE/FIGHTING PATROL		
Cover/Fire Group	**Close Recce/Assault Group**	**ORP Protection Group**

Composition
Task
Position
Route
Formation
Arcs
Opening Fire
Action On:
  Located by Enemy
  Separated
	Composition
	Task
	Position
	Route
	Formation
	Fire Plan
	Opening Fire
	Action On:
	  Fire Group Located by enemy
	  Recce group engaged
	On Assault
	Illumination
	POW
	Casualty
	Separated
		Composition
		Task
		Arcs
		Action On:
		Located by enemy
		Recce Group not return
		Recce Group engaged
		On return of groups

OBSERVATION POST
(Consider the following for both OP and Admin Area/Base Groups)

Occupation	Routine
Composition	Reporting
Route to location	Changeover system
Formations	Task
Arcs	State of equipment
Tasks	Rest
Observation Group	Feeding
Sentry	Latrines
Commander	Trash
Remainder	Action on Contact
Action on Contact	

AMBUSH

Occupation	Routine
OOM	Roster
Arcs of Fire	Relief system
Areas	State of equipment
State of weapons	Rest
Formations	Meals
Lights	Latrines
Arcs	Trash
Time Ambush Set	
Method of entry	
Signal Ambush Set	
Individual positions	
Other signals	
Laying of Lights,	
Mines – nominate	

ACTION ON ENEMY	
Warning from Cut-Offs	Search Procedure
Signal to other groups	Action On:
Signal to spring	Before Ambush Sprung
Illumination	Attacked by enemy
Signal for Grenades/Claymores civilians/refugees	Approach of
Refugees	
Action by Cut-Offs	
Signals:	
Watch and Shoot	
Ceasefire	
Searchers	

ACTION IF AMBUSH NOT SPRUNG
Signal to abort
Retrieve mines/flares (nominate)
Action while retrieving equipment by:
Cut Offs
Killer Group
Action On:
Enemy pre-seen
Enemy Ambush/Contact
Civilians

Note that during these orders, if you are well trained, rehearsed and experienced together as a team, then some of the headings, such as actions on, can be covered by simply stating "As per SOP." However, don't play lip service to this and if there is anyone new or you need to adjust the drills, then cover it in full.

CHAPTER ELEVEN

TACTICAL USE OF VEHICLES

Some of these tactics have been touched on earlier in the book. There is a difference to vehicle tactics used when perhaps initially bugging out to a retreat or moving with your family post-event, to a situation where you are using vehicles tactically. This chapter is primarily concerned with using vehicles tactically as part of your operations post-event, and will form an additional capability to add to dismounted tactics. It is important to note that all the principles that apply to dismounted tactics still apply to vehicle tactics.

There is a big difference between armored and unarmored vehicles. Unarmored vehicles are inherently very vulnerable. Using vehicles will greatly increase your capability in terms of range, speed and load, but they will not provide protection from small arms fire and they will be restricted to routes available. Armored vehicles will give you the same capabilities and disadvantages but they will be far less vulnerable to enemy fire. So, vehicles will both enhance and decrease your mobility, and they will vary in terms of the protection they provide. Thus, it is important to incorporate and deploy vehicles as part of your operations with careful thought given to their capabilities and how best to utilize them to enhance your effect.

If you have unarmored vehicles then you should give careful thought to how you will utilize them tactically. It is not a good idea to fight from an unarmored vehicle if exposed to enemy direct fire, and therefore creating an unarmored technical has limitations. When using unarmored vehicles you should think more in terms of using them for their speed, load carrying ability and ability to increase your tactical mobility over suitable ground.

However, plan to deploy from the vehicles and fight from cover, rather than from the back of the vehicle. An exception would be when you can site a vehicle 'hull down' to allow a machine-gunner on the vehicle to engage from dead ground with the body of the vehicle concealed by the ground.

A simple example would be the use of pick-up trucks to patrol an area, perhaps conducting GDA patrols. You can have riflemen sitting in the back and the roof of the cab can be used to steady a support machine-gun. Unless the vehicle can be placed in cover, if contacted by enemy the personnel should dismount from the vehicle to engage the enemy and the vehicle itself should be driven into the nearest available cover. If you are using pick-up or other types of trucks, then rig up seats in the center of the truck bed, facing out, for your patrol members, rather than having them face in. This way they can observe and potentially return fire as they are being driven around.

You can consider armoring vehicles yourself, if you have access to some steel and the ability to cut and weld. A standard type production B6 (a designation of protection level) armored vehicle is perhaps not ideal as a fighting vehicle anyway, because the armored glass will be degraded by continued enemy fire and you cannot fire out from the inside of most production armored 'suburban' type vehicles.

You can create a fighting vehicle out of a pick-up truck by placing additional steel plate to cover/replace areas such as the side panels of doors, the engine block, the windshield, and to up-armor the truck-bed to protect carried troops or a pintle-mounted support weapon. If you do this, then you will increase the survivability of the vehicle and allow it to be taken into more hostile fire environments, and thus perhaps allow its use as a mobile fire support base (or machine-gun nest). You will need to consider run-flat tires. Don't forget dump-truck style trucks with armored sides! If you can get hold of one of these, armor the cab and install some weaponry and personnel in the back, then you have a formidable armored personnel carrier (APC) that will be able to do some serious damage.

You can also consider military vehicles that may or may not be available to you post-event, it really depends on the nature of the situation. Any Reserve or National Guard location has a motor pool and in there will be parked trucks (LMTV type) and Humvees. Most of the Humvees will be unarmored but they don't require an ignition key and would work great as general use vehicles, with usually a trailer parked behind them. There will usually be at least one or two armored vehicles and they usually just require cutting a padlock to get in. If you can also get into the armory then you will be able to grab support weapons to mount in the turret. An Army center will also have a whole bunch of other useful stuff such as fuel cans, MRE supplies and medical gear. If you could get into an abandoned Reserve Center and bring with you some entry tools, you would be able to do some very useful foraging.

If you have some tactical type vehicles available, preferably with some form of armor on them, then you can boost your operational capability. One of the most useful ways to employ vehicles is as a Quick Reaction Force (QRF). This can be very useful when conducting some sort of area defense where the QRF can rapidly move to a location carrying troops and if armored the vehicles themselves can be used as mobile firing positions. This will give you the capability for rapid reinforcement and maneuver. The following are ways in which tactically employed vehicles can be utilized in the various operational phases:

Patrolling: Both range and sustainability can be increased for patrols if vehicles are employed. Vehicle mounted patrols can be utilized on their own or as part of a foot and vehicle combination, perhaps utilizing the satellite type patrolling as outlined under dismounted tactics. Vehicles increase tactical mobility, which is the ability to move about your tactical area, unless they are employed in an area that is not suitable to vehicle travel.

If you have robust vehicles and the terrain is suited, then vehicles need not be employed on just roads or trails, but they can also move across country with care taken not to get them stuck in difficult areas. You will need to give consideration to vehicle logistics, including carriage of fuel and spares. Vehicles can be used to allow longer distance patrolling and also the carriage if heavier weapons systems if you have them available.

You can move to an area in vehicles to a muster location, which is like a patrol base for vehicles, and then leave a guard force in place while moving on foot to accomplish a patrol. You can also give consideration to employing different types of vehicles, such as ATVs, horses, bicycles and pack mules to increase load carrying ability, tactical mobility and range. Vehicles can also be used imaginatively when patrolling, such as to aid you in establishing TCPs by blocking roads and providing mounting locations for covering weapon systems.

Offensive Operations: some of the applications for vehicles in the attack are similar to the employment under certain types of offensive patrolling. If you have heavier weapons then you can carry the weapons and additional ammunition in vehicles. You can also extract casualties in vehicles and conduct resupply of the troops. An ATV with trailer is very useful for distributing ammunition to dismounted troops and also extracting casualties.

If you have heavy weapons systems such as machine-guns and mortars with heavy ammunition then you can move them in vehicles to a fire support location before carrying out a deliberate attack. If you have vehicles that are armored and set up as 'technicals' then they can actually become your fire base, if perhaps you can maneuver them to a location where they can bring fire down on the enemy. Alternatively, use vehicles to carry personnel and equipment close to the fire support location and pack it in from there.

Defensive Operations: the main utility in defense it to use tactical vehicles as a QRF to rapidly reinforce and counter-attack the enemy. You will be able to rapidly deploy personnel and firepower across your defensive area. If your retreat area is more extensive than a simply house retreat with garden, then you should utilize these hobo armored vehicles to move about and reinforce as necessary.

Contact Drills: For an unarmored move then even though the purpose of the patrol may be offensive, there is little utility in vehicles trying to fight it out on the X. Vehicles should rapidly move off the X to rally and cover as per the drills covered for moving protected personnel. The difference might be that infantry personnel riding in the vehicles may be dropped off into cover to fight and assault the enemy and the vehicles will move to a rally or muster point close to the action, where they can support as necessary, deploy any heavy support weapons or assist with the conduct of resupply or casualty extraction.

For 'hobo' type armored tactical vehicles with mounted weapons systems there is increased survivability and although they should not stay on the X simply for the sake of it, they have an increased ability to maneuver on the enemy and provide support with their mounted weapon systems. Therefore, hobo armored tactical vehicles should maneuver to fire support locations to support any assault by the infantry component onto the enemy positions.

In all cases where the patrol is not designed to fight, then whether armored or unarmored the vehicles will employ break contact drills and conduct bounding over-watch to escape the killing area and rally prior to making further moves. The difference here between armored vehicles and unarmored vehicles will be the increased survivability of both personnel and the vehicle itself provided by the armor, and also the increased ability to return fire, in particular if you have mounted weapons systems in the truck beds.

Halts: you must use your imagination to adapt dismounted tactics to fit the use of vehicles, whichever type you are using. It will be harder to move vehicles off the road to concealed patrol bases but you will be able to find ways to conceal your patrol base. You can circle vehicles to provide a harder perimeter or you can use an alternative formation such as a box or if space is tight perhaps on a small trail then you can use a linear formation.

Ensure that when parking vehicles you always reverse them in to face out (i.e. 'combat parking' - no 'nosy' parking) so that they can move out in a hurry if needed.

You can use the mounted weapon systems on 'technicals' and man them as sentry positions.

If you are stopping you can temporarily rest in the cab and truck beds of vehicles or you can set up your patrol admin base within the vehicles and string up tarps, even off the side off vehicle: but make sure that you use the same battle discipline and the vehicles are ready to fight from and move at short notice.

You will need to plan for breakdowns or vehicles otherwise immobilized and decide if you are going to cross deck the gear and personnel or tow the vehicle out and home. You will need a plan for either.

CHAPTER TWELVE

OFFENSIVE OPERATIONS

"To close with and destroy the enemy with bullet, bomb and bayonet."

Introduction

For many preppers, conducting offensive operations will likely be very far from their minds, perhaps even in the 'inconceivable' or even 'repulsive' box. However, none of us really know what the situation will be post-event and how long it may drag out for. Offensive operations are one end of the use of force continuum and there may be multiple circumstances where you may decide that you need to conduct, and wished you had the capability to conduct, such operations.

A discussion of offensive operations is intended to move beyond the scenario that we started with at the beginning of this book, where we were staying in place or moving with our family. Offensive operations are not family friendly activities! The situation envisaged is one where you have a trained tactical team, squad, platoon or larger, and you need to take some form of action.

Some of these options have been covered already under patrolling such as fighting patrols, ambush and raid, but the specific mechanics of deliberate attacks and ambush have not been covered. Perhaps a family member has been kidnapped and is being held hostage, maybe you were raided and had food supplies taken, or maybe a domestic or foreign invader has taken advantage of the event and invaded, creating an American insurgency, and you have decided that you are going to fight.

If you are fighting in such an insurgency, then the techniques outlined here under defense, patrolling and offense are your bread and butter, together with access to, or the ability to build or liberate, heavier weapons.

Let's first look at some of the theory behind offensive operations, or the attack. We define **success** as achieving our end state which is to terminate or resolve conflict on favorable terms. To **defeat** the enemy we will diminish the effectiveness of the enemy, to the extent that he is either unable to participate in combat or at least cannot fulfill his intention.

All conflict has political, economic, ethical, moral and legal constraints; this places limits on the freedom of taking military actions and as such a direct attack may be costly or counter-productive. There are three alternative or supplementary approaches that can be taken to avoid or limit those costs:

- **Pre-emption**: seize an opportunity, often fleeting, before the enemy does, in order to deny him an advantageous course of action.
- **Dislocation**: deny the enemy the ability to bring his strength to bear.
- **Disruption**: attack selectively to break apart and throw into confusion the assets which are critical to the employment and coherence of his fighting power.

Cohesion refers to a desired state of unity, or operational integrity, on our side which can be brought about by:

- Selection and maintenance of the aim
- Concentration of force, and its application to our main effort
- High Morale

In order to attack the cohesion of the enemy we will utilize:

- **Firepower**, which destroys, neutralizes, suppresses and demoralizes.
- **Tempo**, which is a higher rhythm or rate of activity relative to the enemy.
- **Simultaneity**, which seeks to overload an enemy commander

- **Surprise**, where the enemy is unaware or aware too late to react effectively.

The core functions that will allow us to do this are:

- **Find**: locating, identifying, assessing.
- **Fix**: deny goals, distract, and deprive of freedom of action.
- **Strike**: maneuver to a position of advantage to threaten or apply force. Hit, unexpectedly with superior force at a point selected in order to defeat the enemy.

Principles of Offensive Operations

- Concentration of Force
- Seek surprise
- Maintain security
- Seize key terrain or targets vital to influencing perceptions
- Achieve superiority of fires and other effects
- Exploit maneuver
- Concentrate the effects of force or the threat of force
- Plan to exploit success
- Keep it simple

Advance to Contact / Hasty Attack

The squad advance to contact and hasty attack was covered above as part of the description of squad battle drills. Here we will go into greater detail for large formations, based around a description of a platoon hasty attack. For a platoon operation, which is based around a three squad platoon with a platoon headquarters split into two elements, one containing the platoon leader and the other the platoon sergeant, the squad battle drills still take place within the larger overall platoon battle drills.

Platoon Quick Attack Battle Drills:

- Preparation: including signals and formations to be adopted
- Reaction to any squad coming under effective enemy fire
- The Attack: broken into the approach, the assault and the fight through.
- Reorganization

Movement: A platoon can move in various ways depending on the terrain. If it is a platoon sized fighting patrol then it may well be moving in concealment and will adopt the best formation to the vegetation and ground, which may well be a linear file or single file formation: 'platoon snake'. The platoon leader will usually slot in behind the first squad with the platoon sergeant at the rear. If you have the ability, put out scouts and flank protection to reduce the risk of stumbling into an ambush. You may or may not decide to put in a tactical bound between the first squad and the rest of the formation. In close country it is often better for command and control to simply move in a long snake.

For movement in more open country, and also where the platoon is deliberately advancing to contact, the way to move is more like the way described for satellite patrolling, just with the bigger squads rather than the smaller teams described. You can move with the squads dispersed either 'two-up' or 'one-up'. This is a loose triangular formation with the platoon leaders group located in the center. You can also move dispersed in a travelling over-watch column. The two-up formation puts most of your strength on the front foot and could be used if you expect imminent contact and want to have two squads right up there, one to provide fire support to the other while the third is behind you in reserve.

The one-up approach is more circumspect and allows you to bump the enemy with the point squad and then have two squads back to deploy as necessary. What is really useful is to have the additional asset with the platoon leader of a gun group or two that travels with the platoon leader and can be directly deployed by him to influence the battle.

Usually the platoon leader will travel with a radio operator. The platoon sergeant will need some bodies to help him with ammo carriage and resupply, and if the platoon has a light mortar team (knee mortar) it will travel with, and be deployed by, the platoon sergeant at the rear.

The squads themselves will usually travel in a half attack formation, rather than file, which puts a fire team on the left and right of each squad formation, which can be opened up to arrowhead or even extended (skirmish) line as needs be.

Reaction to any squad coming under effective enemy fire: This used to be 'reaction to point squad' but the drill was re-written to take account that even on an advance to contact you could be hit from the flank or rear, which is why it is useful to move in the loose triangular formation. We will assume that we have been moving 'one up' and for ease of presentation we will also assume that it is the point squad that comes under effective enemy fire. The following will happen:

- The point squad will react as per squad battle drills. They will take cover, maneuver off the immediate killing area into cover, locate the enemy and return fire to gain fire superiority and win the fire fight. The squad leader will make a decision as to the strength of the enemy and whether it is possible for him to assault as per a squad quick attack. We will assume that he cannot.

- Simultaneously the platoon leader is moving up and to a flank to a position of observation where he can do a combat estimate on the situation. He will decide here that it is a platoon attack and he will assess the enemy and ground and make a plan for the attack, including whether to go left or right flanking.

- Simultaneously the platoon sergeant will muster the remaining two squads in a rally point and hold them there.

- The platoon leader will communicate a warning order to the squads. He will designate the point section as the fire support and at this point he can deploy any gun groups he has to fire support locations to assist the point squad and help to suppress the enemy. He can use the radio or if not then he will have to use a runner. He will then either move back to the rally point to brief the squad leaders and platoon sergeant, or if he thinks it is useful he will take the squad leaders up to his position of observation to show them the ground.

- The platoon sergeant will also deploy the light mortar, if you have one, at this point. High explosive (HE) can be used to help suppress the enemy and smoke on the enemy position will facilitate movement, either of the point section as it tries to sort itself out in the fire support position (which is on or close to the X) or the move to the flank or assault of the main body. (If you had any indirect fire support, then this is the time to have the fire controller call it in. Unlikely in a post-event situation, but possible.)

- The platoon leader will issue Quick Battle Orders (QBOs) to the squad leaders, who will quickly brief their men. This is a drill, so it should not take long.

The Attack:

- The Approach: The two assaulting squads will move to the flank on a designated route and move into the FUP. The platoon leader can lead this move, but in case of contacting further enemy on the route to the FUP, or in the FUP, it is better if this move is led by a squad, with the platoon leader in the center, followed by the other squad and the platoon sergeant. A lot of this will depend on how professional the platoon is and how much 'leadership' the platoon leader needs to give them. He may have to do a 'follow me' type move, or if the troops are hardened professionals they will be able to move in formation as described. Remember that we are not in a military situation and the platoon leader is likely to be the most experienced person there, so it is not the typical military caricature situation with a 'wet behind the ears' lieutenant having to prove himself to his men. Once the platoon reaches the FUP they will deploy into it as designated by the platoon leader. It is likely that he will designate an echelon style attack with one squad responsible for the 'break-in battle' onto the enemy position, with the other squad following in reserve until they are called forward to exploit further onto the position.

- The Assault: If it is a two-up style attack then the platoon leader will situate himself between the two squads to control the fire and movement of the two formations. If it is a one-up echelon style attack the platoon leader will be behind the assaulting squad. The platoon leader should only become directly involved in the fighting if the attack reaches a critical point where it may fail and the personal example or leadership of the platoon leader is required to tip the balance. The assaulting squad will cross the line of departure and conduct a squad attack in microcosm onto the enemy position, whether it is a building, bunker or enemy in the open. The fire support squad and any additional gun groups remain at the fire support location continuing to provide support and escalating to rapid fire as necessary, followed by switching fire away from the assault to flank and depth positions.

- The Fight Through: once the first squad has conducted the break in battle and fought to the designated limit of exploitation (LOE) it will go firm and begin to suppress enemy in depth on the remainder of the position. The platoon leader will then push the following squad through in an echelon style attack to fight through the position to their designated LOE. Until that time the following squad is controlled by the platoon sergeant who is reading the battle and anticipating the needs of the platoon leader. He will release the squad to the platoon leader when required.

The Reorganization: Once the position is captured, the two assaulting squads will go into all round defense while the fire support elements are called in to join them. Positions will be adjusted as they come in and each squad will be designated a slice of the clock face as their sector to cover. The platoon leader will be moving about the position allocating sectors of fire and ensuring that there are no gaps in the security. The platoon sergeant will be redistributing ammunition and making sure casualties are taken care of. The position will be checked and cleared for wounded and dead enemy as per the squad attack.

Deliberate Attack

The deliberate attack was partially covered under the patrolling section simply because a deliberate attack or raid is a form or patrol. It has also been covered under quick attack drills simply because the principles are the same. More detail will be covered here.

A deliberate attack is a planned operation that will require reconnaissance and information to locate the enemy in order to plan the attack. You will have a reason for needing to conduct a deliberate attack, whether that is just to wipe out a particularly nasty group of marauders who have established a camp in your vicinity. Once you have that reason, you will seek the information you require to plan the operation and put it into play.

You may have been attacked by a group, perhaps even several attacks by the same group, and you have followed them back to their base, conducted surveillance, and then you plan an attack to wipe them out. Potentially, you are also operating as an insurgent band and have located an enemy installation, perhaps a command and control hub, rebroadcast communication station or ammunition or fuel supply dump and you plan to attack it.

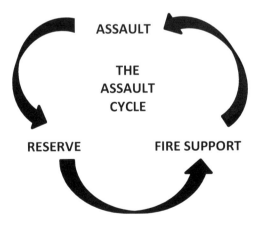

Figure 33 - The Assault Cycle

The assault cycle is how sub-units (i.e. squads, or platoons in a company level operation) will rotate through roles during an attack. They are the three main roles that will be played out during any attack.

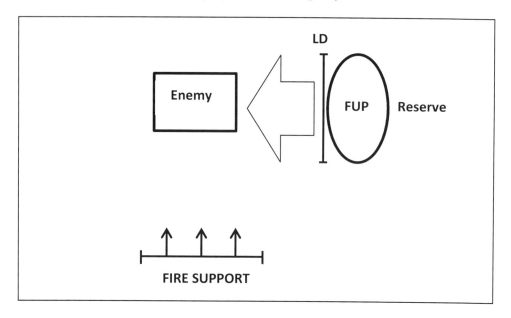

Figure 34 - Deliberate Attack Schematic

Under patrolling we covered the move to an ORP followed by occupation of fire support and assault positions. Ideally, the assault forming up point (FUP), the forward edge of which is the line of departure (LD), will be at right angles (90 degrees) to the fire support position. Attacks from the rear are often talked about, and this is great as a more strategic option, but this is not advantageous tactically within the sphere of this single attack because this would mean the assaulting forces are advancing into the fire from the fire support position.

Similarly, if the assault force advances from the fire support position, then it will mask the fire from the fire support position. This can vary depending on the ground and the availability of hard cover and dead ground to mask direct fires, but generally it should be adhered to. Attacks from the rear are very useful to unbalance the enemy, but they would have to be separate attacks occurring with their own integral fire support and assault teams.

Fratricide

A factor that is very important to consider is fratricide ('blue on blue') contact and the necessity for control measures to avoid this. During daylight this is not as much of an issue as at night, but it needs to be seriously considered. The fire support elements need to be able to switch fire in front of the approach of the assaulting teams, but they don't want to do it too early and have the assault teams lose the benefit of fire superiority.

Depending on the ground at the enemy position, and the real world is neither perfect nor a billiard table; it may not be possible to see all of the assault as it goes in. Control measures and communications are essential. This is also an important factor when determining if you are going to conduct a day or night attack.

A night attack would be great if you had sufficient night vision gear, but that is probably unlikely. The old school and probably most effective way of conducting a night attack, without night vision gear, is simply to 'go noisy' and attack with speed, aggression and surprise utilizing parachute illumination both from rocket type flares and also from mortar illumination if you have access to it.

For daytime operations you could use some form of flags or markers that can be laid out to show the progress of the assault. For nighttime operations, and we are assuming here that you don't have enough night vision IR capability to effectively utilize assets like glint tape, then you will need to think of other low tech ways. The use of illumination will light up the objective enough to see what is going on, while still providing shadow and darkness to not totally negate the advantages of a night attack.

You could utilize partially taped cyalume sticks on the backs of certain personnel's equipment, but this fails if the enemy has a view of them from the rear angle! You could also use cyalume sticks or flashlights to throw out or place down to show the progress of the clearance.

A control measure that can be used is control lines or labeled objectives; so that progress can be reported over the radio and fire switches away to beyond the next phase line or to the next objective, but these must be identifiable to the fire support group and to the assaulting team. This works well with scattered buildings, perhaps in a compound (for instance on a camp attack), when the assault goes in on the buildings in a set manner with fire support switching from building to building as the assault progresses.

Factors

The dawn attack is an age old tactic that is effective because you can approach the objective under the cover of darkness and initiate the attack in the pre-dawn utilizing illum, hopefully when the enemy is unprepared (hence dawn stand-to!) and then it will get light to enable exploitation and control. A dusk attack is perhaps not as helpful because the enemy will still be awake and light conditions will be deteriorating. A full night attack at around 3am is very effective so long as you have night vision or illum capability because the enemy's spirit is at its lowest ebb at that time.

For a night attack tracer is useful to indicate positions and objectives to suppress and will give you some idea of where your personnel are. For this reason, to ensure that tracer is not a double edged weapon, NATO tracer does not light up until 100 meters from the barrel of the weapon, so you can't trace the source all the way back to the firer. Check the manufacturer's directions for any commercial stuff that you purchase.

You will have to tailor your assault plan depending on the nature of your mission and also the type of location and the defenses that the enemy have. Assaulting a built up location with multiple buildings will be covered in more detail below. If the area of the enemy camp is generally an open area or with no significant buildings then it can simply be carved up into phase lines with squads attacking through to pre-designated LOE and then going firm to provide fire support and flank protection as the other squads push through.

If it is defended with a bunker or fire trench system then these bunkers will need to be identified and allocated as objectives for each squad. Isolated small buildings can be treated like bunkers and cleared accordingly.

If it is a linear 'Soviet style' trench system, then the technique is to place down your fire base and then conduct a 'break in battle' to establish a breach into the trench system. Ideally, this will be at the end of the trench system but this may not be possible. Therefore, once the squad breaches in to the system they will establish security and blocking positions; subsequent assaulting squads will push in one direction and continue the clearance while the other direction is blocked.

Once one way is cleared, clearance can progress in the other direction. Squads will push through the trench system using grenades and explosives to fight their way around corners and destroy any bunkers. If the system splits, perhaps with communication trenches, then one way is blocked while the clearance continues down the other way. This needs to be communicated back to leaders via link men so that assets can be allocated to blocking positions and assault teams. Be aware to the possibility of enemy counter attack either coming through the trench system or over the open ground from a rear position.

If a position is defended by wire and obstacles then you will have to consider how to breach those obstacles before you can get in and conduct the break in battle. A 'Bangalore Torpedo' is a length of metal pipe filled with explosives that is pushed out and fed under wire entanglements. It is then detonated and the shrapnel from the metal will cut the wire. Such devices can be made from two metal pickets taped together and filled with explosives. Push the device out from cover, utilizing inert extensions to get the device to where it is needed, and then detonate it. There will also be a partial shock effect from the explosion and if this is combined with rapid fire support and smoke you should be able to breach the obstacle and follow up by rapidly assaulting into the trench system.

The problem is as always mutually supporting and depth positions and if you cannot adequately suppress these with your fire support base then you will either be unable to prosecute the assault without unacceptable losses or you will have to find a way to crawl up in some sort of dead ground in order to break in to the trench system. Smoke is a great asset, but be careful to use it sensibly so as not to mask your fire support – it can be a double edged weapon. If you don't have smoke grenades then you could think of other ways to create masking smoke, such as brush fire or burning oil barrels if you can place them upwind of the objective.

Recalling back to earlier in the text when we discussed the Hollywood and historical vision of running assaults against the enemy compared to what you actually want to be doing, you need to plan and drill to absolutely minimize losses. There cannot be any movement without effective fire support. There may be times when you have to rush across an area, but remember slow is smooth and smooth is fast. Think about an attack in terms of fire and maneuver with the pressure steadily increasing on the enemy as you maneuver to the flanks and increasingly closer, bringing down effective supporting and accurate fire and continuing to steadily maneuver closer and to the flanks, maybe crawling or moving steadily in the available cover and dead ground.

When the German army broke the stalemate in the trench warfare in the First World War with their 1918 spring offensive, they had learned that to get across no-man's land they had to do so in short rushes, the early learning stages of fire and movement that we do today. They trained units of 'storm troopers' whose job was to assault in such away and then clear Allied trench systems, breaking out and turning the previous four years of stalemate into maneuver warfare again.

You cannot assault enemy defensive positions as a mob running at them. You will be shot down. You have to utilize momentum to bring effective fire support onto the enemy thus allowing steady maneuver and flank assaults to close with the enemy. Stop thinking about attacks as running about and charging, think about crawling and flanking and moving steadily with momentum.

Cold Steel

If you have the capability to utilize bayonets on your assault weapons, then do not underestimate it. Bayonets should be fixed in the FUP as a ritual prior to crossing the line of departure. Once in the FUP the leader will look left and right at the line, draw his bayonet and hold it up prior to fitting it to his rifle; the assaulting riflemen will follow suit.

Statistics from wars show that actual numbers of deaths and wounds from bayonetting are very low. However, the secret to this is that the enemy will usually break and flee if they see you forming up to assault with the bayonet. The great thing about bayonets is that if you fix them and begin to prosecute an attack, you will likely not get close enough to actually have to use it because the enemy will flee. That is the secret of the bayonet.

Bayonet training has been taken out of U.S. Army basic training and bayonets are not issued for the current GWOT.. Apparently we will not have to close with and destroy any bad guys in the future?

Bayonet training is usually conducted as an activity all on its own. It is a form of conditioning in savagery. Recruits will undergo a bayonet assault course which will be as muddy and horrific as possible, preferably utilizing any actual animal blood and guts you can get hold of. The recruits will run the assault course under a barrage of abuse from the instructors, with as many battle simulation explosions as possible. They will be crawling under wire and over obstacles and through mud. Think 'tough mudder' with bayonets. They will have to assault and stab both hanging and prone realistic dummies as they go, while preferably having to crawl through actual animal guts and have those guts hanging out of the dummies. Horrific, extremely tiring, great fun and training value!

Gurkhas from Nepal, who have served the British Army faithfully as mercenaries for centuries, do not use bayonets: They have their traditional curved and wicked kukri on their belts and will charge with extreme ferocity when in close contact with the enemy. If you cannot use bayonets, consider perhaps utilizing some other form of weapon, like a machete or hatchet that you keep on your belts and can use in an emergency. Once this gets out, the enemy is not likely to want to engage in close range combat or stand up to a close range charge.

This does not advocate the use of mechanical weapons over the use of your assault weapon or backup handgun at close range, but it's something to think about in sowing fear amongst your enemies. The Native Americans back in the Revolutionary period utilized standoff weapons such as bows and muskets/rifles but I am sure their adversaries such as the British redcoats and the French had nightmares about a close range assault with a tomahawk.

Raid

A raid is a deliberate attack that is carried out as a form of patrol and will usually have an urgency or time limit about it. You will want to get in and out rapidly, assault the objective and get away perhaps before any enemy reserves or reinforcement show up. It could be that the enemy has an indirect fire capability (mortars and/or artillery), or perhaps even helicopters or attack aircraft that can be deployed to follow up as a QRF.

If the enemy has indirect fire capability they will likely call down fire on their own position once it is overrun. This means that you will have to reorganize off the position, occupy enemy bunkers or get your entrenching tools out and start digging! If they have some follow up capability, then you will need to get away off the objective into some sort of cover, such as the canopy of the trees, before the QRF gets there. For both ground QRF and 'Airborne Reaction Forces' (ARF) you should consider the use of hasty ambush on your route away from the objective.

If you expect helicopters, you could for instance leave a couple of machine gun teams in a tree line on a ridge to engage the helos as they came in, with some sort of withdrawal route in dead ground. For a vehicle follow-up, think about ambushing or booby trapping the approach routes, followed by a withdrawal. For foot follow-up you can also utilize hasty ambush and perhaps put in a claymore (or improvised device) or two on tripwires on your withdrawal route. A claymore and/or hasty ambush will certainly make a pursuit more circumspect and have to take more care, and will mess up any trackers that they are using.

Cut-Off Groups: If you are conducting an offensive operation and you want to be able to kill or capture any enemy that are escaping from the objective, or you simply have a destroy mission and do not want anyone to get away, then you can consider the use of cut-off groups. These will be groups in addition to the usual mechanics of a deliberate attack and they will be situated as a blocking or ambush force on likely enemy withdrawal routes.

This is similar to an area ambush and you will have to give detailed consideration to the siting of these positions: given that they will be on enemy withdrawal routes, they may also be to the flanks and rear of the objective and thus you will have to ensure that they are not in the beaten zone for your fires. You can utilize terrain features for this, ensuring that they are in dead ground to the assaulting and fire support groups, or combine the use of such dead ground with allocation of specific sectors of fire – i.e. right and left arcs of fire.

If you are really serious about conducting deliberate attacks then ideally you would get hold of weapons systems such as 240B with tripod mount and also mortar systems, such as 81mm mortars. All these systems can be man-packed in with suitably fit and robust personnel. If you want to increase ammunition carriage then consider use of vehicles to move the equipment closer to the objective. Also, ATVs can be used, with noise consideration, but they can be moved closer to the firing line once the attack begins, and you could also consider the use of various types of pack animals to move equipment over difficult terrain.

You can effectively use the 240 in the 'light role', but if you mount it on its tripod, it becomes a different animal. The stock of the weapon is replaced by a plate and the weapon sits on the tripod and is used in the sustained fire role (SF role). This is a skill for trained machine gunners in the same way 81mm mortar crews are trained. You can even fire an SF role Gun in a map predicted mode and in the direct role it will fire effectively out to around 2000 yards. The gunner sits by the weapon and fires it simply with his thumb and finger, traversing it slightly on the mount; this creates the effect of a 'cigar' shaped beaten zone that is like a fat cigar and can be laid over the objective to suppress it.

Such a weapon can also be sited in defense to cover approaches and can be laid on specific approaches to provide 'FPF' or 'final protective fire' as well as recording specific 'DFs' or defensive fire locations, that are recorded and the gun can be laid on to these recorded locations just like a mortar, using an aiming post off to the side and a specific sight. If you had 81mm mortars, or even 60mm, you would be able to deliver great fires onto the objective, to include HE (high explosive), illum and smoke. This would significantly even the odds.

To have such equipment post-event it would have to be liberated from the military and operated by trained personnel, which may be an option depending of the circumstances post-event. Both of these weapons systems are also excellent defensive assets. If you are using mortars then they can only fire if they either have a view of the objective, which is not wise, or you have a fire controller who can view the objective and communicate fire control orders and corrections to the mortar line, which will be located in dead ground.

Ambush

An ambush is an attack from a concealed position where you lie in wait for the enemy and hit him hard when the ambush is initiated. An ideal ambush would be situated to hit all enemy within the killing area within moments of the initiation and allow none of them to escape. Thus, an ambush is a mechanism for killing the enemy. You could attempt to use an ambush for a capture mission, but that would require excellent fire control, unless you were able to block the enemy in and threaten with weapons in such a way that you 'had the drop' on them and were able to capture without any shots being fired. This section will concentrate on conventional ambush.

An ambush is a form of fighting patrol and will take place based off information and intelligence on the enemy, plus a map recce followed by a ground recce. You will need the required numbers to establish the relevant ambush groups and you will have to patrol out to the ambush via an ORP. The types of ambush are as follows:

Linear: this type of ambush will establish a killing area on some form of linear feature such as a track, road or river. The main body of the ambush will cover the killing area and they will be known as the kill group. Rear protection will be provided by a group left at the ORP. There will also be two cut-off groups. The cut off groups are situated to the flanks of the killing group and have the dual roles of being early warning and act as a cut off to prevent enemy escaping along the trail from the killing area.

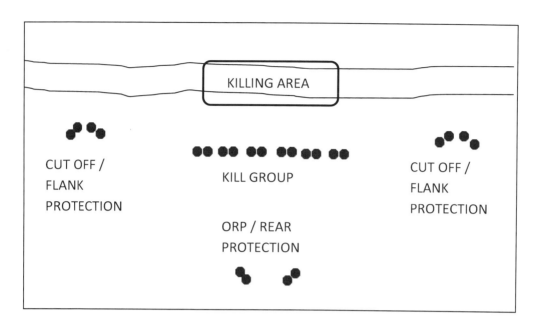

Figure 35 - Platoon Linear Ambush

Triangular: a triangular ambush is similar to a patrol base but by the nature of ambush it will be more covert. A triangular ambush provides excellent all round defense and is an excellent formation if you either expect potential follow up by large numbers of enemy, or you have to

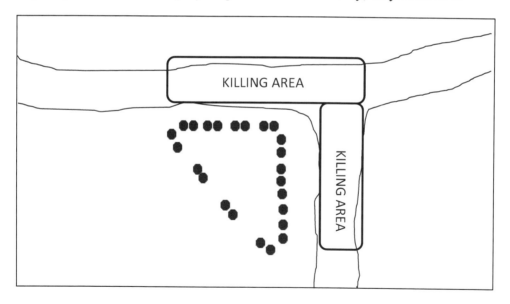

Figure 36 - Triangular Ambush

cover multiple routes. For instance, you could situate a triangular ambush next some sort of track junction with at least two sides of the triangle covering the trail junction and the trails coming in. The disadvantage is the lack of cut-off groups for early warning and cut-off.

L-shaped: an L shape by its nature is very simple and the main killing group is the long part of the L with a sort of dual killing/cut off group provided by the short foot of the L. This utilizes the natural 90 degree angle that we try and achieve and will catch the enemy in a cross fire. It is best if you definitely know which way the enemy is coming from and have the short foot of the L farthest from that, otherwise the enemy is approaching from the rear of this group, may compromise them, and may be behind them if not all the enemy is in the killing area upon initiation of the ambush. You have a cut off group if the enemy tries to run towards the foot of the L but not if they run the other way. This is a popular insurgent tactic because of its simplicity and effectiveness if deployed right.

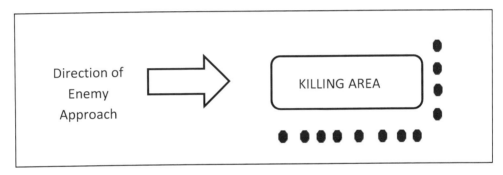

Figure 37 - L Shaped Ambush

Area: an area ambush has a main location of the ambush, which may be at some form of main track junction and may either be a linear of triangular ambush. In addition to the main site there will be satellite sites that are in effect larger cut-off groups. These groups have to be well sited so that one part of the ambush does not threaten another element with its fire. Terrain and sectors of fire can be used to achieve this. An area ambush will cover a wider area and multiple enemy options, and will have a greater effect in cutting off their escape.

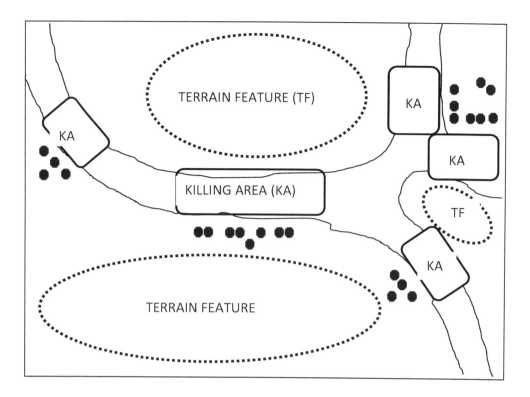

Figure 38 - Area Ambush

Mechanical: this is an ambush used when you are low on manpower but high on explosives. A mechanical ambush is something like an IED but it needs to be a big device or devices that will engulf the killing area and devastate it. This could be something like an improvised huge barrel claymore, multiple claymores strung in the trees, or a fuel device that is going to destroy the immediate area. This type of ambush can be initiated by a reactive OP that stays behind to watch the site, or it could be set to blow by victim operation or even a timer so as to allow you time to get away. It depends on the situation.

Hasty (Snap) Ambush: this is an unplanned ambush that goes in as a drill. It can be done as part of the drill for occupation of a patrol base, and can be linear, L shaped or triangular. A simple hasty ambush would be useful when you are facing an enemy pursuit or perhaps you pre-sight the enemy. In which case the patrol will move into a simple ambush formation, perhaps a simple linear or L shaped ambush, maybe even at squad level, in order to rapidly ambush the enemy and then perhaps to break contact and withdraw. Think of it as belting a pursuer in the face, knocking him back, before taking off and creating some distance.

Duration: An ambush will also be either short term or long term. A short term ambush is generally up to 12 or maybe 24 hours and as such will not involve much in the way of routine, perhaps just some buddy napping in place if it goes on. A longer term ambush will have to involve routine and once this starts happening it may be necessary to rotate personnel out of the ambush to an admin area at the ORP, in a similar way to an OP. This then requires more people in order to have personnel resting while fully manning the ambush.

Depending on the elements and the training of your personnel, you can stay in position for 24 hours on hard routine, with perhaps a 50% napping routine in place, eating hard rations and if really necessary crawling to the rear to take a dump. If you snore, don't expect to be allowed to nap in an ambush.

Sequence: The sequence for an ambush is as follows, within an overall patrol plan:

- Occupy ORP
- Recon of Site
- Occupation of site
- Work Phase
- Ambush 'Set'
- Routine
- Spring or Collapse
- Search
- Withdrawal to ORP

As part of the orders and plan the patrol will move on the route out to the ORP in a certain Order of March (OOM) that will relate to the role that the elements will have in the ambush. They will then move into the ORP and adopt a herringbone formation and probably stand to and conduct a listening watch. After a suitable period of time the leader will gather his recce group and move forward to confirm the site.

The leader will conduct a recce and identify the required locations for the various groups. He will take security with him and will lay down a representative from each group in the various positions. For this example we will assume a linear ambush.

Once he has identified the location for the killing group he will first move to the cut off group location on the side where it is assessed the enemy is most likely to come from. He will leave security there, then at the opposite cut off group location and then move back to the ORP. There he will gather up the remainder of the patrol and lead them in and place them down in their positions. A group will be left at the ORP as rear security.

For the occupation, he will first place out from the main body the cut-off group in the direction of expected enemy, then the one furthest away, and then the kill group; the purpose of this is to establish security to the flanks and in particular the main direction of enemy threat first, to cover the rest of the occupation. As this is happening, the patrol is queuing in herringbone at the rear of the kill group location and moving up as the PL takes each group in turn and places them out.

Once the site is occupied the leader will move along and check the position of each individual and whisper to him his sectors of fire. As part of the plan comms cord is usually strung between the various groups to allow covert communication and also mark out the track plan.

The work phase is then conducted which will consist of the patrol building up the concealment of their fire positions. Depending on the threat and situation you may or may not dig shell scrape fighting positions. Any early warning systems and booby traps will be put out at this time, including trip flares and claymores. You will have to be careful of doing anything on the other side of the killing area because that will involve crossing the trail and could leave sign and compromise the ambush, so most preps will take place on the near side of the ambush.

If you are putting out any device such as a trip flare, claymore or IED the idea is to have it command initiated, not simply on a victim operated tripwire, the reason for this is that you want to retain control of the ambush initiation and it may be that a group walks into the killing area that you do not want to spring the ambush on, so you can't have the area set up for victim operated booby traps. The exception to this would be any devices that you put out, if any, across the trail on the far side to retard the efforts of the enemy to get away from your killing area.

If you do put devices out there, you will need to erase any sign you made crossing the killing area. If you set out trip flares, ensure that they are masked from the kill group by something like the ground or a tree trunk so that the light goes forward to illuminate the enemy but does not blind the kill group. For parachute illumination flares, the same principles apply as for any other use: make sure whoever is firing them does so from cover due to the large smoke signature generated when they are fired.

You may or may not be digging the ambush fire positions in but if you have the opportunity, and it will not compromise the ambush, you should do so for protection. Remember that an ambush is a covert affair and a lot of effort needs to go into camouflage and concealment and remaining undetected, but conversely an ambush is sited to wait for enemy to move through it and as such will likely be on a route somewhere, so as long as there are no enemy right there right then, you should have the ability to dig in if you have to. You will need to place sentries out beyond the limit of sound, as per a patrol base, if you are going to do so.

Once the work phase is complete, the leader will need to 'set' the ambush. This has to be done carefully, particularly at night, because it has actually happened (at least once) where a commander was killed by setting the ambush and then moving back through the killing area by accident. Preferably you will not use a radio in case of detection, so if you are doing it physically the way to do it is to use the comms cord to find your way and move out first to the cut off group nearest the expected enemy direction, and then move back behind the killing group to the other cut off.

Tell each man 'ambush set' and then move back to the rear protection and finally the killing group, telling each man. At this point the ambush it set and ready to be sprung. The routine will now begin, which will have been organized depending on whether it is planned to be a short or long term ambush. For a short term, you will simply lay there in place for the duration. For a long term there will be shift changes and an admin area at the ORP to the rear, and changeover will have to be done carefully to maintain concealment and also make sure no-one wanders into the killing area by mistake.

In fact, an ambush should never be sprung arbitrarily, but this is a failsafe to not have people walking about. It is always possible that someone will open fire. The ambush should be sprung by the commander. If the enemy comes into the ambush he will receive a warning from the cut-off group either by radio or by tugs on the comms cord. He will wait to identify if the right number and type of enemy are out there and wait until they are at the right place in the killing area.

An ambush should always be sprung by the use of lethal force, never by a harmless signal such as shouting "Fire!" or blowing a whistle etc. The commander will usually initiate by firing his own weapon or perhaps another pre-planned act such as detonating claymores or an IED, or perhaps signaling a machine-gunner to fire – if he does this it must be an unmistakable signal such as squeezing his shoulder twice or similar.

Upon springing the ambush there must be an instant 'ambush weight' of fire into the killing area. If you have automatic weapons a useful technique is to have every other man fire on auto and the others fire on single shot, to generate the weight of fire but also ensure that everyone does not have to change magazines at the same time. Hopefully the shock of the sudden ambush and the weight of fire will decimate the enemy in the killing area.

If any enemy try to run out the cut-off groups will engage them. The kill group will continue to fire at the enemy until they are no longer moving and the commander will then make the decision to cease fire, by shouting something like "CEASE FIRE!" "STOP!" or blowing a whistle. It needs to be heard over the sound of fire. Once the ceasefire is given the killing area will continue to be observed, what is called the "watch and shoot" phase, and any enemy that were shamming and take the opportunity to run will be shot.

The commander will then give the signal for searchers to go out. It is imperative that all hear this signal so that the searchers are not engaged: pass it down the line through the link men. There are various techniques that can be used at this point. One technique is for the cut-off groups to remain in place while the killing group gets up in a skirmish line and fights through the killing area, which is very effective particularly if there is a lot of dead ground and hiding places out there which need to be cleared.

The method discussed here will be for a couple of buddy pairs to go out as search groups. They will usually be from the kill group and nominated in advance. They will move to the cut of group opposite of the way the enemy entered the ambush and skirmish out into the killing area, sweeping the killing area and searching the enemy dead.

The purpose of an ambush is to kill and as such it is ok to clear the ambush with fire as they search through, to ensure that no enemy are shamming. They will take any information or equipment of value from the enemy and continue to move until they get even with the opposite cut-off group, who may have to let them know by voice or signal when they have reached their limit of exploitation, at which point they will move back in through the cut-off and return to their positions.

If the ambush is not sprung, then at a certain point, maybe a certain time depending on the orders or mission, the ambush will collapse and move back to the ORP and then home. For an ambush that is not sprung the order should be to collapse the killing group then the cut-off groups to allow flank security to remain in place for as long as possible. Leave no sign of your ambush.

For an ambush that is sprung, once the searchers are back in the commander will give the signal to "WITHDRAW!" and the cut-offs will collapse back in to the killing group and then back to the ORP followed by the killing group peeling out in pre-designated order. It is useful on a dark night for the rear protection at the ORP to do something like shine a small red penlight so that the ambush team can see it and home in on it as they rapidly move back to the ORP.

An ambush is like robbing a bank – once it has gone down you have to get out of there as quick as possible and clear the area to avoid enemy follow up or indirect fire. The ambush group will move back to the ORP as per the pre-designated plan as rapidly as possible and once there a head count will be taken.

The patrol will then form up and move out at a rapid pace to the next RV. Once they get sufficiently clear, the pace will slow down to a patrol pace. If it is felt there is a need, booby traps and possibly a hasty ambush will be placed on the extraction route by a rear guard group.

From the previous description it should be apparent that in planning an ambush patrol it is very important to be detailed in the orders. Rehearsals are very much key and every person has a specific place and role. Rehearsals need to be thorough and detailed and of the noisy and silent type so that there can be no doubt as to every person's place at the various phases. To a certain extent it may seem to be simple for the rifleman because he just has to be in the right order of march and be placed down in his position, but it needs to be drilled in by training and rehearsal. There is no place on an ambush patrol for a cluster or for raised voices trying to fix a situation.

Fighting in Woods and Forests (FIWAF)

Fighting in woods and forests (FIWAF) will modify some of the offensive drills that have already been covered. Depending on the type of woods, it may be that your drills can remain pretty much the same, so long as they are not too thick and there are plenty of clearings. But in dense forests or woodland, including jungle, you will have to amend some of your techniques to take amount of the thick cover and concealment.

FIWAF is a casualty intensive activity if you are up against a determined enemy. There is a lot of concealment provided by the trees and vegetation and a lot of cover provided by the tree trunks. There is also the additional dimension of the trees and the ability for snipers to get up them and engage from up in the canopy.

If you are fighting from outside of the forest into it then you will conduct a conventional 'break-in battle' by establishing a fire support position to engage enemy in the tree-line and then assault onto the objective in the trees. The issue when in the trees is the limited visibility which impacts on the ability to conduct flank attacks. It is not the ability to go to the flank that is affected, but rather the ability for the fire support and assault teams to see each other which then increases the risk of fratricide in the trees. This may not be an issue depending, as previously stated, on the thickness of the vegetation and the amount of clearings. However, in extensive and thick forest you will likely have to revert to a more old school method.

If you are a platoon advancing through the trees then you are more likely to have to go with two squads up in an extended skirmish line. You will use your third squad as flank protection, with a team on each flank. Think bush warfare in Africa, where you will be advancing in a skirmish line and engaging the enemy as you come across them and fighting through their positions.

This is similar for a camp attack in the woods. If it is in a nice clearing then you may be able to do a 90 degree attack and also use the wood line to get close, but if it is in the trees then you may well find yourself advancing on it in skirmish line. This reduces the effectiveness of your support weapons.

FIWAF is pretty much the same as the jungle. The difference in the jungle in a nutshell is the conditions of humidity and wildlife and the fact that you have to make different sleeping arrangements by getting off the ground. This will become relevant in some areas of the States such as the swamps in the south and if you are operating in these areas you are going to have to become comfortable with jungle warfare; you will want to get hold of some hammocks and learn how to construct an A-frame to make yourself comfortable.

It is also traditionally true that you should not move at night in the jungle, due to the difficulty of movement; however, there are many areas where it is not true jungle and you can move about if necessary – you will have to assess your environment and the possibilities in your area.

Roads, trails, clearings and firebreaks in a woodland environment become almost like the streets in an OBUA environment and they will become areas for ambush, killing areas and fields of fire. Vehicles will be limited to moving on trails and firebreaks and therefore this is a great opportunity to ambush them. Be aware in offense and defense that trees can be felled to block routes; this can be done in advance or explosively as part of the ambush. It is easy to bog vehicles down in a FIWAF environment and as such conducting an area defense in a forest environment gives many advantages to the defender, to include the concealment afforded by the wooded terrain and canopy.

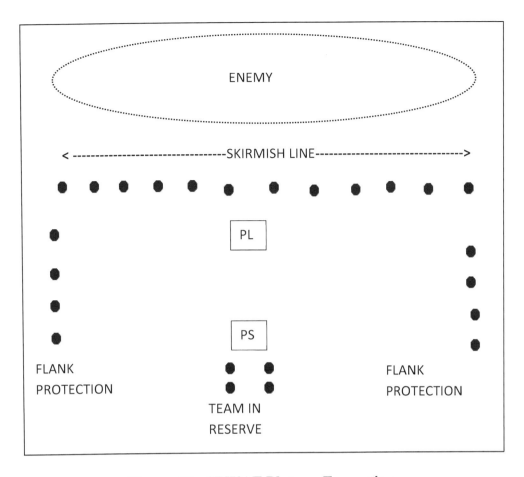

Figure 39 - FIWAF Platoon Formation

Offensive Operations in Built Up Areas (OBUA)

If we move our operations into urban areas, then we do not forget all the principles that we learned so far, but they have to be adapted to the specific challenges found in an urban environment. The simple presence of buildings does not create an urban environment, but the OBUA techniques can be applied to single or small groups of buildings, even if you are operating otherwise in mainly rural or wooded terrain. However, some types of structure do not really qualify as a building and therefore these techniques would not really be applicable; such as lean-to or small sheds or something similar.

What is very important to remember throughout any OBUA is the type of structure that you are working with. Most OBUA techniques work best in strong structures where there is some protection provided by the structure of the building, but in many types of building there is no real hard cover available. This is because the structure of the building will not stop ballistic threats. Many houses in the US are made from wooden studs and plasterboard and will not stop bullets. Be aware of this, which comes back to the previous point about some structures not really requiring OBUA techniques simply because they can be 'shot to pieces' and cleared as an afterthought.

TV and Movies also have a lot to answer for in our conceptions of urban warfare. It is also true that the nature of warfare in Iraq and Afghanistan over the past decade has taken us away from true OBUA (which the U.S. Military calls MOUT, Military Operations in Urban Terrain). This is because a lot of the operations in urban and village areas are more about arrest, search and capture. This, along with the assimilation of techniques from police/SWAT type entities has led to the current teaching for MOUT.

In simple terms the current techniques are broadly 'SWAT' style techniques which concentrate on breaching through doors and flooding a building to overwhelm the occupants, capture and search. This is what is behind the 'stacking' technique where a team will set up outside the door of a property, breach the door and rapidly pile into the building. This is dangerous in an OBUA environment because stacking outside a door puts you all together, not dispersed, and vulnerable to fire, which is good for a stealth raid but not if you are in a fight. The door is not an ideal entry point into a defended building, it is a 'fatal funnel'. Also, you are rapidly putting four men through a door into the unknown and if it blows, then you lose four.

It is also true that a lot of what is termed here as "SWAT" techniques has filtered down from Tier 1 Special Operations Forces CQB (Close Quarter Battle) raid techniques as part of arrest or capture missions over the last ten years or so. Such forces practice 'ad infinitum' for such techniques, usually surprise raids onto compounds, structures or buildings containing the target personnel. Such CQB has become a specialized industry and techniques have been refined specific to these tasks. That's high speed stuff and requires intensive training, equipment and support.

Although the police 'SWAT' techniques alluded to look similar to the military dynamic entry stuff, it is also true that the police CQB techniques are more suitable for use to breach, enter and subdue occupants for arrest. If there is a real threat of armed resistance in a building, SWAT does not usually go in. They wait it out and negotiate.

The actual US Army drills for MOUT are closer to what is covered here, which diverge a little from the CQB techniques you may be familiar with from the media. In a non-permissive kinetic urban fight, you have to approach, breach and clear buildings with slightly different techniques. This does not mean that SWAT style CQB drills do not have use if you have to enter rooms, just be aware of the dangers.

It may be appropriate, in particular with large rooms, to put four men in through a breach. You should also consider using two man assault teams. Depending on what you are doing, a useful technique for a four man team is to have two men breach into a reasonably sized room, followed rapidly by the team leader to assess the room, with the fourth man in the corridor covering down it and also acting as a link man to the rest of the force.

So, although these urban CQB techniques are effective, and are very effective as SWAT methods, they are not ideal for full offensive operations and will be amended here. Another issue is the portrayal of SWAT and military teams moving in the 'half crouch' technique with their weapon sights jammed into their eye sockets, moving the weapons around in an exaggerated manner with every movement of their heads. There is a certain amount of sarcasm here but it has become such a common portrayal that it has become almost taken as the right way to do things.

It is true that you should have your weapons up in a ready position, and that your weapons should move with you and in the direction that you look, but that whole half crouch and weapon in the eye socket thing is not ideal. Just don't overdo it. It is better to be moving comfortably, in a position where you can engage and if necessary walk towards the enemy as you do so, but realistically it is better to stop and engage rather than try and walk onto them while doing so. This does not preclude the use of the 'toe heel' style walk that you may use to steady your weapons as you advance down a corridor, for example.

Also, have the weapon at the ready but be alert, both eyes open and looking over the top of the sights (exceptions are use of ACOG type optics techniques with both eyes open). At close range you will engage instinctively by pointing the weapon anyway, and the TV portrayal creates far too much tunnel vision.

In terms of entry, any entry point that you use such as a door or window becomes a 'fatal funnel' where you will be silhouetted as you move through it. If you do go through a door, move out of the way as rapidly as possible. The following are good principles to abide by for making entry into buildings:

- Enter the building as high as possible. It is better to fight down than up: To get to a higher entry point, consider how you will do it. You can move over neighboring roofs, use ladders, use parked vehicles or bring in your own vehicle and climb off the roof, using a ladder/vehicle combination if necessary. Assault ladders should be carried in an OBUA environment, and can be used even for simple stuff like getting over walls or fences.

- Create alternative breaches; avoid use of doors and windows if possible: you can breach walls utilizing mechanical methods such as sledgehammers, breaching tools and even vehicles. You can also use mouse-hole charges, which is a cross shaped wooden device with arms about a yard long each with explosives taped to the end. This is laid against a wall and blows a hole in the wall, also shocking and killing those inside the room. If you want to use an anti-tank rocket type weapon, think carefully: an RPG, AT4 or LAW type weapon will create devastation inside the room but will only make a small hole in the wall, unless it is very flimsily constructed, because it is designed as an anti-armor weapon. You will probably not be able to gain access through the hole created with such a weapon. A SMAW-D bunker buster would be more appropriate. You should also consider making alternative routes through the interior of the building by breaching and mouse-holing the wall rather than going where the enemy expects you to go.

- Clear the whole floor you enter on, before moving to other floors: This will aid command and control and also ensure you do not leave enemy behind you. Preferably you will be clearing whole upper floors and moving down, but if you did not get in at the upper floors you will clear your whole entry floor and then pick the next floor to make entry to.

- Use explosive or stun devices to grab the initiative before entering: This will depend on what you have and if you expect there to be any friendlies or neutral civilians in the building. If you have it, grenade a room before entering: be aware of the construction of the wall before taking cover behind the wall.

Squad Level OBUA

Let's now look at the way a squad will conduct an attack onto a building. As previously discussed, your techniques, numbers and methods can be altered as per the circumstances. We will assume a two level building, ground floor and an upstairs. For OBUA purposes our eight man squad will break down again into four two man teams as follows:

Charlie Fire-Team: Assault Team 1
Squad leader plus link-man

Delta Fire-Team Assault team 2
Fire Support/Assault Team 3

The squad will approach the building and establish Delta team in a fire support position. They will identify a blind-side approach or alternatively an approach that can be successfully suppressed by the fire support. If there are multiple buildings that need suppression, this gets beyond a squad attack into a platoon or company task. We will assume a lone building for purposes of demonstration.

The squad will use some sort of code to identify the four sides of the building for target indication and directional purposes; something like red = left side, green = right side, white is near side and black is far side.

Under cover of fire support, dead ground and possibly smoke, the assault fire team will move up to the building. The squad leader and link man will stay back in cover and provide fire support while the breach team moves to the building. They may be aiming for a window; they may have a ladder, a mouse-hole charge, sledgehammers or maybe a vehicle. For this demonstration, they will make entry by a ground floor window.

Assault Team 1 approaches the window and tosses a grenade in, and then takes cover as the grenade detonates. As soon as they grenade goes off they will be through the window.

Once they enter the room, one will go left or right and the other following will key off him and go the other way. They will sweep the room with their weapons to identify any targets and engage as necessary, as they move away from the entry point to the corners of the room. They sweep the room with their weapons from the center out to the corners as the move in.

They will engage any enemy in the room and if you are going full out with no possibility of friendlies they will fire rounds into any available cover in the room, such as sofas and wardrobes. Once they are sure the room is secure they will call out to the squad leader: "ROOM CLEAR!"

At this point the squad leader and link man will move into the room, if the squad leader is not in there already, and the second assault team will also be moving to the breach as a domino effect. During the initial breach the squad leader was ready to support the assaulting team as necessary, but did not breach at the same time in case of booby trap and to maintain command and control.

Once the squad leader gets in, the assault team 1 will tell him where the exits are from the room and the squad leader will make a plan as to where to move next. The link man will now be positioned either inside or outside the room by the entry point and his job is to be with the squad leader in the best place to relay messages. He will call in the second assault team and the squad leader will rapidly push them through to clear the next room or corridor.

Assault team 2 will clear their next objective, at which point the assault team 3 (fire support) will have been briefed to either continue in support or to move into the building.

Using the three assault teams at his disposal the squad leader will leapfrog through the house until all the rooms on the floor are clear. By this time, the whole squad should be inside the building. At this point, for a platoon assault the squad would usually call in another squad (via the link man) and they would clear the upstairs.

OBUA is very manpower intensive. For a single squad attack they would have to make a breach to the upstairs and systematically clear that also.

Assaulting buildings in OBUA is a violent and aggressive activity and you should really get away from the idea that you can somehow 'black ops' your way through with night vision devices and stealth. You will be kicking doors in and fighting through. If it is nighttime it will be doubly hard and although the use of white light is usually discouraged because the flashlight on your weapon will give away your position, you will need weapon mounted flashlights (white light) and use them selectively for room clearing

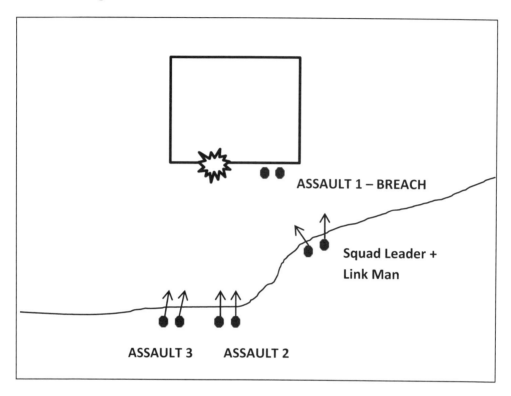

Figure 40 - OBUA 1 – BREACH

.

The advantage is to a defender if you are assaulting a room so you really want to have the ability to do something that will put them off balance, onto their back foot, and allow you to regain some of the initiative as you make entry. Explosives, grenades, stun grenades, gas or making entry via a place other than the door are all techniques that can be used. If a house is not strongly built, be aware of rounds coming through walls and you can use that to your advantage if you are assaulting.

When entering a room one man will go one direction and the other will key off that movement and go the other, both sweeping the room with their weapons barrels and moving to the corners. If you have a stoppage, then shout out and get down so that your buddy can engage. You may end up in a physical hand to hand fight if you are breaching rooms because it is easy for someone who is in the room already to get close to you so ensure that you are acting aggressively and are prepared to fight.

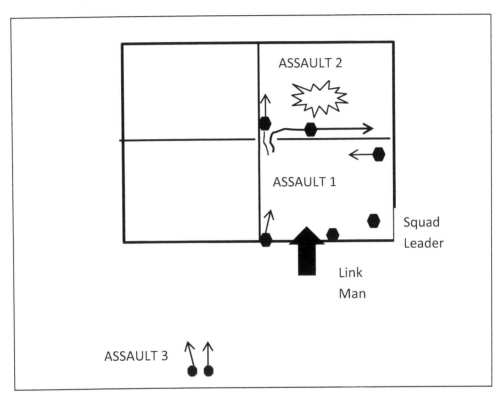

Figure 41 - OBUA 2 - CLEARANCE SCHEMATIC

One of the uses of a sling is to keep a weapon on you while you are doing some other task. The other reason is to make it harder for an assailant to take the weapon off you. If your weapon is grabbed retain control of it but rather than getting into a 'to and fro' over it do one of the following or both: maneuver the assailant so your buddy can shoot him, or go for your backup with one hand and shoot him yourself.

If you are fully geared up in body armor, helmet and equipment, which you will likely be if you are do this sort of thing, you will have formidable momentum when entering a room anyway. Of course, you may also trip over unexpected furniture and fall end over tip! But if you get into a fight, you need to rapidly overcome the opponent. You can hit him with your rifle barrel, your helmet or whatever. Just remember that it is about overwhelming him, not getting into a fight.

If you have the capability to use full auto fire then don't. Use rapid single shot when clearing rooms. It is more accurate and will not waste ammunition or put excessive rounds through the walls to potentially hit your buddies.

Platoon Level OBUA

At platoon level, we simply build on the blocks we already have for the squad level. The platoon leader will make a plan to organize the mechanics of the break in battle, or breach, and the subsequent sequencing of the assault onto different buildings with fire support as necessary. For a platoon level assault we can imagine perhaps a small cluster of buildings, a farm complex, compound or camp.

It is useful if the buildings are labeled in some way that everyone will understand, preferably on a diagram or schematic that they can carry, so the fire support and assaulting sequence can be coordinated. At platoon level, we have another two squads that can potentially provide fire support to allow the first assaulting squad to breach into their first objective.

Once they are in, link men are used to coordinate the platoon, with the leader situating himself in the place where he can best visualize the battle and coordinate. Squads will clear floors of buildings before calling in other squads to push through and clear other floors. Once buildings are clear, the squads in them will provide fire support while those not engaged will move through and assault/breach into the next building in sequence.

If you are fighting up a street then it may be that you end up taking a complicated route through the buildings, using explosives and mechanical methods to breach walls and blow mouse-holes. You want to stay out of the open street, which will be a kill zone for the defenders. This route needs to be marked and link men will provide communication.

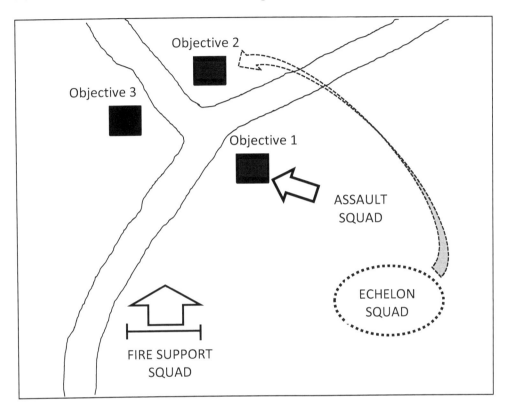

Figure 42 - Platoon Level OBUA

Ammunition re-supply will have to go forwards, and casualties will be evacuated back, though this tenuous cleared route. If you have armored vehicles you can use them to either approach buildings to allow a breach, perhaps from the roof into an upper floor, or depending on the relative strength of the building and vehicle you may actually be able to breach into the building by ramming with the vehicle. You may even be able to knock a big hole through the building or even knock it down, depending.

Company Level OBUA

There are multiple ways that a company commander can sequence an OBUA offensive operation. A simple way to show the sequencing of a company level attack would be to describe a clearance assault along a street towards an objective.

Let's assume that we have a street of semi-detached or detached houses that leads up to the objective, which is a strongpoint. We can't go up the street because that is a killing area so we are going to move up through and over the buildings towards the strongpoint.

A company commander will have three platoons, so let's assume that he has one platoon assault one side of the street and the other assault the other. The third platoon will be in reserve behind Company HQ.

If you refer this to the OBUA defense chapter you will see that a good enemy will make the streets no-go 'sniper alleys' and force us to fight through the buildings, where they will fall back to their strongpoint for the final defense (note: if they have several mutually supporting strongpoints then their hand is a lot stronger).

Each platoon will breach into the end building, using fire support as necessary. They will then continue to breach up their respective row of houses clearing as they go. The difference here is that coordination at company level will ensure that although on separate sides of the street the platoons will leapfrog each other: one platoon will provide fire support across the street at allow the other to break in and assault, then the supported platoon will repay the favor.

Once both platoons have fought their way to the end of the row they will get into fire support positions and the reserve platoon will be sent through to assault the strongpoint.

In simple terms that is how a company level operation could mutually support itself in an OBUA environment.

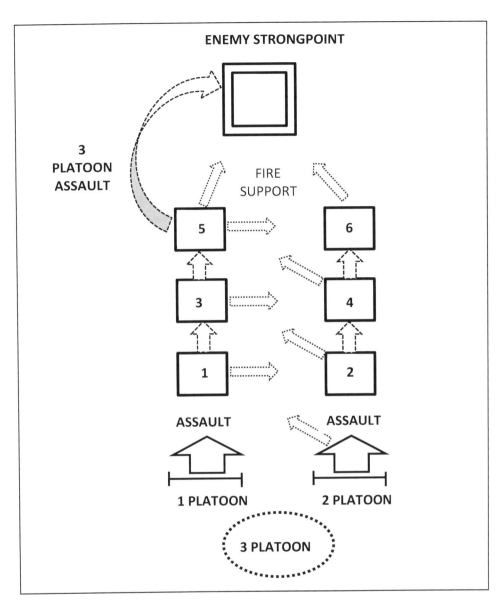

Figure 43 - Company Level OBUA

CHAPTER THIRTEEN

WITHDRAWAL

Introduction

A tactical withdrawal, or retreat, is a potentially difficult operation that you will want to plan for and put into effect before you are pushed off by the enemy and it becomes a rout, with the resulting high and potentially catastrophic casualties. In planning for a withdrawal, you should identify, brief and rehearse routes, ERVs and equipment such as ready grab bags of essential gear.

The sooner you do actually withdraw, the more equipment you are likely to be able to take and the better order you are likely to be in. It is feasible to adopt a strategy of 'stay in place' in covert and/or defended locations and then draw a line in the metaphorical sand that, once the enemy reaches it, this will trigger a withdrawal. This could simply be levels of mob and looting activity, organized raiding gangs, or even simple discovery of your location if your defense philosophy is based on concealment.

The simple moral is that the sooner you withdraw, the better off you will be, but realistically this must be balanced against practical ability to withdraw, options of where to go, and the need to defend life-essential assets.

There are two types of withdrawal, that of withdrawal out of contact and withdrawal in contact. The latter is the most dangerous. They involve separate but related techniques.

Withdrawal Out of Contact

For a withdrawal out of contact, it is essential to ensure that the enemy does not know you are leaving. When we say 'out of contact' this still assumes an enemy presence, probably keeping your position under observation. If they get wind that you are leaving, this will likely trigger a pursuit response and you will suddenly find yourself in a withdrawal under fire.

The principle for a withdrawal out of contact is for the rear elements to move first, leaving the 'front line' in place to conceal the move until these final elements move out. If you can conceal the move until even these elements have left, then you will be successful.

Historically, there are many good examples of this. On the withdrawal from the defended position at Gallipoli in the First World War, the Allied forces left behind deception in the form of rifles attached to water gravity devices that would fire at varied times once the receptacle had filled up. At the withdrawal from Arnhem of the movie 'A bridge too far' fame, the paratroopers left behind wounded comrades that they were unable to move to give the impression that the defense was in place; the wounded were subsequently captured and humanely treated by the Germans.

You will need to establish control measures. What should happen is that each element has a check point immediately behind its position. The elements will move through the checkpoint and be accounted for before moving back to an RV at the next higher formation, where they will be accounted for again at a checkpoint and moved back to the next RV in line, until the whole formation is together and moving back to their next location. This could also involve a rally point and pick up by vehicle for the move to the next location.

Withdrawal In Contact

For withdrawal under fire, you change the method. This is very similar to a break contact drill and you will have to fire and maneuver out of your positions and away from the enemy. If you can identify withdrawal routes that incorporate cover and concealment then you will be better off.

When withdrawing in contact you will move the front elements first, and they will fire and maneuver back with fire support provided by other elements that have appropriate fields of fire. So, this method collapses from the front, rather than leaving the hollow shell of the withdrawal out of contact.

If you try to use the out of contact method, you will likely have your forward stay behind elements overrun and destroyed. This would work if the circumstances were that you were using a sacrificial rear guard, but then you would be about losing people, which we want to avoid as much as possible. This may be an option of last resort if protected personnel and kids are at stake, and then you need to take notes from the Spartans at Thermopylae!

When withdrawing in contact, you will need as much fire support as possible, and preferably indirect fire support from in depth at the rear also. You probably won't have this. You need to attempt to knock the enemy back, give them a bloody nose, in order to create space to move and break contact.

It may be that a limited counter attack or other offensive operation will work to create this space. Another technique would be, once you had moved off the main position and in order to discourage pursuit, lay a hasty ambush to knock the enemy back with sheer 'ambush weight' of fire as they pursue.

Remember that if you take casualties, you will have to carry them out with you, so have a plan and some equipment to allow you to do this. It may be that you are fighting back to vehicles and can then evacuate in those.

Exfiltration

An alternative to your force gradually amalgamating into a single force and moving back as a group would be to use exfiltration. This is simply the reverse of infiltration and would see you splitting your force into smaller elements to make their way separately back to a consolidated RV. This would be useful in an area where there was no 'front line' as such and where you see risks of trying to move through hostile territory as a big group. As with infiltration you will have to balance mutual support and strength versus the need for concealment. If you choose to exfiltrate, your elements will break down into smaller elements and move covertly via separate routes to a main RV.

Vehicles

Another option to consider with withdrawal, which would be better than a dismounted option if you could pull it off, is to conduct the whole withdrawal in vehicles. This may in effect make the operation more of a break out than a withdrawal, simply because your escape routes options may be minimized, but will amount to much of the same thing except that if you are moving in vehicles it is likely that rather than moving away from the enemy, you are likely to be having to attack towards them to get through, simply because if they are vehicle mounted they will have come in on the roads and will be located on or close to them and seeking to block them. An exception would be if you were lucky enough to have a suitable trail out the back of the property that they had not cut off and allowed you access to the hinterland, and hopefully other navigable trails.

Break Out

If you are moving out in vehicles and have to fight through a blocking force, then you will need maximum firepower and protection. This is where armored technical vehicles would come in very useful. What would be excellent if you had one would be some sort of heavy protected vehicle such as a dump truck preferably with a plough on the front.

You would need to break down into a first moving group and a follow up group. The follow up group would provide fire support for the first moving group, who would break out in armored vehicles with the protected personnel cocooned in some sort of protection. Their job would be to smash through and move away, where elements would then go firm and provide fire support for the second group to mount up and move off.

You would likely have a protection detail for the protected personnel, who would continue to move to an RV out of contact once they had broken out.

The remaining two elements would move in vehicles using bounding over-watch to suppress the enemy and move to the RV. If the enemy continues to follow up then suitable ground should be selected for a vehicle mounted ambush to push them back before moving to the RV and getting mobile away from there. Once moving on from there, you are back to vehicle mounted mobile tactics when moving on the roads.

Alternatively, if you were less well equipped with perhaps unarmored vehicles and perhaps lower in numbers, then you would have to use some form of deception and/or surprise to enable the breakout. Even so, you should do what you can to protect the vehicles, in particular the ones with kids in, with added hobo armor and keeping them low on the floor.

You would want to consider moving at night with either stealth or a distraction plan, maximum use of smoke, whether from smoke grenade or by burning something, and try to take the enemy by surprise.

If you have a trained tactical element then perhaps they may be able to conduct a night attack onto the enemy camp while the escaping group prepares to get out in the ensuing chaos. The tactical group will have some plan to escape, whether it be moving to a pick up point or even exfiltration; some of your options will be extreme depending on the nature of the enemy you are facing and it may be that the tactical team has to take a lot of risks in order to give the escaping group the space they need to get out.

The tactical team will have a plan to survive and hope to do so, but may be against heavy odds. This is an example of the sort of decision you may face, and hard choices will have to be made for the safety and survival of your family.

CHAPTER FOURTEEN

CONCLUSION

There is a considerable amount of tactical information included within this manual and it would take an allocation of considerable amounts of training time to assimilate and train in all of it. The best advice is to work on the basics and apply the principles that are described to your personal situation. Application of the principles and techniques will allow you to improve your situation or make plans to change it if you assess that as necessary.

There is certainly a sliding scale described here, from basic tactical movement and use of weapons in self-defense all the way up to company level offensive operations. There is a point at which the techniques move from being something that you will do to protect your family to something bigger, requiring a tactical team of varying size to accomplish tactical operations.

In the event of a total collapse of society these tactics and techniques will come into their own as a means to allow communities to defend themselves against roving marauders and other threats, even against the neighboring town, community or rampaging gang.

In the event of total collapse, there will be a time period during which defending your supplies and conducting limited forage will suffice. After that, it may be two seasons before food is able to be grown again and the 'die off' is largely complete.

In order to be able to survive in the long term, you need to be able to do two main things:

1) Is to be able to survive the short term as the collapse happens and the violence and mass starvation continue; you have to be able to hunker down and defend your family or group while this madness washes over the country. There will be huge die-offs. Ultimately, all but the most avid of food collectors will run out of stored food in the end.

2) Is to be able to survive the long term when the resources have been eaten out and most of the population has died off. This will require a sustainable program of food production, which is a community activity.

Throughout all of this the constant is the need to be able to protect yourself, your family, your group and your community. In the long run you are better off finding yourself part of a sustainable community that can produce food. If you were not part of one before the event, you will have to protect yourself through the disaster and whatever movement you have to make to get to that situation, and prove to that community that you are worth taking onboard.

Whatever the exact situation you find yourself in post-event, you will have need of the basic tactical skills to protect your family and for the more advanced tactical skills to form a community defense to protect your people and resources in a lawless land.

If you require further clarification or explanation of the contents of this manual, have training or consultancy requirements, or would like to discuss or debate the TTPs in this manual, please contact the author.

Max Velocity

Email: info@maxvelocitytactical.com

Web: www.maxvelocitytactical.com

Blog: maxvelocitytactical.blogspot.com

Are you ready?

Made in the USA
San Bernardino, CA
11 April 2013